# DARK CORNERS

# DARK CORNERS

**Gerard Mac Manus**

MERCIER PRESS

WHAT YOU NEED TO READ

MERCIER PRESS

Cork

www.mercierpress.ie

Trade enquiries to CMD Distribution,
55A Spruce Avenue, Stillorgan Industrial Park,
Blackrock, County Dublin.

© Gerard Mac Manus, 2008

ISBN: 978 1 85635 585 8

10 9 8 7 6 5 4 3 2 1

A CIP record for this title is available from the British Library

 Mercier Press receives financial assistance from the
Arts Council/An Chomhairle Ealaíon

Printed and bound in the EU.

# Contents

To Uncle Paddy.

Sorry it took so long.

'Uncle Paddy' or Francis Mac Manus, is the author's uncle and one of Ireland's most venerated writers. His influence on this writer's childhood resulted in this book.

# 1

# THE THEN TIMES

It was early morning with a crisp chill in the air and the fog was lying heavy on top of and around the woods they called Tippings, which rose up the gentle sides of the mountains they called Mourne. In between the mountains and me ran the wide, strong-flowing Dundalk river, now swollen with heavy spring tides going in and out every day. The surging tides brought in heavily loaded merchant ships, low in the water on the in-tide, and high in the water when sailing away on the out-tide.

From my bedroom window, which directly overlooked the river, I was close enough on a clear, quiet day to hear the deck-hands talking and joking as they prepared their ships to dock or depart. They sounded happy either way – to get ashore on the way in, and to go to new places on the way out. As these ships surged past my window, the sounds of steel hitting steel, men shouting, chains rattling, engines straining, all sharply echoing off the mountains of Mourne, overwhelmed me with the magic of it all. These sailors were on their way to exotic places like France, Holland, Africa and who knows where.

In an old invoice book my father gave me, I used the blank backs of the used pages to maintain a log of the ships coming to and going from Dundalk harbour. It was not always coal they were carrying: many carried molasses, and they were my favourite because of their sweet smells. The molasses ships were always clean; their engine rooms sparkled with polished iron, steel, and brass gauges, with their mysterious numbers in red and black on top of hissing boilers. That is not to say I did not love the coal boats with their black-faced workers and the coal dust everywhere – up their noses, into their lungs, in their ears and eventually saturating every pore in their body so the blackness never went away, even after their wives scrubbed them down with a hard floor-cleaning brush. These men went down every day into the suffocating holds of the coal ships and I would see the same men in our bar in the evening, smoking and coughing up black spit, then gasping down their pints so they could clear their throats.

My father had me throw sawdust around the bar, especial-ly where the men sat on the stools and spat. I was too young to know then the significance of what was happening: these men were dying of black lung disease, just like the coal miners around the world. That said, it was a day's work at a time when a day's work was hard to come by; and at the end of the day, a hot meal on the family table, with a little pride in their hearts for providing that meal, was enough for the coal workers.

My grandparents lived just four doors from our home. My beloved grandfather, Francis O'Dowda, Dundalk's postmaster, was the wellspring of my imagination. He had a vision of the world that far surpassed his own life's experiences, and it was a wonderful vision, yet nobody knew it except me. He had a small library of books that included Zane Grey, science fiction, and books about war and America. When I spotted a new ship I would hurry over to him and tell him what country it was from and he would take out his worn atlas and tell me about the wonders of that country; and then he always ended up tell-ing me about the great world out there, and that I should go out and see it for myself. He talked of America with wistful eyes, of great deserts and cities, many races, of a place to grow and prosper. He told me to go there and see the wonders of it, and come back and tell him what I had seen because he would never get there.

My grandfather, who never travelled farther than Cork City, fuelled my young mind with his vision. To this day, he remains a great man and a visionary to me. I often wonder what he would have accomplished if he himself had made that journey he dreamed about. I was but a child then, yet the die was cast: I was going to see that wonderful world out there, and I was going to touch it all, and have it touch me, and that is what I did.

I would sit on the jetty at the end of the Navvy Bank, day-dreaming, as the ships steamed by, the sailors waving, less than thirty yards away. The Coastguard Station where we lived was at the end of the Point Road. Except for Christopher Taylor, there were no children my age, which was all right. Christopher was a good friend. Our only problem was that he was always on a tight rein. His parents, Jessy and Len, kept a close eye on everything Christopher did. I now know that they were transplanted English protestants, and were probably somewhat nervous living in Dundalk, an operational IRA town close to the border. Over time, they grew more comfortable with Christopher and myself being friends, sitting around reading our Dandy and Beano comic books.

The issue of religion never arose between us and frankly neither one of us could have cared less. He was dragged to a protestant church on Sundays and I was dragged to a catholic church. My parents allowed me the freedom of running the fields and fishing the waters all around us, while Christopher had to remain within calling range. That put the Navvy Bank and the Sally Gardens off limits and that is where everything happened. We got out there sometimes when his mother would pedal her bicycle to town. It was only years later that I came to realise just why Christopher's parents did not want him to venture to the forested Sally Gardens. The men in black conducted weapons training there and I am sure that they knew that.

When Christopher was eighteen he travelled to England, and following his family's tradition, joined the British Royal Marines Commandos. Just as we had talked about so often, he was off to see the world, fight his wars and win medals. That he did, but never came home again: the IRA knew where he lived and he was a marked man. We communicated when I also was serving in an army, first the Irish and then the American, and we made plans to meet some place where it would be safe, and we would talk the way we used to talk at the end of the Navvy Bank. It was there, on a trip home, that I was told he was dead. He had had inoperable cancer of the brain.

I named my son Christopher, then was sorry I had done so, for each time I call my son's name, memories flood back. He was a good friend and a brave soldier, a father of five sons with a loving wife. Life is hard to figure out sometimes – who or what makes those decisions as to who should live and die?

Back then I would venture out on the jetty at low tide and risk going down the seaweed-covered, slippery slope, getting as close to the rushing incoming tide as possible, and then hoping that I could get back up, and not drown, for that is where I could get closest to the passing ships. It was risky behaviour, perhaps an indication of my future. On a clear spring day, with the river flat, but swollen and calm between the incoming tide and the outgoing tide, it was a sight to behold. The mountains with their greens, purples and yellows were majestic, reflected on the quiet river's blue-mirrored surface. And in the silence you could hear in the parking lot of the Blue Anchor bar, all the way across the river, people talking as they enjoyed a Sunday pint in the warmth of the sun.

The river between the Coastguard Station and the mountains was a virtual echo chamber on a quiet day, and even more so when the tide was out and the river was flat to the mud, and it was there I first experienced war. I was sitting down on the bottom of the jetty, close to the water's edge, waiting for the incoming tide. It was a quiet day and the echo of metal on metal was like the sound when you ping fine crystal in a silent room. It was hushed all around except for the cry of a curlew once in a while. This was a place that was at peace with itself, a blue sky, a fog-cloaked mountain, and a river between tides. Then a monster came up the river towards me.

To this day I remember I was not afraid; I just could not move. A German fighter-bomber, on its way to the Belfast shipyards, came roaring up the river bed trying to elude two British Spitfire fighter-planes. The German bomber passed so close to me I smelled the pungent smoke from its exhausts, and I saw many canvas patches on its fuselage. The noise was deafening and then I saw the pilot's face – he was that close. In that instant, I saw him lift his left arm a little bit and nod his head, and then he was gone. Behind came the British Spitfires, their engines screaming as they passed. I saw their faces too – faces just like the German pilot's. The doomed German bomber tried to climb over the mountains with his engines straining, and it was there that they got him. I could not see the encounter, but I heard the loud explosion.

That night my father came home and told us that the police had found a flying helmet, with an ear inside, at the crash site. I had seen all the pilots' faces, and they had seemed old. Now, with the wisdom of age, I know they were very young – children killing children because of one madman. I know now from my own experience that children fight and die in wars, led by old men, who have forgotten that they were once young.

Ireland was neutral during the Second World War, but suffered at the hands of the German Luftwaffe, who bombed our small nation. Not many young Irish men and women are aware of Hitler's interest in our country. He had plans to occupy Ireland, starting in the west, and then attack England from its vulnerable western flank. It would be logical to suppose that after hundreds of years of British brutality against Ireland, Hitler would have expected some support from the Irish.

It is hard to believe for some, but 180 aircraft crashed in the Republic of Ireland during the Second World War. Some were German, some American, and – the biggest mystery of all – many were British planes. The big question is: what was the British RAF doing flying sorties over neutral Ireland?

Just as strange is the fact that Germany bombed neutral Ireland. Apart from Dublin, they bombed 'targets' that have puzzled war historians for decades. They bombed counties Wexford, Wicklow, Carlow and some other places, such as Carrickmacross and Julianstown, that defied explanation at the time. These bombings made as much sense as, say, bombing the Sahara Desert when your real target was Rome.

Well, decades later, I was to discover the real reason for the bombings, and in of all places, Germany. I was stationed there with the American army as a Sergeant in the 3rd Mechanized Infantry Division on the Czech border from 1961 to 1964. The 3rd is the same division that fought Hitler's armies all across Europe during Second World War. More recently it was the spearhead of armoured infantry that stormed into Iraq twice. This division was no place to go if you wanted a nice military pension. One would be better off defusing sophisticated bombs while drunk on Jack Daniels, which to my great shame, and even greater relief that I survived, I once did. In my defence, if there is any, I was alone at the bomb site, and who in their right mind would ask an Irishman to defuse a bomb on St Patrick's Day at eleven at night, I ask you?

I was undergoing Ranger training. This is basically a sophisticated series of extreme military challenges that the American army dreamed up to produce a super warrior, the army Ranger. It is not unusual for candidates to die during this training. A few did in the swamps of south Florida – from hypothermia they said. My own take on the cadre who are assigned as instructors for Ranger training is that they are battle-hardened veterans who are closet sadistic monsters recruited from insane asylums for the military, and I am only half joking.

The Ranger training was conducted in the dead of winter near the Czech border of mountainous southern Bavaria. While our personal conditions rapidly deteriorated due to the harsh blizzards and freezing temperatures, I was struck by the extreme beauty of the place, for there were stunning vistas of unspoiled wonder. One night I sat under a pine tree and saw a herd of deer that must have numbered in their thousands, pass in the bright moonlight across a broad valley. The bucks' antlers were so big and wide that they seemed unreal, but nobody hunted them. A gunshot here could start the Third World War. There were no hunters or tourists, just the soldiers of two world powers, on nuclear hair triggers; quiet, almost invisible villagers; and a suffocating dangerous silence. This vast Rhine Valley area was under a tight Cold War lock-down, and had been since the First World War.

During the course of one training exercise, on a clear frosty evening, I saw a village in the distance, and it looked like something out of an old Bavarian oil painting. It was dusk and the small chimneys of the cottages emitted a light white smoke from their wood fires. The windows were aglow with oil lanterns and looked warm and inviting. Since we were on an escape-and-evasion course I had no map and was alone. I knew that the town of Loer was nearby because I had studied a map of the area during the pre-exercise briefing. I also knew I was going to return to that magical little village isolated in the beautiful Bavarian Alps. I really wanted to meet these villagers who had suffered through two world wars, farmed their lands, raised their children, knowing that at any moment they and all they cherished could dissolve in a nuclear nanosecond. If ever I saw the utter futility of war, it was that night in that beautiful Bavarian valley, and its quiet village.

When my training was complete and I had received my Ranger certification, I returned to our base in Schweinfurt. I felt drained of all energy and took many hot showers and slept deeply. I know that the personal brutality of such training is at times worse than actual combat itself; or maybe the instructors had intended it to be that way. The cadre were dressed in Soviet uniforms, and when we were in the simulated prisoner-of-war camp, they did everything within their power to break the 'detainees'.

The American army was condemned by the world for the torture of prisoners at Abu Ghraib prison in Iraq. But in my opinion, the accused and jailed American soldiers were conditioned to render torture in training camps like mine; it was not their fault, and they should be turned free, and their generals jailed instead. They knew exactly what was going on in their chamber of horrors. The generals wanted results, and they knew how to get them. The low-ranking jail guards got the message through their immediate superiors, who were low-ranking officers and sergeants. While no direct order on paper was ever transmitted, a nod and a wink was clearly accepted as tacit approval for their tactics.

There is a chain of command in the American army that is fluid, yet rigid, and leaves no doubt what the upper echelon wants achieved. To understand why torture of enemy prisoners is routine in the American army, you only have to look at the conditions in the simulated prisoner-of-war camp where I was confined during my Ranger training: they were brutal. The Geneva Convention clearly forbids countries from training their military in prisoner-of-war torture techniques. The Pentagon had a solution: escape-and-evasion training. I realise this statement will not sit well with many people; however, that is the harsh reality of the truth, and sometimes the truth is the bitterest pill of all to swallow. To qualify that statement, I should say that the training is necessary and is designed to teach pilots and naval and military personnel how to survive if captured, or if they find themselves behind enemy lines. A segment of the training is how to resist enemy interrogation. There is no doubt that the exercises are critical if one is to refuse to divulge military information.

I believe that this type of training is vital and should be continued. However, there is one aspect of it that will stay with those who have endured it: being tortured. The training is normally undergone by career military personnel, sergeants and other officers. To rise in rank within combat-oriented units, you have to display intestinal fortitude, and these kinds of intense courses accomplish just that.

Some of the techniques that were used in the simulated prisoner-of-war camp I was confined in were far worse than those portrayed in photographs smuggled out of Abu Ghraib. My experience was this: thirty senior soldiers were released in the harsh winter of the Czech border with no equipment or food. They had to escape and evade capture and reach an objective in a certain period of time. The chances of evading capture were slim, as was intended. I escaped and was captured, then escaped again and was captured again. They had had enough of me and so put me in an armoured personnel carrier to transport me to the prisoner-of-war camp. It was dark, bitterly cold and snowing, and when the carrier stopped outside the camp, the soldiers exited through the rear ramp, while I exited up through the command hatch, and was gone again.

This time they threw a cordon around the area and caught me about a mile away. They bound and gagged me to make sure I was not going anywhere. The first thing I saw when we finished the bumpy ride was a brightly illuminated camp with what appeared to be Russian soldiers yelling in a strange language at American 'prisoners'. It was chillingly realistic. We were not to know that we would soon begin to feel like real prisoners, and it did not take long.

The camp looked and soon felt like a real POW camp. So much so that the cadre often got carried away and went beyond their scripted techniques, which were harsh enough. We were already exhausted and sleep-deprived. That was step one. We were disoriented and that was step two; but, so far, no problem for any of us. Then things began to get a little crazy. We were forced to stand naked in the snow and hold a heavy log up in our arms until the log dropped, and then we were kicked. Suddenly it was no longer a game: they were hurting people. Some prisoners were stuffed naked in a hole, one on top of another, head to butt, head to butt, and it was always one black soldier and one white soldier. I got to know parts of a black man's anatomy I never want to see again, and, I'm sure, vice versa. I knew that Ranger training was not intended to be a walk in the park, and that was all right with me – I could handle whatever they had in mind.

I was the last to be 'captured', so the other prisoners had been in the camp for some time. I had no idea what the conduct of the 'guards' had been in the earlier stages of their interrogation, when I arrived it was not reassuring. However, I figured that was just part of the scripted plan. Yet I began to sense that something was wrong, terribly wrong. The guards seemed to be taking their roles very seriously. A sergeant I knew began to scream incoherently after about an hour in an open-ended steel drum with a guard beating it with a steel rod, and I always thought he was a hard case. He seemed to be in disbelief at the harsh treatment, even though he was a veteran.

I myself was brought into a tent where a large tub of water was boiling on an oil stove in front of a metal folding chair. I was ordered to sign a paper that listed clothing that had been confiscated when I arrived at the camp. I knew it was onion paper and, once it was peeled apart, I would find I had signed a war crimes confession; so I refused. A guard yelled at me and told me he was going to stick my naked feet into the boiling water unless I signed the document. At that point I knew that there was no way in hell that was going to occur on a training mission, so I refused and was blindfolded. But then I felt somebody lift my legs and plunge them into the boiling water: the pain was excruciating. I felt the skin bubble up in blisters and peel from my legs. My scream of horror must have scared those prisoners outside in the worst way, then I mercifully passed out from the searing pain.

I awoke outside lying in the drum, behind the tent, and away from the other prisoners. At that point we believed we really were prisoners, and that is what they intended us to believe, which was impressive in itself, but there was something else going on. As I lay in the drum, with the maddening insanity of loud steel on steel pounding into my brain, I realised that the only thing wrong with my feet was that they were icy cold. Later I was to learn that after I was blindfolded they switched the boiling water for a tub of ice water mixed with broken ice. The human brain tells the body how to react to whatever crisis it encounters, so I experienced my feet being plunged into a tub of boiling water, and the pain seemed real to me. It had been a mind game, and an effective one.

We experienced other torture techniques in that camp which I will not detail; I believe the reader will have got the point by now. We were being trained to resist torture. However, we were at the same time learning to administer torture, simple as that. Something was obviously wrong in the camp because the guards were beginning to get personal with their prisoners. Racism and other aspects of man's psychological make-up came into play as the 'guards' began to act more like real guards, not role players. For whatever reason, the vast majority of the sergeants in the American army at that time were from the deep south, and it showed. Their attitude towards black soldiers was intensely unpalatable and their attitude towards me was similar because of my accent, for they assumed I was a yankee from the northern states. Race, religion and skin colour played a major role in the American military back then. As for today, I have no idea – I hope it has improved.

This was not my first army, so I knew the best way to survive within the military itself, if things went wrong – and they were going wrong here – was to keep a low profile, which I did. When we returned to base, so many complaints were made by the participants about the abuse that the coveted Ranger certification was being withheld: that was the end of my low profile. I had not filed a formal complaint; I wanted my certification. Even when some plain-clothes types asked me about the alleged abuse, I just shrugged and shook my head. They did not want the truth and that was obvious. But withholding my Ranger certification was too much for me to stomach; I raised hell internally. To this day I have my faded Ranger certification locked away in a box.

This first cold-weather Ranger training was conducted at the height of the Cold War. Normal initial Ranger training tended to be Vietnam-oriented, jungle warfare. Now, with the Russians threatening to surge down the Rhine Valley, Ranger training underwent a drastic transformation, and we were the first candidates, and the last.

For whatever reason, the US army abandoned the training

after our camp. I met a senior Ranger who was a jumpmaster and mountain warfare instructor in Dahlonega, Georgia, in 1996. I discussed the abuse and he winced, so I knew it was still happening. As recently as August 2007, the Marine Corps charged an instructor with 225 criminal charges involving the corps' recruits. These were not minor infractions but brutal physical assaults with tent poles and heavy metal flashlights. Two other sergeants were brought up on similar charges. To reiterate, the administration of torture at Iraq's Abu Ghraib prison by American soldiers was learned behaviour.

Going back to my personal experience in Bavaria, when I had recovered from the Ranger training I took a few days off and caught a train in the general direction of the small village that had so enthralled me. This time I had a map and stopped at the town of Loer, and I knew that my hamlet had to be close by. After wandering around and getting rides from friendly but puzzled Germans, I found the place. It had begun to snow, so I asked around for a place to stay and was guided to a small hotel, where I was met with more perplexed looks. It was obvious that the residents of this small town were wondering just what an American was doing roaming around in the snow in Bavaria. It was almost like I was an alien presence, which I was, I guess. The elderly owner, a tall stern woman, was coldly polite, but efficient. On the registration form I wrote 'Irish' as my nationality, which it was, legally. Then she smiled, and from then on it was open arms!

After settling into my very cosy room, I started to explore the tiny town. Word apparently spread fast and I was approached by a number of Germans who told me about the great times they had had in the west of Ireland fishing for salmon. As it grew dark, I found myself outside a small restaurant that looked inviting. It was warm inside and the décor was antique in nature with low lighting. I found a table at the back, where there was only a lone man at the adjoining table. He was eating sauerkraut and bratwurst, which looked and smelled good. I ordered the same from the waiter, a small, gentle older man, who turned out to be the owner.

There were few people out and about, what with the snow beginning to blanket the town. Now that I was actually inside the hamlet, I could see that it was exactly as I had imagined it to be when I was out on the slopes during Ranger training. Each window had a warm amber glow, and there was white smoke wafting out of all of the chimneys. It was truly relaxing there. I ordered a beer and the owner brought me a stein and a cold flip-top bottle of locally brewed beer. He also set on my table a basket of freshly baked bread and nodded to the man at the next table. 'That is Heinz, he is my brother. He was a prisoner of war in Ireland during the last war. He talks often about how much he likes your country.'

I was taken aback – a German prisoner of war in Ireland! I had heard a little about that, but now I had an opportunity to sit down and have a chat with a POW. Heinz waved and asked if he could join me when I finished eating. 'Of course,' I replied, glad for the company, especially after what I had just heard.

The meal was delicious and when I had finished Heinz joined me at my table. He was a heavy-set man in his early fifties with a round jovial face. He had crashed his bomber in the west of Ireland, and then spent the rest of the war in the Curragh army detention camp. From his account, he certainly did not sound like he had been in any distress during his prisoner-of-war days in Ireland. In fact he sounded like a typical Butlins holiday camp resident. I just had to ask, tongue in cheek: 'Heinz, was it not the sworn duty of all German officers to attempt to escape once captured?' He began to laugh so hard tears ran down his cheeks. 'For what? To get killed for that crazy wallpaper-hanging corporal, Hitler? No, I wanted to come home alive. Besides, everybody knew we would never win that stupid war with the Americans involved. No, I was happy to stay in Ireland.'

Word was sent out and two more former 'Irish prisoner-of-war' veterans arrived, with wives and a few teenage children in tow. We drank and swapped stories, and I told them I was a sergeant in the American army. They apparently liked Americans because they 'liberated' them from the Nazis. It was apparent that Hitler had little or no support in that part of Bavaria. I spoke a little German and they spoke a little English, but after a few drinks it did not matter any more. They would not let me pay for my meal or drinks. We sang 'It's a long way to Tipperary' so many times that I couldn't get it out of my mind for months.

The wives and children stayed for a while but left when the snow started to get heavy. It was then that the conversation began to get interesting, and they told me the true story of Germany and Ireland during the Second World War.

Yes, the German Luftwaffe did bomb Dublin. Everybody knows that, but why? It's an odd thing, but every German I ever met always fought on the Russian front; nobody seemed to have fought the British or Americans. As the alcohol loosened everybody up, the truth came out. Many of the bizarre bombings that took place in Ireland were done mistakenly by defecting Luftwaffe pilots. They were deserters and it was as simple as that. Although desertion does not sit well with me, considering the pilots' extreme circumstances, being answerable to a maniac, it made sense. The idea of these deserters provided an explanation for the Luftwaffe bombings. Some pilots got lost, and ended up over Ireland. It has been convincingly asserted that the British deflected the German homing signals, thus causing the bombers to target Ireland. I have no idea if that was the case. However, it is a plausible explanation for one reason: the British have such a long history of effective counter-espionage that I would not put it past their capabilities or motives.

As to the reason for the other bombings, Heinz said that many German pilots got lost and found themselves over the west of Ireland or some place far removed from their intended target. Rather than risk the flight home with a full load of bombs, and the need to explain why they had failed in their mission, they looked down at the pitch-dark Irish countryside and jettisoned their bombs. These were tragic decisions but sadly understandable. The electrification of rural Ireland was still not a reality, and much of it was indeed pitch dark at night. I remember well furiously pedalling my bicycle from our business in Dundalk down the dark Point Road to the Coastguard Station, sure that every goblin in hell was lurking in the bushes as I sped past. All the Luftwaffe pilots saw was what appeared to be uninhabited countryside as they unleashed their deadly load.

As for the bombing of Dublin, my German companions suspected that the intended target had been the Belfast shipyards. Due to poor navigation or as a result of those deflected signals, the pilots found themselves over shipyards. They dropped their bombs and that was 'mission accomplished' as far as they were concerned.

I found myself reluctant to dip my quill into this murky ink and write about these matters. All I have are the stories of a few former German pilots in a bar. However, what they said rang true with me; they had no reason to lie. As for the German pilots who had ended up being interned in Ireland, they obviously had no intention of dying for Hitler's war, so they just opted out. Where should they go? That also was simple. Being a POW in England did not appeal to them, after what the Luftwaffe had done to the civilian population in their bombing campaigns. Ireland was the only alternative. Heinz had dumped his bombs over the Irish Sea, then looked for a safe place to 'crash land' his bomber. He said he had no argument from his crew. So there it was – the truth in a small restaurant in a remote Bavarian village. Not much to it really, just normal people making decisions to survive; no conspiracies, no secret plans, just people's natural instinct. That evening seems like a long time ago.

Growing up in the Coastguard Station was a magical experience. While we often – sometimes dramatically – embellish or debase our upbringing, mine was privileged. Not because of money or power, which we did not have; but I was privileged by being a member of a close and loving family. My younger brothers, Terry and Canice, were, and are, the best siblings anybody could have beside them. Canice is a practising lawyer who has defended republican causes in the north. Terry became a respected senior executive in the aviation industry in Ireland and abroad. My sister Marna has a heart of gold; she is a great parent and a successful businesswoman and I am proud to be her brother.

My mother and father implanted in me a strong sense of where I should go with my life, and provided me with the courage to reach those objectives. My father's early life was cruel. Both his parents died at an early age and he missed much of the joy of a happy childhood, like the one he provided for me. He went to work at a very early age, hard physical work that would break many a grown man. When he was old enough, he fled his native Kilkenny and rarely returned. He was a good man, a good husband and a good father.

My mother was a dynamo of a woman. She had limitless energy for life all around her. She was a beautiful woman, a talented painter and clothes designer. I remember well her deep frustration at not being able to develop her talents because of economic constraints and severe social stratification, but she doggedly persisted. Today her paintings hang in famous homes. The late Irish president Eamon de Valera's family still has the oil painting my mother made of him many years ago.

I still have a photograph of my parents in formal wear taken at the Shelbourne Hotel years ago, when they were young. They were a handsome couple. I realise this sounds like a sanitised version of a family's life. Every family has problems. That is the way life is, and dwelling on the bad times is not a healthy thing for anybody. I believe that it is better for any member of any family to look back at the blessings that their families have given them, because soon we will all be dead, and it just won't matter any more. So I write about my family as I remember them – good and decent.

I was exposed to a startling dimension of my parents' personalities when they visited me in America. I shouldn't have been startled, but I was, considering the circumstances. When they flew to Washington to pay me a visit, my good and dear friend James 'Duke' Short and his beautiful wife Elaine went to great lengths to see that my parents saw Washington in the best light possible, and they were just the people to do that. Duke was the chief executive of the powerful US Senate Judiciary Committee. This group of senior senators chose judges for the US Supreme Court and all the judges within the federal judiciary. This gave them considerable power since these judges' decisions impacted on every aspect of American life. Senator Strom Thurmond, a staunch Republican, was the committee's senior chair and Duke was the senior member of his staff, which in turn gave Duke a lot of power. In fact Senator Joseph Biden, a Democrat and presidential candidate, admiringly called Duke, in open session, 'America's non-elected fifty-first senator'.

If you met Duke, he would probably strike you as a humble yet gregarious man, a man you could trust. I can honestly say that in the four decades that I have been a close friend of Duke, that opinion has never changed; if anything my affection and trust for him has grown. I know now what the definition of a true friend is, and Duke refined that definition, through good times and bad times for us both.

Duke, Elaine and I met my parents at the airport in Washington. It was their first visit to America and my mother's first comment to me as we walked to Duke's car was a classic: 'My God, Gerard, there are so many foreigners here in America, black and brown and Chinese.' Coming from the Coastguard Station and our then insular Irish society, it must have been a shock to be exposed to the melting pot of humanity that is America. I quietly reminded her not stare at all these 'strange' faces as she called them. It was only later that I fully understood her fascination with their faces: she was an artist and was entranced by all of the exotic people milling around her. I had to keep a close eye on her every time she visited America because she would begin to stare at some unsuspecting person with an interesting face. Needless to say she left behind some uneasy Americans in her wake.

How did my parents fare in Washington? To my great pride they moved around like they belonged there, even in the White House. We stayed with Duke and Elaine in their Virginia home and they were gracious hosts, treating my parents like visiting royals. My parents later visited me in Atlanta and Florida and captivated all those around them, and it was not my imagination. I am a hard-core realist, the sort of life I have lived has made me that way. So, when it comes to parents, I could not have wished for any better. I am very proud of them, coming out of our simple Coastguard Station in Ireland, yet being comfortable in their skins around the most powerful men and women in the world.

I have often wondered how far they would have gone in the

New World if they had made it there; probably very far. The Coastguard Station was and is a small place next to the water. My grandparents' home was a large house surrounded by eight others. The houses had been occupied by British Dragoons in the 1800s and their stables had lain behind my grandparents' home. Each house had property that extended at least a hundred yards back to the sea wall. My grandparents' place was separately walled. It is surmised that this was the home of the Dragoons' commanding officer.

The stables, long abandoned but still used as storage, were a place of mystery and excitement for me. They were filled with what adults called junk, but to a five-year-old with a fertile imagination, this 'junk' was mysterious old boxes and books covered in dust, treasures to be explored. Only one stable was off limits and that was where my uncle Vincent raised mushrooms. He had apparently read an article in one of my grandfather's handyman magazines on how to set up indoor mushroom beds. He really worked hard building the beds, much like bunk beds, with a special mix of soil, and then he sent to England for the actual mushroom-planting kits. Every once in a while he would allow me inside to observe the progress his mushrooms were making, which was not much. Try as he might, the mushrooms never grew beyond the size of tiny marbles.

It was in the big house there that I was to find great role models, and much love. My parents were busy every day trying to make a go of the business, and my siblings did not begin arriving until I was five years old. Even then it would take another two or three years before they were involved in any playful activity. So for a good seven years I was on my own to roam around the Coastguard Station. My grandparents raised eight children there: my mother Maureen and her two sisters, Betty and Ina, and five sons, Frank, Bill, Vincent, Kevin and Brendan. They were a pretty and handsome family, and a strong one. In the always-closed formal dining room was a large credenza laden with tennis, football and other sports trophies, and the walls seemed to be covered with medals for tennis and other sports. They were an active bunch of people and good to be around, especially since I was an equally active child. Weekends were filled with sporting activity in the now-grassed quadrangle in front of my grandparents' home, and I was not excluded.

However, it was Christmas that was a magical time for me, as I was the first grandchild and the beneficiary of gifts from my uncles and aunts. That ceased after more grandchildren arrived, but I was spoiled rotten while it lasted. Yet it was when everybody went to town to visit friends and left me alone with my grandparents that the real magic occurred at Christmas. My grandmother cooked at least eleven Christmas puddings, and I would help. Or so she had me believe. When she ran short of an ingredient, I would pedal my bicycle furiously up to town and get what she needed from my father's grocery. I now suspect that she just wanted me to feel important, which I did. She cooked the puddings the old-fashioned way, wrapped in white muslin and boiled. Never again would I taste moister, tastier Christmas puddings.

The O'Dowdas were a musical family, or at least some of them were. My grandmother played classical music on her piano until late in her life, and there were many musical recitals in the living room, with candles, a roaring fire and a few off-key Christmas carols from my uncles. My uncle Brendan was the only one who could sing. He was the youngest in the family, and went on to gain international acclaim as one of Ireland's most famous tenors. He would sometimes give me a ride on his bike to town, and we were close. However, there were just enough years between us to mean that playing together was rare. That said, uncle Brendan stayed in touch with me throughout our lives, while my other uncles and aunts drifted away, as relatives normally do, when their own lives became full.

Few Irish people know that Brendan O'Dowda could have made a considerable fortune, if he had taken advantage of the opportunities that America offered him. But he chose to stay as close to home as possible. Brendan headlined in Las Vegas in a big way, and when he arrived at the airport, a line of convertible stretch limousines escorted him to his penthouse suite at a luxury hotel, with him sitting in the front vehicle waving to the crowds who had come out to meet him. He showed me a 16mm film of his visit, and it was spectacular.

Brendan sang for royalty at a command performance at the Palladium in London, and he rubbed shoulders with the rich and famous, but he always stayed in touch with me; he was like that. When he came to perform in Waterford, he had his ivory Rolls Royce shipped over. I was at home from America on leave, and we had a great time roaming around. He had me sit in the back and acted like my chauffeur, but nobody was fooled: everybody knew who he was, and waved, and he waved back.

Brendan knew how to connect with people. Many years later, in 1998 while I was the managing director of the Irish branch of the international security firm, ADT, he flew over from London. We dined at the Shelbourne Hotel in Dublin. It was a long way from pedalling his bike up and down the Point Road in Dundalk with a few pennies in his pocket, and he was glad to have them at the time, as I was.

The real curse of immigration, I believe, is the break-down in communications within one's family. Many members of my beloved family passed away, and I would receive a letter when they were long cold in their graves. Today, the world is a much smaller place, but back then we all seemed to be living great distances apart; I might as well have been on the moon.

The art of 'progging' is a refined form of stealing other people's apples while they are still on the tree, which is practised at great risk and with considerable skill. I was a progger, and one of the best, if I may say so myself. There were many apple orchards in and around Dundalk, but the most challenging one was right next door to our home. George Elliot grew championship-grade apples in his small backyard. He only had four really choice trees that produced the juiciest red and green apples, but they were beauties, and he protected his apples as if they were virginal daughters living next to a naval base. No nicer man has ever existed, but in my childish mind, he turned into Count Dracula when his beloved apples grew close to maturity.

Progging time was known by everybody, which increased the risk for the progger. One can't pick the apples when they are too young and their taste has not fully developed, which provided a very limited time-frame for the progger's illegal operations. And to compound my problems, Mr Elliot always seemed to show up around our house just as his apples ripened, ostensibly to admire my father's roses, but I knew better. He would fix me with his snake charmer's stare and say to my father: 'Looks like I will have a nice crop this year, Peter. I am on the look-out for those boys from town.' As he spoke he never took his gimlet eyes off me. To me he was issuing a challenge, a dare, or at least that is what I imagined. He'd thrown his gauntlet down, and I mentally picked it up. He suspected that I had progged his orchard for the past four years, and he was right. He had also always suspected the boys from Clements Park, so he would sit in the front window, which left his back wall free and clear for me to make a quick raid. I think that after four years he began to suspect that the progger was closer than he had thought, like next door. So he erected additional defences and shifted his surveillance to the back of his house. This presented a major challenge, but he was on to me and had dared me to give it a try – at least it looked that way.

Mr Elliot had nothing to fear during the week, since I was in school. It was the weekends he had to worry about. Close to the fateful day when the apples would be picked, the tension grew. He knew that I was poised to strike, so he was on full alert.

One fateful Sunday, there was some weekend sporting activity going on in front of the coastguard houses. I walked away from them and positioned myself at the very rear of the sea wall. I could clearly see Mr Elliot watching the wall on his side, close to his apple trees. He was convinced that the progger would have to cross that wall to steal his apples. He did not move for hours, and I knew time was crucial. He had told my father he was going to pick his apples that day, knowing that I was standing there, listening.

I had been reading some of my grandfather's war novels about prisoners of war. The prisoners discovered that if they did something totally unexpected, the German guards seemed not to notice it. For example, they planted gardens around the camp commandant's hut at least three feet high. There they grew vegetables and flowers. Soon the other officers and guards ordered that the prisoners do the same for them. The camp became one big botanical garden comprised of the soil the prisoners had dug out of the ground to build their escape tunnels. It was so obvious, yet none of the guards paid any attention, until their prisoners were discovered missing.

So, in a similar vein, I did something unexpected: I sidled along the side of his house, right under his bedroom window. I was so close I could hear him cough. While he was concentrating on his wall, I walked straight through his garden gate, right under his nose, but out of his direct line of vision, and progged his orchard. I loaded up the front of my sweater with a dozen of his choicest apples, then walked back out undetected, mission accomplished!

That evening, I asked my parents if I could sleep in my grandparents' house, which was a regular event. My logic was that there was safety in numbers, because when Mr Elliot discovered he had been progged, all hell was going to break loose. It did not take long. I was hardly settled in my room, eating a delicious red apple, than there was a loud pounding on my grandparents' door. I heard angry voices, including my grandmother's and Mr Elliot's. I ran into my grandfather's small library and concealed the rest of the apples behind a bookshelf, then beat a hasty retreat to my room, and bed. I heard Mr Elliot say: 'I know Gerard took my apples just now; I want to wait until he gets here.' Apparently he had waited out the day and had gone down to pick his apples at dusk. My indignant grandmother declared that I had been upstairs in bed for hours. He was having none of that; he just knew I had sneaked out and raided his orchard. He demanded she check my room, sure that he had me. The only thing she saw when she switched on the light in my room was my angelic face composed in deep sleep. Mr Elliot left in a sour mood, certain it had been me, but helpless to prove his case.

The next morning my perfect crime began to unravel. My uncle Brendan volunteered to give me a ride to school on his bicycle, which was a little bit unusual. All was well until we got up on top of the hill next to the Dalys' house, then he said: 'I heard you eating apples in your room last night – they wouldn't be Mr Elliot's apples would they?' All this as he reached into my schoolbag and extracted two big juicy red apples. He stopped pedalling and put me on the ground. He asked me how I had done it, since he and his brothers had tried and been caught so many times they had given up. I explained how Mr Elliot had been looking straight ahead, and I had walked through the garden gate, unobserved. He never expected that anybody would be that foolhardy as to walk through his garden gate with him in the bedroom window upstairs. Brendan confiscated my two apples and I confessed where the rest were hidden.

That night when I got back to my grandparents' home the remainder of the apples were gone. I hope those hard-earned juicy apples helped his singing voice. Decades later, on a visit home, Mr Elliot paid me a visit at my parents' home to pay his regards, or so I thought. He asked about America and my other travels, as he sipped the tea my mother prepared for him. When we were alone, he dropped his question on me like a thousand-pound bucket of wet sand. 'Tell me Gerard, was that you who progged my orchard?' There was not much I could do but confess, which I sheepishly did, and me a big-time homicide detective in America – busted on my own turf at that! He grew excited and wanted to know the details of my escapade, so I told him the *modus operandi* of my heist. He laughed and could not wait to tell anybody who would listen just who the phantom progger really was. He seemed pleased that he had solved the case with a confession. If the truth be really known, I believe that he enjoyed the challenge of protecting his precious apples. I figured that out because each time I returned home he would come over to our home for another retelling of the story. He was a worthy adversary for the chief progger.

I was not to limit my nefarious activities to apples, for as I grew older, I discovered there were more exciting adventures out there: salmon adventures, or rather, illegal salmon adventures. There was not one plump, delicious salmon in Ireland that was not owned by a 'somebody', who always raised his eyebrows when emoting with a pseudo-British plummy accent. I have conducted business and socialised with this strange breed of Irishmen, who are neither Irish nor British, but can become one or the other when it suits their needs; I find them a singularly creepy bunch. These estate owners employ what best can be described as zombie wardens who protect their waterways, and their salmon. These grim guardians, who apparently never sleep, always keep their ears to the ground and can be counted upon to pounce out from the most unexpected places at the most unexpected times in the dead of night.

I always thought that the salmon in our area were so out of reach that even thinking about poaching them was unrealistic. Then I began to talk to Peter the poacher when he would come into our family pub. That is not his real name, but his sons and family still live in and around Dundalk, and it would serve no purpose to reveal his true identity. My father never said anything, but I sensed he did not like a convicted poacher frequenting our pub. But Peter was quiet as a mouse, and the other customers liked him, so that was that. For me, he was a Robin Hood, and when my father was not around, we talked. By then I was an accomplished fisherman and hunter, and had put many ducks, geese and fish on the family table. Terry, my younger brother, who went on to achieve major success in the airlines industry, was a constant corporate diner. He always said that my wildfowl had introduced him to that page of the menu many people avoided, but which the corporate diners relished. While I put wildfowl and fish on our family table, I never provided a cherished salmon, which I knew my mother and father craved.

Peter the poacher, as long as I knew him, was a decent caring person. My gut instinct told me to trust him, which I did, and he never let me down. I am reasonably certain that some reading this book will recoil from my description of Peter as 'decent', so please allow me to explain. Under British occupation, which was harsh to the extreme, times were difficult, food was not as plentiful as it is today and many went to bed with the ache of hunger in their bellies. And during the Famine when millions of Irish people died of starvation because of a potato blight, England actually shipped food out of the country.

Like rice to Asians, the potato was the staple food for the

Irish. The horrific sight of starving, dying people lying everywhere with green foam pouring from their mouths from eating grass did not move their British rulers to offer more than paltry help, like a few soup kitchens in Dublin. They had their motives, land consolidation and greed.

Every time an Irish farmer and his family died of starvation, their small holdings were added to a larger holding. These holdings were more productive and the proceeds were sent to their English landlords. There is another term for it today: ethnic cleansing.

While Irish people starved to death, they were surrounded by the large estates, castles and manor houses of their British occupiers. Within those guarded estates ran rivers filled with salmon, and their grounds teemed with fowl and game. Imprisonment or deportation was the penalty if one were caught poaching, and sometimes worse. Poaching became a necessity if a man was to feed his family. It was either that or sit watching your wife and children's bellies swell up and see the green slime and foam pour out of their mouths as they died in great pain and anguish.

I am also reasonably certain that some readers of this book may ask when we Irish are going to stop blaming the British for our problems, past and present. We are not blaming them, we just let the horrific facts of the brutal British occupation of Ireland speak for themselves, and our dead.

Peter poached not because of the long-gone British or hunger, but because he loved to poach and it was in his blood. His father and grandfather poached under British occupation; and they passed on the skills necessary to be a good poacher to Peter, who became an even more successful poacher. No British to blame there; Peter was just a natural-born poacher. He took his knocks gamely when the police and wardens grew tired of estate owners' complaints, and all fingers pointed at Peter the poacher – who else? Perhaps he should have adopted a less incriminating nickname.

Back in the marshes and fields around the Sally Gardens I would encounter Peter at work. He would sneak onto private lands and set rabbit snares, then bag them and wait for darkness to make his way home. He was not opposed to picking up a few potatoes and vegetables as side dishes for his pan-fried rabbit. He paid no attention to me, knowing I presented no danger, as I watched him go about his work. Actually the farmers appreciated some of Peter's work – the rabbits were a constant pest – and they did not begrudge him a few spuds and carrots now and then. It was when he ventured further that this cosy relationship soured.

Peter was to open up to me the mysterious world of poaching. He was to teach me hunting, tracking and concealment skills that later in life were to prove invaluable. They probably saved my life on many occasions – no, not probably, they did – not only in jungles, but also in the concrete jungles of major cities, where the rules for basic survival are the same. While many of his poaching skills were fascinating, none compared to his pheasant-poaching technique. Pheasants, the most luscious of all game birds, were always on the estates of the plummy-voiced people, with their game wardens who never slept and who guarded the pheasants as if they were the Christ Child. Pheasants are intelligent birds, especially those imported from Asia. They seem to fully understand that while people admire their magnificent plumage, it is for their broiled flesh, set on a tray and surrounded by choice vegetables and roasted potatoes that they are really prized. So pheasants have tended to be a cautious lot.

For Peter the first step to poaching a peasant was to drop by our local brewery and fill a sack with the discarded grain and hops, all saturated in alcohol, which are beloved by fowl everywhere. Then he went off to the flour mill where he would fill a bag with leftover grain. His last stop was at the horse market. There he secretly plucked some horse hair from some highly indignant horses' tails. When he showed me his technique, it was like watching a scientist at work. A little odd to be sure, but ingenious. In the privacy of his home and his kitchen table, he selected the best grains from the flour mill and placed them in the wet sour mash from the brewery. He covered the container, and let them sit in a dark closet for a week.

After a week he would remove the sealed container and take an appreciative whiff as if he were smelling a fine wine. He would lay out the horse hairs and the swollen corn on a newspaper. With a pair of sharp scissors he cut the horse hairs in three-quarter-inch lengths and then push the hairs through the damp corn. The last step was to allow the corn to dry in the sun for a while so that the hair was sealed inside the corn. The odour of the alcohol was not lost in the process, and that was important, for it was the alcohol that would attract the pheasants. He placed about fifty of the hair-filled corn grains in a plastic bag with some more of the grain mash. The only other equipment he needed was his trusty burlap, or woven cloth, poacher's bag.

One fine sunny day, when my parents were shopping in Dublin, I officially became a poacher. The night before had been an almost sleepless one; I was beginning to feel uneasy. It was one thing progging a few apples, which was almost a rite of passage in any boy's life in rural Ireland. But this poaching thing began to make me feel that I was crossing over an invisible line. I was graduating from a boyhood prank into more dangerous and illegal grounds. Anyway, I managed to shake off my feeling of unease as Peter and I pedalled towards Ravensdale, and an estate which he told me was 'crawling' with pheasants.

I knew the area from the far side of the woods, but had never been around the back. We crawled through the woods and bushes and made our way to an open area that Peter signalled was the location of the pheasants. My excitement by then had overcome my unease and nervousness. Years later I was to experience the same feeling, but then I had a gun, and it was men I was hunting.

Peter was right, there were pheasants everywhere. Plump, cocky, ring-necked pheasants strutted around in all their feathered glory, safe from predators because they were guarded night and day by apparently homeless zombie wardens who never slept, or so the pheasants thought. They were not to know that when the time was right, these same wardens would round them up for an afternoon 'shoot' for the landowner and his landed gentry friends. That sport was about as sporting as shooting them in a coop. The pheasants by that time had no fear of man, and had to be agitated by the wardens to lift off and fly. This would give the 'hunter' a clear shot.

At this point we realised that silence and stealth were critical. The pheasants would disappear into the bushes if startled. They were located about fifty feet away from us, and that was as close as we dared go before alerting them to our presence. On pieces of newspaper we laid out about fifty pieces of the corn and scattered about some of the sour, soggy grain, then withdrew to wait. It took about an hour for the first ring-neck to detect a whiff of the booze-soaked bait. He decided to investigate and brought some friends with him, all cocky, strutting, plump males. They spotted the grain and pounced, at the same time letting all the other pheasants in the area know that dinner was being served.

It seemed like hundreds of almost frantic pheasants converged on the grain; those birds certainly liked their booze. Almost immediately they started to run in giddy circles, and it was not from the alcohol, but the horse hairs. The hair stuck in the birds' throats and this confused them, so they could not fly. Pheasants are ground runners but get easily distracted. We gathered up twenty birds and beat a hasty retreat. Already we could hear whistles blowing and loud shouts, but they faded as they went in the direction of the main road. We decided to split up and make our separate ways home. That was easier said than done since it was broad daylight. I took four big males and Peter took the rest. I have no idea how that short, wiry man could shoulder such a load, but he did it effortlessly.

Peter kept four of the pheasants for his family. He dressed and dissected them so the meat looked like chicken, guarding against nosy, big-mouthed neighbours. My parents still had not arrived home, so I had time to pluck the birds and place them in the outside game chest. My father had constructed it in the wall of the house so that the cold air could circulate through the box and keep the game fresh.

Peter shipped the remainder of the pheasants to a five-star hotel in Dublin, who were regular customers, paid cash, and asked no questions. Years later I was a guest at that hotel, and had a delicious pheasant dinner. I wondered if Peter the poacher's sons – and he had four – were the providers; they probably were.

I went over to my grandparents' house and told my grandfather of my good fortune. I said that four pheasants had wandered off private property onto public land at the Sally Gardens and had become fair game, so to speak. He gave me a strange look, one I had never seen before, then rummaged around for an old cookbook. As I was leaving, he said quietly: 'Gerard, I can always hear you when you shoot over in the Sally Gardens, I did not hear you today. That is strange, don't you think?' So there it was, he knew all right, but never mentioned the subject again.

I made a hasty retreat to my home and ran back to him with the biggest pheasant. I did not tell my mother and father what type of wildfowl the three big birds were, but everybody enjoyed them immensely. Since neither my parents nor my siblings had tasted pheasant before, the meal passed without comment. Strange as it may seem, my grandfather and grandmother never uttered the word 'pheasant' in my family's presence. So, there you go; sometimes submission to delicious circumstances, however suspect, is the best road to travel.

My family and grandparents had some fine Sunday dinners of 'duck' while the going was good. Now that I had our pheasant supply chain established, it was time to expand and refine further my family's taste for fine dining: it was time for Irish river salmon. I have fine-dined all over the world, and tasted the world's best salmon, and none compares to our own. That should evoke yells of protest from the wild Alaska Sockeye and Atlantic salmon folks. I agree they are extremely delicious, but the delicate taste of freshly caught Irish salmon is beyond compare.

Peter the poacher, for some unknown reason, was reluctant to introduce me to salmon poaching. He knew I was an experienced fisherman. I persisted and he finally relented, but it was going to be a night operation. That actually presented no problem. By then I was serving in the FCA, Ireland's reserve defence force – equivalent to America's Reserve Officers' Training Corps (ROTC) – or as we were called, 'weekend warriors'. Later I was to realise that FCA training was excellent.

So, the problem of being away from home overnight was solved by my participation in the FCA. I told my parents I would be in Gormanstown camp for the weekend, and that was that. We made plans to liberate some tasty salmon from the estate of what we considered then to be some plummy-voiced lord of the manor and his soulless, sleepless game wardens. Peter referred to them as pseudo-Brits and said we were within our rights to poach their salmon. I had no idea what all that meant, but if Peter the poacher said that was so, then it was the truth. I had no idea that my secret little world with Peter was about to come crashing down on top of me in the worst way possible.

What I was not to know until much later was that Peter had used that justification to poach, which is a romantic word for stealing, on decent and good Irish people's land, and that the wardens were just decent hard-working men trying to do a difficult job.

At our last meeting, Peter's last words had been, 'This is going to be dangerous, Gerard, are you sure you want to go?'

If anything, that only piqued my interest. My excitement grew as we met at the bridge heading north that night. It was cold and raining. 'Better concealment,' Peter said. I followed Peter on my bicycle and we travelled about six miles or so, then the area began to look familiar, even in the darkness.

I asked Peter if it was going to be same estate as where we poached the pheasants, and he said no, and not to worry. But a growing feeling of unease began to envelop me, and I did not know why, and in retrospect, I wish I had known.

We concealed our bikes in some bushes and I followed Peter through the trees. He was carrying two large burlap sacks, one filled with something with sharp edges. We arrived at the river and followed it until it looped into a deep dark pool.

The rain abruptly ended and the moon began to light up the river. Peter started to grumble, only increasing my tension. He began to set out his equipment which was comprised of the components to make a carbide bomb. He assembled the bomb, inserted some kind of fuse, lit it and wrapped the bomb in a plastic sheet, weighed it down with rocks and threw it into the pool of water, all in a matter of seconds.

This had happened so fast I was stunned, then he grabbed me and said, 'Run, and when the bomb goes off grab all the fish you can and then run like hell.' A violent muted eruption in the pool indicated that the bomb had detonated. We ran back to see about a dozen big dazed salmon floating on top of the water. We grabbed them behind the gills and dumped them in his sacks, then we were off. This time I heard another sound aside from the whistles and the shouting: the sounds of gunfire. Somebody was shooting what sounded like shotguns, and they were close.

We ran to our bikes and peddled furiously for about a mile down the road, then Peter swerved into the trees. A vehicle was coming! We lay behind some trees and saw a Land Rover with four men in it, waving flashlights, and shouting that we had to be close. It began to rain again and eventually they ceased to patrol the wood line where we were concealed.

Still, we waited for a few wet chilly hours until we were sure they were gone for good. Then we broke up and headed home. He gave me two salmon and kept two for his family. He then shipped the remaining eight to the big hotel in Dublin. Everybody was still asleep when I got home. I concealed the salmon out in a shed and changed clothes, then left a note that I was going fishing on a river in Drogheda.

Instead, I walked over to the Sally Gardens. The rain had cleared up and the sun had come out. I lay in the sun and thought about what had just happened. I don't know how I thought Peter would catch the salmon, but a bomb! I was still mentally numb from the experience. As the morning stretched to noon I had plenty of time to think about things. What we had done was wrong, very wrong. And deep down in my heart of hearts, I was ashamed.

There was no excuse for my involvement in those crimes, and crimes they were, serious crimes. Whatever else happened that past night, I know that inadvertently Peter the poacher had taught me a critical lesson about honesty during those hours. I should have known better and my age was no excuse.

I swore that in some way I would make retribution to the people I had harmed, not really knowing how. As I lay there feeling the warm dampness of the ground on my back, I was not to know that the nightmare that I had participated in had just begun.

I decided that the best thing to do was not throw away the two salmon, but to give them to my parents and grandparents. I rationalised that it would be a bigger sin to waste the magnificent fish. I returned home the back way and picked up the two fish. I told my parents that they had strayed off private water and into the Annagasson River, which was public, and so was fair game. I then brought one big salmon over to my grandfather and told him the same story. I will never forget him sitting in his chair slowly stroking his moustache, his eyes boring holes in me, and then he said, 'Better take it back home.'

The short walk home was one filled with shame, but it was to get worse. The police came to our pub and told my father that I had been seen with Peter the poacher many times, and he was the chief suspect in bombing the river, the river of a member of my own family!

It was the property of a family member, someone I was not all that familiar with, but still my family. My father barred Peter the poacher from ever setting foot in our pub again. There is no sense in narrating his sad discussion with me. Suffice to say, my shame deepened.

The worst part of it all was that I had made my family complicit in my poaching by bringing the spoils of my illegal acts into our home. The next time I saw Peter the poacher he was shuffling down the street on his way to his menial job at Clarks shoe factory. I hardly recognised him, all bent over, and with his head down. The life had gone out of him, and he had aged badly, yet he was still a relatively young man.

This childhood experience forever branded into my heart

and soul that stealing and corruption were evil. I was not to know this credo would forever alter my life as I would embark later on careers that were corruption-ridden in law enforcement and corporate America.

Those life-altering experiences left me with nowhere to go in those circumstances, they gave me no grey areas, no room to bend the rules, and that was to impact upon me in dangerous and violent ways when I eventually ventured out into the world. But that was later.

# 2

# A GOOD BOY

I remember the day an American walked by our home on his way to the Navvy Bank for the scenic walk by the river. How did I know he was an American, even at my early age? I have never been able to pin that one down. I think you know an American instinctively. It's not the clothes; everybody wears the same clothes in this global world we live in. Maybe it's the skin, with the touch of a tan; but people vacation all over the planet now. If Americans open their mouths, that's a giveaway, but even if they don't, you can still tell.

My grandfather told me that you can always tell an American by the way they 'held themselves', which didn't really help me. So I do not have a clue. Oddly enough, even after years of working in America as an undercover policeman I have never been taken for an American, and this has saved my life. We are all animals, I guess, and like those in the wild, we can tell our own species.

Anyway, the American outside our home stopped and studied the plaque on our gate, then motioned for me to come over to where he stood. He asked if he could speak to my parents. I knew my mother was washing her hair so there was no way I was going in the house, so I shook my head. He smiled and removed the cap from my head. He fumbled with it for a short time and then placed it back on my head at a different angle – I've worn my hats like that ever since. The name of our home was 'Watergate'.

It was only when I was asleep that my mother discovered the hundred-dollar bill inside my cap band. Times were hard then, and a hundred dollars was a lot of money. Many years later as I stood waiting for my Aer Lingus flight to take me to America, my mother pressed the hundred-dollar bill into my hand: 'I knew you would go to America, so I saved this for you.' With my last hug, I stuffed the bill into her purse. Times were even rougher then, and a few pound notes and some coins in the till of our business was a good day's work.

By the time I reached the streets of New York City all I had left was five dollars. Not keeping the hundred dollars had been a mistake, a really big stupid mistake. New York at any time is a very expensive city, but in the dead of winter with snow on the ground, it was no place to be with just five dollars in your pocket. Today they arrest people like that and call them vagrants. If the truth be known, I could not have cared less: I was in America and could feel the ground under my feet, and it felt good. As long as I had my health there was no obstacle I could not overcome. I honestly felt that way as I stood in the blowing snow taking in the sights and sounds of this wondrous city. Taxis, limos and private cars were honking and people were blowing whistles and yelling at everybody and everything for no apparent reason – and it's the same this very day.

I soaked myself in this giant city; its sights, sounds and smells intoxicated me. As soon as I saw the skyline of New York glowing through the snow, I knew I had arrived, and nothing else mattered. Well, something did matter: where was I going to stay? It's not that I had not given that some thought – I had. The military attaché in the American embassy in Dublin had looked at my Irish army papers and said the American army really needed people like me. He said he would transmit the information to the New York US army recruiting office and all I had to do was go there and they would immediately process my enlistment papers.

I soon learned that from point A to point B in America is sometimes not a straight line. Come to think about it, probably not anywhere. Without going into all the comical, frustrating and dangerous moments I experienced, I made it into the centre of New York, still with my five dollars. I slept the remainder of the night in a very warm subway, just getting nudged once in a while by nosy people and cops. Since I had my suitcase, everybody assumed I was waiting for a train or something. It gave me some degree of respectability, I guess.

The next morning I went to the army recruiting office. They looked at my paperwork and had me fill out more paperwork. I was asked where I wanted to be assigned after basic and advanced infantry training. Since I had had some communications training, I chose Fort Monmouth in New Jersey for communications training. They asked what my second choice was, and I chose Europe. I was not to know you always got the second choice. I assumed that I would then begin the entry process but that was a wrong assumption. The grizzled, medal-bedecked sergeant told me it would take at least a week to process my papers and that I should check back every day or so. That news presented a new set of challenges because five dollars in New York would not rent a cardboard box. I asked him if I could store my suitcase in his office. He just shrugged and told me to put it in a back room where he stored his promotional material.

I took a change of underwear and my overcoat and went out to see the city. I roamed around and was absolutely amazed at the height of the skyscrapers. I stood on a street corner and looked up at the wonder of it all. There was so much noise and so many people, everybody going someplace in a great hurry, and nobody looking at anybody. I wanted to buy a hot dog from a street vendor, but that would have depleted my remaining cash, so I started to get serious about my current situation, which was not good. That said, I was happy to have my papers processed and all I had to do was survive for a week or so, on five dollars, in New York City.

One thing I discovered about Americans was that you have to pick the right one to ask for assistance. I was in the middle of the financial district when I stopped two well-dressed men. I asked them if they could assist me. Without breaking stride both reached into their pockets and handed me some coins; they thought I was a beggar. I was stunned and ran after them trying to give them their money back. Both of them backed up and one handed me a dollar, obviously intimidated and believing that I was protesting at the small amount they had initially given me. I pushed the money at them and took off at a brisk pace, red faced. My first day in America and I was a beggar!

After that illustrious start in my new world, I decided I needed to observe a little more before venturing into further communications with these Americans, so I just roamed around. After all these years and having had the best New York has to offer – food, Broadway shows, luxury hotels and fine dining – the city still awes me. This giant metropolis was built by immigrants, many of them Irish like me, who toiled to raise this marvel out of the ground. It's not Paris, London or Rome – it's the New World.

As the day wore on, I decided I had to find some place to sleep and buy some food. I saw a policeman standing by a newspaper stand and approached him. He was stocky and Hispanic, and friendly. I decided the best approach was just to tell him the truth. He listened and gave me the address of a public shelter where I could stay and get a free meal. I thought about that for a minute. I had already been mistaken for a beggar, now I was to become a vagrant! I asked if there was a park nearby and where I could buy some cheap food. He just shook his head and wrote down directions to a surplus food store and a park, then offered me a dollar.

Right then I knew I had to improve my social profile in America. I found the surplus store and bought two loaves of day-old bread and two pounds of suspect sliced baloney for a dollar and a half. Then it was on to the park, or famed Central Park. I was reasonably well dressed so nobody paid much attention to me as I roamed around looking for a place to sleep. I found my new home: it did have a ritzy address, with an impressive view of some of the city's most beautiful buildings, but it was a stone bridge. It was snug enough underneath this small scenic bridge. However, I knew that as night would fall soon, and snow flakes would be swirling around, I had to find insulation if I was going to survive. I already knew where to find it. On chilly nights when I finished working at our bar, I would pedal to our home at the Coastguard Station. The wind would cut through you like a knife, so I stuffed a newspaper down the front of my sweater and did not feel a thing. On the way into the park I saw many large, wire trash baskets brimming over with fast food containers and newspapers. I commenced my rounds and by the time I had dug through three baskets I had been approached by no fewer than four people with sad eyes who offered me money. I politely declined, but began to wonder if a career as a professional beggar in America was such a bad idea.

The oval interior of the bridge was about ten feet across, with bushes at either end. I cleared an area for my resting place and laid out my many newspapers as a bed. I knew already that if you shaped the dirt you were going to lie in to the contours of your body, it was a remarkably comfortable place to sleep (all this compliments of the Irish army). Covered in newspapers and my overcoat, sleep came easy. I figured that all this was part of the package, lots to learn along the way, something here and something there – learning the ropes, life's hard and easy lessons. But I was here, the first step of my journey, and I was happy.

I roamed around the next day and walked into the New York Broadway district. What an experience! Broadway shows were being headlined and I saw many actor types shaking papers at each other and reading out loud. I was to learn these were aspiring actors on the way to readings, looking for a shot on the most famous stage of all. London's West End and all of the other famous theatre districts of the world may present stunning stage performances – and I have attended more than a few – but Broadway has the glitz. If you are an actor, here is where you get the attention if you are lucky enough to grace the boards.

All in all, I still had three dollars, and I was living rent free in New York; I had no reason to complain, except for my diet. The bread was holding up well because of the frigid temperature; however, the baloney, which was a little green around the edges to start with, was beginning to become a culinary challenge, and an ingestion one. I had candles for light, and now I needed something to cook with. I made my daily trip to the army recruitment office and was told not to worry and that it was just a matter of time. The sergeant allowed me to live out of my suitcase. He had a monthly quota to make or he was back in the trenches, so he could not have cared less if I lived under his desk. He knew I was living 'rough' as he called it, so I asked him where I could get a frying pan. He told me to sit in his office for a few minutes. He left and did not return for an hour. No potential recruits came through the door and it occurred to me that I might have been be a precious commodity in the sergeant's life.

When the sergeant did return he had an army sterno cooking stove and ten cans of sterno fuel. He also had matches and an army knife, fork and spoon, and a mess kit. There was no way he was going to let anything happen to his Irish recruit. I suspect he went to an Army & Navy surplus store and splurged a few dollars.

I returned to my bridge and rearranged my abode – it was becoming 'downright cosy', as the Americans say. I had blocked off the ends of the bridge with plastic bags, and my space was tolerable enough for me to be able to sleep in with just my overcoat on. I set up the sterno stove and had it going in no time. I placed the small frying pan on it and fried some baloney. That was after carefully trimming the green mould off the edges. There was enough fat content in the baloney for it to fry well. I then fried two pieces of bread in the remaining fat until they were crispy and brown. That evening I feasted on the first hot meal I had eaten since arriving in America; I felt warm and wonderful. The aroma was rather nice and after a very short time it attracted a stray dog who sat and whined outside my abode. She was a mongrel and had big eyes and was shivering in the cold. I let her in and made her a sandwich; she was obviously starving and exhausted. Immediately after eating she went to sleep on some newspapers. I decided to call her Molly Malone. The smell attracted more than just Molly, because soon after I had fallen asleep I felt a gentle tapping on my heels, and woke up. I looked out and saw a very big New York City policeman.

'Hey buddy, what are you doing under there?' he said.

'Just trying to stay warm.'

He looked at me closely for a minute and said: 'You wouldn't be from Ireland, would you?' His Irish accent was as thick as butter on a cold morning. He clambered under the bridge and sat on a milk crate I had liberated from a nearby hotel. He was a big man with a strong face, an Irish face.

'What are you doing living under this bridge?' He seemed relaxed and bemused.

'I'm waiting for the army to process my papers. It'll be any day now'.

'What's with the dog?'

I explained that Molly had come by when she smelled the food. He examined her and shook his head. 'You better not get attached to Molly; she has a collar and the owner's phone number is on there.' He wrote down the number and said he would call the owner tomorrow. He also explained that few if any homeless people ever came to Central Park; they normally hung around the Bowery or the docks. The only reason he discovered me was because of the smell of my baloney. We talked far into the night about Ireland. He had come to America with his parents when he was ten, and had not been back since, what with children and a home to pay for; but he was going back to retire there with his Moira. Dennis Murphy was his name, and he was a nice man, a good man and probably a good policeman.

The longer we talked the more we both missed home, and our eyes welled with tears. He invited me to stay in his home until my papers were processed, but I declined. I was close to the recruiting office and I probably only had a few days to go. He insisted that at least he pick me up early Sunday morning for mass and Sunday dinner.

Sunday morning I cooked Molly a batch of fried baloney and she seemed content with that. She was a good dog who fretted when I left to visit the recruitment office and seemed genuinely glad when I got back to what was now my home. She snuggled up to me at night and, to be honest with you, I was glad for the company. True to his word, Dennis drove by in a station wagon with wooden side panels. It was meticulously clean and waxed to a high sheen. I had never been in an American car before so the station wagon felt like I was in a Dublin bus. He was dressed in a suit and just shrugged at my clean but far-from-a-suit clothes.

Dennis drove over to the Bronx and I entered the world of the Irish American. His wife Moira looked like any one of my aunts, and their four children were not shy like Irish children, just curious and polite. They lived in a four-bedroom apartment which they owned. I am not sure if it was a flat or a condominium by today's standards, but they possessed the title and that was a source of great pride. We all got into the station wagon and Dennis drove us to St Patrick's Cathedral. This venerated place, I later learned, was soaked in Irish American history. They did not normally attend mass there but just wanted me to see the church.

After the mass, Dennis picked up some Sunday papers, including a week-old *Sunday Independent*. (Aer Lingus was good enough to bring a stack over on their daily flights.) The two boys, in their teens, badgered their father to drive by a gym supply store. After much grumbling Dennis parked in front of the store, and the two boys jumped out, dragging me with them. In a side display window, two voluptuous girls in bikinis were doing some erotic weight exercises as a growing crowd looked appreciatively on. If ever I needed justification for leaving Ireland, it was in that window – and on a Sunday! Moira cuffed the boys and that was that. Such a display in Ireland would have had the bishops and the parish priests burning buildings and screaming heresy. On second thoughts, a few priests I knew well just might have enjoyed a glance, strictly for religious purposes, I am sure. It was obvious that this first-generation Irish American family had elevated themselves from the 'dirt poor' existence both of them described back home.

Dennis was a highly decorated police officer whose job routine had changed after he slighted a UN diplomat who, like many other diplomats, had hundreds of illegal parking tickets. It appeared that the diplomat's wife or mistress had been constantly blocking a fire hydrant – a crucial apparatus in a metropolis like New York – with her car, using diplomatic licence plates. After the area fire station commander had written a series of complaints about the blocked hydrant, Dennis found his captain breathing down his neck. Enough was enough, so Dennis had the diplomat's Mercedes towed to a police impound lot. All hell broke loose as the UN ambassador from some remote tiny country lodged a formal protest. The next thing Dennis knew was that he had been reassigned for a month to a walking beat in Central Park, and I was glad of that.

Supper at the Murphys' consisted of Irish potatoes, boiled cabbage and ham, and it was the best meal I have ever tasted. It was a nice easy evening and we drank a few American beers, and they were not bad, all things considered. Dennis regaled me with stories of police work and said: 'When you get out of the army, come back here with us and I'll get you on the force.' He said that a George Mac Manus was chief of detectives and that would not hurt, since we shared the same name.

Dennis and Moira drove me back to my bridge. I guess Dennis failed to mention my living conditions, because Moira threw a fit. She was outraged and wanted me out from under the bridge. I tried to explain my situation but all she did was grow angrier at Dennis. Finally, when she realised I was not moving out from under my bridge, she gave up and they left, she still berating poor Dennis.

For the next week, when I returned from my visits to the recruiting office there would be a hot meal and a thermos full of soup awaiting me. Dennis would drop by to pick up the empty thermos and we would chat. He had contacted the owner of Molly and she was distraught. Apparently she hired a dog walker to exercise Molly each day, and the dog had broken loose in the park. Frank brought the lady by the next day and once again I was introduced to something I had never experienced before: a wealthy American dog lover. The elderly lady had a nurse and what appeared to be a man-servant with her. Dennis brought Molly up from under my bridge and you would have thought Molly was her long-lost first-born. She gave me a few suspicious looks until Dennis explained that I was a good person. She told her man-servant to give me a hundred dollars for my trouble. I refused until Dennis stepped in and said: 'The reward is actually a thousand dollars, take the money.' I had recently declined another hundred dollars with disastrous results, so I took the money.

That night I was settling in to sleep when I heard a familiar whine outside – it was Molly. She slept well that night and the next day the woman and her staff came back and reclaimed her. For the next four nights Molly always returned and had her sleep, and her now thoroughly-miffed owner would pick her up in the morning.

Dennis and Moira and I stayed in touch, but communications then were not what they are now. I know they returned to Ireland on a holiday to visit Donegal and their old home and that they were sorry they had done so since there was nothing or nobody left. I never did join the New York City police department, or even try to: my life's winds took me on a different course. Dennis and Moira evaporated from my life and I truly wish they had not.

Decades later, when I was an executive with ADT, I would travel to New York to their executive offices atop the World Trade Center, and eat at Tavern on the Green and other up-market restaurants. But when I was alone I would take a taxi to Central Park and my bridge. I would sit under my bridge and think about those days, so long ago, and Molly, Dennis and Moira. My life was blessed by them being in it – there is nothing surer than that – and I miss them. It's always that way in life, it seems; the good people you wish were still either alive or still close to you are gone.

I never really talked about my first days in America, because there were no family members around for a while. Years later when I did talk about living under my bridge, it was not a sad tale; it was just life. I can tell you that in later years I sometimes wished I was back under that bridge! If ever there was irony in my life, it was that bridge. It is called the Trefoil Bridge and is located along the park path near the boathouse and the lake. When I stayed there it was closed for some repair work that I never saw happening – council workers are the same the world over. There is a shamrock cut out of the stone on the bridge, which is where the Trefoil name came from. If you can rent a copy of actor Jack Lemmon's classic movie *The Out-of-Towners*, my bridge was a central backdrop.

I am dwelling on that bridge for a reason because it was there that I began to know myself. In the absolute silence that existed under the bridge, I had time to think about my life, and how it had been. I thought about my home at the Coastguard Station which I had just left, and it came into clear focus: a house set against the backdrop of the mountains of Mourne and the sea that made the house, on certain sunny days, seem to be like a three-dimensional photograph. Then, on other wet, dark, rainy days, it all sank into itself. The magic of Ireland lies in its incredibly deep civilised history. Perhaps that might explain our collective interest in our own history. Charley McCarthy, who bought my grandparents' home, conducted extensive research on the Coastguard Station, and it makes for fascinating reading. Our home, the venerated 'Watergate', used to be a bawdy public house, or bar, in the 1800s. No wonder I heard strange, ghostly noises at night when I was a child.

If there was a negative about living at the end of the Point Road, it was the drunk drivers. The road came to a dead end at our front door, and I mean our front door. During my early years, blind-drunk drivers tried to drive north. Their only problem was that our home, the river and the mountain stood in their way. They could have taken any number of roads to get home, but the Point Road was not one of them. My father had an oval wall constructed around the front of our house; even then some drunk took a shot at his wall.

Down that same road for hundreds of years came smugglers, emigrants catching a boat to Liverpool, and men in black on their way to tear at the shanks of the British army, just a stone's throw away. The Point Road and the Coastguard Station have a thousand stories to tell, if only they could talk. The emigrants and sailors drank in our house before they sailed, and for those who had to stay overnight due to bad weather, there was the Daley boarding house just up the road. Directly behind our home was the large stone boathouse with a slip, where the passengers stored their luggage if they stayed overnight.

Paddle steamers like the *Magdalina*, captained by sailors like Tom Jordan, made the trip to and from Liverpool, ferrying people twice a week for two shillings. These ships weighed 109 tons and, on a good day, could get up to forty horsepower. Due to the hard times then, I suspect there were more vessels going than coming. I have always associated paddle steamers with Mark Twain and the Mississippi River, but Charley McCarthy's research showed that they used to dock in a boathouse behind our home, yards from my bedroom, long before I was born.

It was once in that big old boathouse that I nearly died, in the stillness of a warm summer's afternoon. That's the problem when you are a child – people thinking you will be fine roaming around close to home. I had squeezed through a loose plank in the back door of the boathouse and entered a magical world of interesting smells and sights. The afternoon sun pierced the darkness through holes in the wood covering the windows. These bright shafts of yellow light illuminated an old lifeboat, overturned on wooden blocks, and sea-going things were everywhere, and there was a sweet smell. There were old rusted anchors and thick ropes that smelled of tar, and a few old rotting sails, and a wooden box on a shelf. I pulled at it and the box came crashing down on top of me, spilling its contents onto the hard stone floor. I was not to know, as a child, that I was in mortal danger. The wooden box contained eight-inch sticks of very old dynamite.

That day in the boathouse I came as near to death as I ever have done. When the wooden box came crashing down on me, blobs of a yellow substance struck the floor. It was nitroglycerine and extremely volatile. While it would normally require a detonator to detonate the dynamite, the nitroglycerine itself was susceptible to explode if violently jarred, which it just had been. There was enough dynamite in that box, if it had exploded, to destroy the boathouse and our home. Each stick of dynamite was wrapped in oily wax paper which was weeping nitroglycerine. I smelled the clear yellow liquid and dipped my finger in it for a taste, because it looked like toffee. It had an oily taste.

I decided to take two sticks to my mother. When I reached our home I could hear my mother screaming for help: her ring hand was stuck in our new electric washing machine's wringer. I threw the two sticks of dynamite to the floor and helped her free her hand. I saw her eyes widen in horror, then she grabbed me and we fled our home she had spotted the two nitroglycerine-bleeding sticks of dynamite. To this day I do not know how my sainted mother was instantly able to recognise unstable dynamite, but I have my suspicions. She was a staunch supporter of republican causes, and it's best left at that.

What followed is a blur in my memory bank. My father arrived on the scene with a policeman, soon followed by an army truck. My grandmother came and brought me to her home, tut-tutting all the way. My grandfather brought me back to his clock repair room in the back of the house; nothing was said, and that was that.

If that was a close call, there was worse to come, much worse, and all within hearing distance of our home. That is why, when raising two sons, I have never taken for granted the safety of our home. At best it is a false sense of security; things happen, and sometimes they are bad things. When the sky was clear blue on a chilly spring day, the incoming tide created an almost picture-postcard scene, what with the mountains in the background. I had constructed an imaginary boat out of stones at the water's edge, and I'd sit there until the incoming tide eased me out, wet and shivering, while in my mind I had sailed far away.

One morning I was late and when I arrived at my 'boat' I discovered that I had company. It was a massive black round thing with prongs sticking out of its sides. It was a German sea mine, capable of sinking a large ship upon contact. It had escaped its sea anchor and had drifted into Dundalk Bay – directly behind our home. I started to pound on it with a large rock – too young to realise the danger I was in. I was determined to discover just what was inside this massive black thing. I guess, as children normally do, I tired and went home, unaware of just how close to death I had been as I pounded upon the deadly high-explosive device. Later in life, when I became an expert in explosives, I would often shudder at the thought of my narrow escape. The next day it was gone.

It was with memories such as these that I passed time under my New York bridge, thinking about things, about my life, and dreaming of where I would go. I thought about our family pub and grocery store, and the magic of it all. My mother and father had built two solid businesses during hard times. There was not much profit at the end of the day, but we lived well. Everybody assumed that we were wealthy, as busy as we were, but it was all about buying and selling and keeping food on our table and meeting our financial obligations. It takes a lot of guts to leave the security of a regular salary and strike out on your own and open a business. My parents left me that legacy and I needed it in later life.

The grocery is long gone, but our pub is now one of Europe's most famous watering holes, thanks in a large part to one of Europe's most famous singing groups – the Corrs. I remember those beautiful girls working part time in the pub when I returned home on vacation, and Andrea pulled me a pint of Harp once or twice. Andrea released her first solo album, *Ten Feet High*, in the latter part of 2007 and it flew off the shelves as expected. Born and raised in Dundalk, the entire family can best be described as remarkable. Musically talented, they were, and still are, hard-working, nice people. I cherish a signed photograph of the Corrs, sent to me by their mother, Jean, in January 1996, saying she was sorry for not sending a picture earlier but her children had been out of the country 'until Friday last, 23/1/96'. Sad to say, she went long before her time. Our family sold our pub to the Corrs' aunt, Lillian McElarney, and when the money was finally good, the Corrs bought it from her. As the eldest in the Mac Manus family I wish to thank Lillian and the Corrs for keeping our father's name over the door because that was a nice thing to do.

Workers, musicians, scholars and poets, writers, sports people, doctors, debaters and just about every kind of human being feel welcome there. The sign over the door spells Mc Manus instead of Mac Manus because the original sign painter forgot the spelling, so my father just left it the way it was, and that's the way it stays. That mistake was a bone of contention with some members of our family. The Mc and Mac spellings are serious business to some people. Others, like my father, just don't care.

Our grocery store was not just a place where one would come for the basics. My father had worked for Carlins, which was Dundalk's largest wholesale importer. When he sent me there to buy supplies for our shop, the exotic smells from the coffees, teas and spices were almost intoxicating. It was a wonderful place for a young, wide-eyed boy. One of the men, with curly red hair, who had worked with my father, always treated me well. He would stop what he was doing and get me what my father needed. He said my father was a good man and I wish I could remember his name.

With the contacts he had at Carlins, my father stocked our shop with some odds and ends not available in similar small shops. He had grapes delivered in wooden kegs, packed in cork pulp; bananas from Jamaica; oranges from Africa; and teas from Ceylon. I truly liked working in the shop. It was a respite from school, where my performance was dismal at best. I just could not get interested in the drone of teachers who were trying to teach me the basic skills I would most certainly need in later life. They did their best, but I was just not there; I was oceans away, academically a lost cause.

My father's shop delivered groceries and other things. Although he had a delivery boy, he also had me to make special deliveries on my bike, taking envelopes to the families of jailed republican prisoners. When I knocked on those doors, a woman – it was always a woman – would say: 'You are a good boy Gerard.' I now know I was delivering dollars from America. While the police kept an eye open for such activities, nobody paid any attention to a very young, snotty-nosed boy delivering groceries on his bicycle. I did what I did because my father told me to do so.

While the Coastguard Station in itself was a fine place for a young boy to grow up, it was the back banks where all of the really interesting things happened. Few people took the time to cross the fields to reach the long dam that stretched all the way to the next town of Blackrock. Without the dam, the spring tides would have flooded the farmlands. Behind the dam were the Sally Gardens and a few small rivers, an area rich in wildlife.

On the sea side of the dam is some of the best wildfowl hunting in Ireland. It was there that I first met 'Cobie' or James Coburn, who, without a doubt, was one of the best shots and wild fowlers I have ever encountered. While I had Christopher Taylor to pal around with on the front bank, I now had Cobie on the back bank. I still have a photograph of his one-day take of wild ducks, probably thirty of them.

It was there on the back bank that I saw men do things I did not understand; but I do now – they were training to engage the British army. Later in life I became a so-called internationally recognised expert on terrorism. Nowhere have I witnessed a more cunning, effective and frankly hilarious example of 'terrorists' coexisting with their own society than on that back bank.

Halfway along the dam is a large Irish army rifle range. It is utilised on a regular basis by the regular and reserve forces. The long firing range faces towards the sea, and the army engineers constructed a deep, tall earthen backdrop to absorb the incoming bullets. It was directly behind the earthen backdrop that the 'men in black' – I call them the 'men in black' because I used to see them pass by our house in black combat gear, on their way across the river to avoid roadblocks – practised their marksmanship.

For years the government could not figure out just how the shadowy army managed to train its members in firearms. Ireland is a very small country with strict gun laws. In rural areas everybody pretty much knows who is shooting at what, not that there is a lot of shooting. Well, it was right under the Irish army's nose that the men in black conducted their firearms training. The firing range's earthen backdrop was perhaps a hundred feet high from top to bottom. The soldiers of the Irish army could fire at it from a hundred to three hundred yards. The targets were raised and lowered manually by soldiers safe in their bunkers. These 'spotters' would signal each round fired with a black metal disc, placing the disc on the last round fired. This effectively showed the shooter and the trainer where to make adjustments. The shooting was done in barrages, and the men in black were able to join in: all they had to do was to coordinate their firing with that of the military and nobody was the wiser. Their boldness defied belief. A republican spotter would conceal himself on the side of the embankment and signal when the army was about to commence firing. After that the black-clad shooters needed no further signal as the thunderous sound of many .303 Lee Enfield rifles reverberated across the back bank. Nobody ever noticed that the men in black were training alongside the members of the Irish army, or maybe they did and just did not care.

I walked up on the men in black one day while they were training. I instantly recognised them all from our pub. They told me to pick up all the expended shells and empty ammunition boxes, and said they would give me five pence. Once in a while they would let me fire a pistol, and I was surprisingly accurate. All of the weapons were from America: Smith and Wesson and a few US army 45s. They always seemed to have plenty of ammunition, probably from the same American source. What with so many ships plying the Atlantic route to and from America, it was relatively easy to smuggle in a few cases of munitions now and then.

When their training sessions were complete, the men would start to drift away, one at a time, just men out for a walk, a common sight. I would see them later in our pub, quiet men who sat apart from the others in dark, smoky nooks and crannies, always whispering, heads down and close. The other customers never seemed to acknowledge them, not even with a nod of recognition. Those were dangerous times and spies were everywhere.

My job was to pick up empty glasses from the tables, but not theirs; they would keep the same glasses all night and would send me for refills. At the end of the night I would wash their glasses until my hands turned blue under the cold water. I did not know it then, but I was washing off the fingerprints of bombers that the British secret services would have given their eye-teeth for.

Dundalk is a border town and was the launching pad for the vast majority of all republican raids against the British army just a few miles away; and our pub was ground zero for many of the men in black. The pub is frequented now by a much younger generation who have no memory or personal experience of such things. Some of the old timers still come in looking for their hard-earned stools and seats, but mostly during the day when the pub is quiet.

When I walk into the pub today the memories wash all over me as if it were only yesterday that I worked there. I can imagine faces long gone, their voices stilled by their passing. I can feel the warmth of being home, for it will always be my home. I always go to the back room, where the men in black would sit with their heads down, and wonder where they are now. I remember the nights when those men were not in the pub, and I knew then that a spy was in there, and everybody knew who the spy was – a doomed man. Spies would later meet their end on the way north to Newry, which was occupied by the British army.

It was insane to attempt to penetrate the suffocating closeness of our pub, yet they kept coming, and dying. I would be asked by the men in black, who sat in cars down Mary Street, who the spy was talking to. Those people might as well have walked into our pub with a sign around their necks that said: 'I am a British spy.' Although I was an unwitting participant, the memories of those people still hang around in my mind. So much went on in that pub and so few people knew about it. To a stranger our pub was just a friendly place to have a drink and meet nice people. To this day there are former customers and family who will rear back in disbelief when they read these pages. All this intrigue was swirling around them and they did not know; how could that have been possible?

The British intelligence services are the best in the world. Yet, while dominating the tiny country of Ireland for hundreds of years, they never successfully penetrated the republican movement. As a former intelligence agent I can assure you that is totally illogical. The British and the Irish look the same, speak the same language, and republicans should have been an easy penetration target, but they weren't. That is why the republican movement has stayed a closed society, even within families, to this day.

Under my bridge in New York I had, for the first time, the peace of mind to think about my early life. Those days were not all steeped in intrigue because there were also funny times. My small bedroom faced the river with the mountains in the background. On quiet nights I would hear the sounds of muffled oarlocks as people crossed the wide river, and they were not all men in black, but smugglers too. They had to pass by our house to reach the road to Dundalk, and I watched them all. Some smuggled butter and cigarettes, and sometimes a pig or two, squealing in protest. The why of it all and the economics involved escaped me at that young age; but these men were fascinating to watch, struggling with their heavy loads, swearing and grunting all the time. Sometimes the customs service and the police would make a halfhearted effort to apprehend the smugglers, and I would hear them running beside the house, blowing their whistles.

There is no sense in my identifying 'Danny', a regular smuggler, because he is still around, though long since retired because of economics and age. The authorities would watch Danny as he crossed the river and made his contacts. The river was the way to go because the main road had constant roadblocks. I would see them sitting behind the boathouse, waiting for Danny to return, and then the chase was on. Fearful of being caught, Danny would become an Olympics-class speedster and easily outrun the portly police and customs officers, but they knew where to find him – at home. Danny would rush inside and jump into bed with his long-suffering wife. She would answer the pounding on the door and escort the authorities up to their bedroom. Danny would howl innocence as usual, but his wet muddy clothes under his wife's clean sheets told a different story, so off to jail he went.

Danny's arrest got a passing mention in the *Dundalk Democrat* newspaper and everybody appeared to be doing their job, but not so. The police and customs actually did not want to go anywhere near the lane that ran by our house, for it belonged to the men in black. Aside from being unarmed, they just might have encountered a close relative on the way north; it was better to stay away. Arresting predictable, hapless Danny occasionally was good enough and it was safer to man roadblocks. Besides, it appears that everybody but Danny knew the police and customs were going to be staking out the back of our house on a particular night.

There was an incident at the pub involving me that became infamous. I was tall for my age and I began to work behind the bar. I did well enough and learned to pull a more than fairly decent pint of Guinness – a coveted skill. As I worked I began to grow confident, and the regulars treated me well. My father seemed proud of me, until a disaster occurred. At that time Guinness was delivered in wooden kegs. It took a major effort to lift the keg up onto its shelf directly under the television set. Once that was accomplished, the next step was not for the fainthearted – inserting the big brass tap into the keg. The contents of the keg were under enormous pressure, held in only by a small wooden plug. One had to hammer the brass tap into the keg with one mighty swing of a heavy wooden mallet to ensure an airtight seal; there was no room for error. Should you fail, the entire contents of the keg would spew out all over the pub and our customers. I begged my father to allow me to plug a keg, and he always hesitated.

But one evening he nodded his head when the keg on the rack was empty. As if by magic, all the customers moved out to Mary Street for safety. I plugged that keg well and my father was obviously proud. I changed many kegs, hammering in the brass taps with a mighty swing of the wooden mallet, and I was proud as a strutting rooster: mistake number one. Our customers relaxed and began to treat me like an experienced barman, and that was mistake number two. The night of the disaster was a busy Saturday. Paddy Dobbs and Peter Clark were sitting on their regular stools and Jerry Mills, our resident doorman, was close by the stove for heat. Nobody paid any attention when I swung the keg up on its stand: mistake number three. I swung hard with the wooden mallet and struck the brass tap off centre and the keg exploded all over our pub and our customers. The keg gyrated on its stand, saturating everybody and everything.

I am not sure I can describe the carnage and the reactions of my father and our highly emotional customers. I have no idea how many varieties of dirty look exist, but I must have got them all that night. That was to be the last keg I was to tap. It cost my father a fortune in free drinks to assuage our customers' stress and mental suffering, but eventually things returned to normal, and the dirty looks diminished.

The oddest thing about a crowded, noisy pub is the acoustics. If you are a customer, you can barely hear your companion standing next to you. However, if you are behind the bar, you hear everything. Often as not, what a barman hears is more than he wanted or needed to hear. But in the back rooms everything changed, nobody heard anything unless what was said was intended for them, and it was here that the men in black would sit, heads always bowed, speaking softly.

Some of these men had served time in British internment camps and were always of current interest to the intelligence services. They allowed me to sit with them sometimes and they would talk about hunting and fishing. Strange as it may seem, I never liked to look them straight in their cold blue eyes. They would lock me in with those eyes and say, 'You are a good boy Gerard,' and I wondered what they meant. Was it because I knew what they did, or was it because I was indeed a good boy. I always had an uneasy underlying sense of something that made sure I kept my mouth shut. Even a flame-thrower up my rectum would not make me indiscreet.

Later I would sit with them as they planned raids, bombings and murders. It is often asked why they would meet in such a public place to discuss critical information. The reason was that their homes were under constant physical and electronic surveillance, and they did not want to involve their immediate families. When I was in America, I would often wonder about it all, knowing my father knew what those men did and that he had still allowed his son to sit down with them.

I later got the answer on deserted, wind-swept Juno Beach

in Florida. My parents were visiting me, and my father and I had gone for a walk on the beach after dinner. A slow drizzle came down but it was a warm evening. Without warning he began to talk about his political beliefs and in a roundabout way said he was sorry that he had let me get involved. I wished he hadn't started the conversation. Now it was a father and son, facing each other, and talking about things that probably should have been left unspoken, but it was too late. I asked him if he had come all that way to America to make things right for him or for me. Then I asked him about me: where was I to go? I had nowhere to go. I was to pay a heavy price both in America and Ireland for what I did as a young boy because people in the intelligence business never forget.

We went back to my home and my mother immediately sensed that something had happened, I could see it in her face, but nothing was said. The following morning I cooked a big breakfast of farm-fresh eggs, Irish bacon and Donnelly's white and black puddings which I had purchased from an importer. By the end of the meal we were back on track again, talking about what we were going to do that day, glad to be together. When my father left the room, my mother asked me if I was all right in America. I assured her I was, and that was that. But I was not all right: my young past stuck to me like wet skin, suffocating me if I let it, and many times I let it into my soul, and it was as if my childhood were yesterday.

Once-innocent memories, which are now raw and dangerous, having been transformed by my present-day knowledge of what I had seen and done, even as a child, lurk within my heart. They have not gone away, not even to this day, and I know they never will. Now in the grey light of dawn as I write these pages, I ask myself whether I would have changed anything about my young life, even if I could have done so. Yes, I would – I wish I had done more.

I was born and raised in a solidly republican home and raised by intelligent, loving parents. As their first born, I was imbued with their silent anger at the injustice of the British oppression and occupation of Ireland. Their deep and simmering anger became muted as my siblings later began to arrive. When my father's ashes were on the way to the cemetery in a box, held by me, the men in black were there, unnoticed. As our car crossed the bridge into Dundalk, I saw them in the large crowd. Every twenty feet or so they stood at attention, a hand over every heart, their honour guard for my father; and nobody in my family noticed, except me. Yes, at the end of the day I had been a good boy.

# 3

# THE IRISH ARMY, GHOSTS AND PICKING POTATOES

Standing behind the counter with only one customer, I knew we were in trouble, and there was only thirty shillings in the till. The bank manager had already called twice that morning, but we had nothing to give him. The sole customer had lingered over his pint for hours, reading our newspaper and grumbling about the hard times. I was seventeen then and it was 1957. In hard times, the pint glasses had many white rings as the men tried to make their drink last. Then when the times were good, and a few quid were to be made, the lines on the glasses were about three or four, no more. But when there was nothing but the dole, there would be as many as ten or more. It was then that my father's little white book would appear to keep accounts for regular customers. Most paid what they owed when things picked up, but many did not. My father gave away money we did not have. The good customers paid their bills off ten shillings at a time, the others pleaded poverty. Then when times were good the latter would avoid walking by our business by taking the long way around by the Marist College to go drinking at other bars and shop for their groceries elsewhere.

A few years later, I found a number of my father's little white books and recognised all the names. Those books truly reflected the good and bad economic times in Dundalk since our pub and grocery store opened. I then found his second set of books, for the grocery store, and my anger almost consumed me because the people who had not paid had lived free off our grocery store, and were the same customers who had owed bar bills. The worst part of it all was they were walking around now-prosperous Dundalk, acting like they did not know, still avoiding our business. These same people brought my father into bankruptcy, depression and personal humiliation.

During those hard times, the local bank was relentless in threatening to foreclose our family business. I can attest to that, as well as the constant, cold, menacing telephone calls from the bank manager, who demanded some kind of deposit to cover an outstanding balance. I would go up to the bank with a bag of coins and small notes, and that brought a little relief for a day or so, not much more. The manager's tight mouth and cold blue eyes stay with me to this day. My father owned the pub and our home at the Coastguard Station, surely the bank knew that and could have held a credit note guaranteed by the value of one of those properties? But not so: the manager's calls were relentless, almost sadistic, and I took almost all of them.

In life there has to be humour, and during this crisis for my father came black humour – funny now, but not then. My mother, always the trouper, decided to cheer our father up a little with a night on the town, a bite to eat and a play. The meal went well and then we went on to the theatre. To my parent's horror, one of the lead roles was being played by the bank manager.

Understandably, my father became deeply depressed during this period, and began to spend more time at home tending to his tomatoes and flowers. It was not a good time. During that period, Ireland's economy was terrible, unemployment cheques were the bottom line for basic survival, and that was not much at the end of the day. St Vincent de Paul pink food coupons began to show up more regularly and the outlook was grim. The political situation gave little hope and the worsening economy led to a general election being called. Eamon de Valera was elected as Taoiseach for the last time. But to the man in the street it was just more of the jaded same; it changed nothing for those with an empty pocket and a family to feed.

When I was first stationed in Germany, I completed Ranger training and had thirty days' leave on the books. I had saved all of my military pay and was excited to get home so soon, and it was on that trip home that I found my father's little white books. Times were still bad but I had an option, and I took it. I went to the men in black who used to practise weapons training on the back bank and showed them the books. They said nothing, but took the books. They then showed the people who owed my father money the books and the amount they owed. There were no guns or veiled threats, but everybody knew who these men were. The instant injection of cash revitalised my father and the business, and I went back to the American army.

What I wanted to do to those false-hearted people was far worse than what the men in black politely inflicted on them. My father was not focused for a few years, and people took advantage of him. Some employees pilfered at will and as a child I saw them. When they went to the cinema they would drop by the shop and openly fill up with sweets and money for tickets. Back then, that made the difference between profit and loss. I tried to point that out to him as a child, but got reprimanded. It was not that he did not believe me, but my father trusted basically everybody. A case could be made that he was a poor businessman when it came to who he trusted, but I would disagree; he just had a good heart. He built, during hard times, one of the best business establishments in Ireland, one that still prospers with the Corrs at the helm.

Other thoughts were in my mind during those days when I stood in our empty or near empty bar, including: how was I going to get the money to go to America? I knew a way to get the money and announced to my parents that I was joining the Irish regular army. One would think that I had just announced that I was gay, and was getting married to a lusty Mayo sheep farmer. All hell broke loose as my mother went into one of her operatic crying binges, as my father hung his head. To this day I strongly suspect that he was glad that I was making a break for it, one out of the nest and just three to go: Terry, Marna and Canice.

The move made sense to me; there were no jobs available and my family certainly had no money. The army paid a wage with free room and board. I could save enough during my three-year tour for my fare to America. I pointed out to them that my uncle Kevin, my mother's brother, had joined the army and gone on to a successful career in the Irish customs service. And I mentioned that my father's brother, Brian, had served in the army and then become some kind of government official in the labour department.

I was to remember later, as my mother and father waltzed to an orchestra on a luxury boat in Fort Lauderdale, sated with lobster, *filet mignon* and fine vintage wine, my mother telling me – as my father rolled his eyes: 'I was happy the day I sent you off to the Irish army, for I knew it was the beginning of a great journey.' Irish mothers can rewrite family history like no others, and load their children down with enough guilt to sink the *Titanic*, without the assistance of an iceberg; yet we love them so much it hurts at times.

I had already served in the FCA for three years, so induction into the army was routine, then it was off to Dublin for training. Everything went well except for the food, or lack of food.

The meals were reasonably tasty but hardly enough to feed a child. Later, when I became a military policeman, I learned that the sergeants assigned to the kitchens and whose job was to purchase the food were as crooked as corkscrews. They would feed the sergeants and officers like sultans and the privates like beggars. The food they stole was sold to nearby restaurants and stocked their own larders.

When I was on duty at the front gate of McKee barracks, I began to notice a portly mess sergeant always speeding by on his shiny new Raleigh bicycle, smiling and waving. The bike had large bags attached to the front handlebars and under the seat. He would always whip by while I was busy checking truck convoys. So, one warm summer's day, I ordered everybody to stay in line as I slowly checked the paperwork of every vehicle. I painstakingly checked each truck and its paperwork, all the time keeping an eye on the now-sweating, very nervous sergeant. He tried to move out, but I ordered him back in line; he was locked in between a jeep and a truck with no choice but to sweat it out. By the time he reached my checkpoint, blood was dripping out of both of his bicycle bags. I ordered him to open the bags. What a treasure trove of pork chops and lean cuts! I placed him under arrest and thought that was that. That day I was transferred to the military barracks in Kilkenny. It happened so fast that all I could assume was that the pork chop scam went all the way up to the officers.

After serving in both the Irish and American armies, I noticed a marked difference between the officers in the two forces. In our Irish army, the officers tended to be elitists. Perhaps the most striking example was when I was on a late-night bus returning to Collins barracks and found myself sitting directly across from my very tense commanding officer, a lieutenant, and his wife. Within a few stops, we were alone on the bus, just the three of us. He glared at me all the way to the barracks.

We were just feet apart, and his wife was clearly uncomfortable with his behaviour, and I could not wait to get off the bus. The next morning he called me aside and wanted to know why I had not moved away from them.

He was not an isolated example. During my three years of service with the Irish army I rarely encountered an officer who had the vaguest idea what the genuine comportment of a military officer should be. They stayed remote people. The contrast with American military officers was like night and day; they recognised you with a smile and a salute. These men I could follow into battle. Thankfully, today's Irish army officers have changed due to exposure to dangerous overseas assignments and other nations' officers.

The first time we went to the firing range for rifle training they realised that I was an expert rifleman, outscoring the veteran instructors. I was immediately taken out of basic training and transferred to the battalion's all-army rifle team, a high honour and a great relief. The team was led by a Sergeant Barnes, a big quiet man and one of the army's top marksmen. Aside from an initial casual meeting, where he advised the small team that they were only expected to report to a truck to go to the range each morning, our time was our own. I apparently was the only unmarried soldier on the team and had an entire floor of the barracks to myself, while the rest went home every afternoon. It was a surreal situation in a military setting, but that was all right with me.

As I relaxed on my cot in the afternoon, I could hear my former platoon mates sweating it out on the parade ground. They were drilled in bayonet fighting and other forms of military torture the instructors dreamed up. I had already received that training in the FCA and my superiors were comfortable with that; so was I, needless to say. The prize was the annual all-army rifle competition at the Curragh Camp in Kildare.

Any kind of win there would give my battalion officers serious bragging rights at the officers' club. The Curragh Camp is a five-thousand-acre training camp which was first constructed by the British in the 1800s. It has some of the finest training facilities in Europe, and the Irish army Rangers are based there.

One afternoon I awoke to find Sergeant Barnes standing at the foot of my cot.

'You are one of the best shots I have ever seen, Mac.'

He studied me for a short while and then said: 'You're from Dundalk, right?' I nodded and he gave a small smile.

'Well, that makes sense.'

That was all he said as he walked off with a chuckle.

We went to the Curragh and I was the top marksman in the Eastern command, even beating Sergeant Barnes. All he did was give one of his smiles and said: 'From Dundalk?' My home town was nicknamed 'El Paso' by the media, and for good reason.

The next year I did the same, and in the American army I was awarded the expert marksman medal. I guess the men in black did have an effective marksmanship training programme on the back bank, across from my home, behind the Irish army rifle range. There is a lot of irony there, when I think about it all.

Following my experience on the rifle team, I was transferred to the Signal Corps which was based at Collins barracks. I was taught the Morse code and communications. Incidentally, Morse crossed my path in life later on. While I was strolling around Central Park in New York I observed a magnificent statue of Samuel Morse, the inventor of the code, which, in its time, would have had the same impact on civilisation as the internet has on ours today. Also, many years later, while staying at the beautiful mountain home of my dear friends, Sandy and

Bill Hamilton, I happened to pass down a long hallway and observed some stunning paintings, all signed by Samuel Morse. Farther on I saw letters from Morse and the framed original patent for the Morse code. I had no idea that Sandy was a descendant of Morse, and our conversation over breakfast that morning was fascinating. It turns out that Morse was not only an inventor but also a famous artist.

After my training in the Signal Corps, I was assigned one day to teach a class on communications to the military police detachment at Collins barracks. It went well and they asked many questions. Following the class, a senior sergeant approached me with an offer: a transfer to the military police with the rank of corporal. My pay then was that of a private, and my saving plan for America was meagre; the rank of corporal offered higher pay.

The next day I began my military police training. My commanding officer, the one from the bus, gave me a frosty look, but there was nothing he could do to stop the transfer because the head of the military police outranked him. Collins barracks enveloped me in our past because it was so saturated with Irish revolutionary history. It ate me up because for the first time I was being exposed to the other side of the coin, for I was now in Michael Collins' army. The realisation of where I was and how diametrically opposed it was, militarily and politically, to where I had been in Dundalk filled my mind and I became numbed and confused. I just had not considered the ramifications of what I had done. When I was off duty, I would lie on my cot and attempt to put my life and loyalties in perspective. It was not easy because the men in black were on my mind. Not in a bad way, but a good way, and that made it even harder. Each week we had to swear our allegiance to the Irish government, and I wondered about that: were they that insecure? I also thought about Michael Collins who had been a man in black himself, and wondered whether my men in black were any different. I knew the history of the treaty and I wondered why we were fighting amongst ourselves?

Those years I worked in and around our pub in Dundalk were violent times. In December 1956 the IRA commenced what came to be known as their Border Campaign. IRA guerrilla units operating out of Dundalk made a series of raids on military targets in British-occupied Northern Ireland; it lasted until February 1962. The British government lodged protest after protest with the Irish government, demanding that they do something about the IRA. Eamon de Valera was at first reluctant but was forced to act when an IRA unit ambushed a British police patrol outside Forkhill, and all tracks led to nearby Dundalk. Constable Cecil Gregg was killed and Constable Robert Halligan was badly wounded. This was a major tactical error on the part of the IRA: they had killed a policeman, a keeper of the peace! On 7 July 1957, Eamon de Valera introduced internment to Ireland. The political arm of the IRA was, and is, Sinn Fein, which is a legally established political party in Ireland. On the 6 July 1957, while Sinn Fein leaders were conducting their regular meeting at their office on Wicklow Street in Dublin, the Irish police special branch swooped in and arrested everybody, including the president of Sinn Fein, Patrick MacLogan, and the entire leadership of the political party – numbering sixty-six people. The final total of people arrested was 131. The internment camp, the Curragh – the same one they used to house the German prisoners – now became home to Irish prisoners. There was outrage within the Irish American community and in Ireland itself, but the British were appeased. Military policemen were being posted to the camp, and I asked not to be assigned there. The officer whom I talked to just shrugged and said he understood, and that was that. Eamon de Valera's internment of Irish political prisoners ended in

February 1959; it was a sad chapter in our history – a freedom fighter jailing freedom fighters in his own country.

Once when I was home on vacation for a few weeks, my Mother and I decided to drive to Straban to visit my youngest brother Canice. I rarely got a chance to see him as I had left Ireland when he was three. He was a practicing attorney. We took the scenic route over the mountains and the scenery was spectacular. The day was pleasantly warm with a clear blue sky, and very relaxing. We chatted together and as my mother filled me in on all the family news, I realised just how much I was missing at home, and had missed. She talked about the fact England was still in Ireland, and that was a sore spot for my republican mother. I stayed quiet, better that way as she would just get more upset. Suddenly, a heavily armed British soldier jumped out in front of the car. This was in Northern Ireland, just miles from our home. By this time, I had nine years' military experience, so the following comments should be seen in perspective. Why in the world would the supervisor of this jerky, nervous soldier order him to conceal himself and jump out of the bushes at slowly moving cars? We were on a single-lane, scenic road, and a simple wave-down from a soldier fifty feet away would have been effective and appreciated. I nearly ran over the man because he gave me no stopping space; it was insane. What followed was even more insane. The soldier reared back and started to wave his rifle at us in the firing position, his finger on the trigger. A corporal appeared and, sensing they had created this mess, smiled and asked me for my identification.

All this time my mother said nothing; she just sat there in her seat, her jaw set. I knew what that meant: all hell was getting ready to break out. I detected a light machine gun (LMG) emplacement about a hundred feet up on a hill. I was hoping that the gunner was not as nervous as the soldier on the road. I also spotted other camouflaged soldiers on either side of the road. I have often thought if that nervous soldier had indeed unleashed a barrage of shots because of his stupidity, the automatic response from his fellow soldiers would have been a murderous hail of automatic weapons' fire. That's just the way 'things' happen in perceived combat situations, which this was. This enjoyable drive on a scenic road in the mid-morning sun had turned into a nightmare; but it was not over. The corporal, who had been talking on his radio, turned to me and handed me back my American passport, and the smile had left his face. Believe me, I knew the drill, and knew what was coming. 'Wait here for a moment; you will be escorted to another clearance point.' By then my mother's lower jaw began to protrude slightly, and her eyes grew frostier. While we waited to be escorted, I held my mother's hand and implored her to relax. She just sat there and said nothing, her body rigid with suppressed anger.

A British army jeep backed down the road and signalled me to follow them down the road. We were directed to a massive, circular concrete bunker, and waved inside. It was like something out of the Cold War. The interior of the bunker was clearly designed to contain an explosion, like a car bomb, and was deserted. I could see faces moving behind thick, green, explosive-proof glass, then an officer and a soldier stepped outside. The officer was holding my passport and frowning. Clearly he had run my name through their intelligence network and come up with a hit. The soldier, another nervous type, poked his rifle at me through the open car window and ordered me to get out, and the officer did the same to my mother. She refused to move.

Right then and there I knew I had to do something or the situation was going to escalate into a major confrontation, a needless one. I got out of the car after telling my mother to sit tight. I produced my American police identification and gold shield, and said: 'If you touch my mother all hell is going to break loose. As an American citizen and a sworn American law enforcement officer, I demand a representative from the American embassy be contacted immediately. Am I being detained as an American citizen, yes or no?' I remember my words well.

The officer muttered something under his breath but seemed under control as he ordered the soldier to search the back seat of my car and remove the hubcaps. He then returned my passport and went back behind the concrete wall. The soldier was joined by another and they proceeded to trash my car trunk and remove anything that was not permanently fixed to the car, but never came close to my mother. An RUC police officer entered the compound and asked for my papers. After examining my police identification he visibly winced and walked inside the bunker observation post, where the lieutenant was. Even though the sounds were muffled, we could hear well enough that the police officer was yelling at the lieutenant, and saying things that were not polite. My mother began to relax and that was a relief. My car was a mess, bits and pieces everywhere.

The policeman used his radio and four more policemen arrived in a patrol car. They pushed my car through the exit gate and then a nice thing happened: they began to reassemble my car. By then my mother had totally relaxed and was chatting with the police supervisor. She told me later that he said not all Northern Ireland policemen liked the idea of British soldiers manning heavy-handed control points. They all apologised and we went on our way.

We visited Canice and his family and returned back to Dundalk by the same route that early evening. British army checkpoints were everywhere, but nobody stopped my car.

While I was in the process of becoming a recognised anti-terrorism expert in America, the long reach of the British intelligence services tried to destroy me, but failed. While their memories are long, so are the memories of every descendant of Irish emigrants driven from Ireland by brutal British military occupation. Many of these descendants now occupy powerful stations in American life. The British failed while I was in law enforcement, but tried again when I joined corporate America. They came close and stained me, but I survived, at a cost. I truly understand why they did what they did to me, and hold no hard feelings. Why should I? They were just doing their job and doing it well – to give the devil his due. I frankly believe that the American intelligence services could learn a thing or two from the British. However, the British are only as good as they are because the IRA have kept them on their toes for so long. With the IRA they have failed, otherwise they have been magnificent. Perhaps America should consider hiring some effective 'retired' IRA operatives as intelligence consultants; stranger things have happened.

Aside from the Royal Hospital in Kilmainham, Collins barracks is the oldest public building in Ireland. It is one of the oldest military barracks in the world, dating back to 1701. Theobald Wolfe Tone, one of the leaders of the 1798 Irish rebellion against the British, was jailed, tortured, tried and convicted of treason there. Throw into the historical mix thousands of soldiers, Irish and British, and hundreds of years of intrigue, and there is more than enough room for a few ghosts. When I was stationed there I had a few sleepless nights thinking about creaks, voices and strange sounds in the dark. All that said, the gargantuan, granite barracks pales in comparison with its adjunct, Arbour Hill Military Prison, so far as lost spirits are concerned.

I was assigned there as the lone, interior military policeman on the midnight watch, or, as they called it, the graveyard shift. This depressing granite building – a testimony to British prison skills – sits atop Arbour Hill and is impregnable to those wishing to break out and, for that matter, break in and release prisoners; it just can't be done. While there is only one unarmed military policeman assigned inside, the exterior is heavily guarded. The role of the interior guard is to ensure that there are no suicides at night and that medical emergencies are responded to quickly.

When I reported for duty, the prisoners would already be asleep and locked down in their one-man cells. When dawn broke, I would wake the prisoners, open their cells and line them up for an inspection. Apart from threatening stares from a very few, there was no danger, they were broken down young men with no future. They had been charged with serious crimes, otherwise they would not have been in there; in essence their life was over. When and if they got out, who would hire them? There were only twenty prisoners there when I was assigned, and, when I lined them up in the morning, I only had to keep a close watch on three of them, who were classified as dangerous.

Arbour Hill Prison is oppressive by design. It is polished brass, concrete, and wood, and human contact is at a minimum. It is a dark place, and, in a sense, I was a prisoner just like the inmates. While other military policemen avoided the assignment, I was honoured and excited. The leaders of Ireland's 1916 Easter rebellion against the British occupation were interred there, and I wanted to walk those hallowed grounds. Those were not ordinary men. They had answered a call to fight injustice that they knew in their heart of hearts they could not possibly win; but in the end they did win. Those fourteen ordinary men's names are now part of Irish history, and at the time inspired Irish people to stand up and fight against the brutal British military occupation of Ireland.

In a revealing act, General Maxwell, the leader of British occupation forces in Ireland, ordered the prisoners be taken to the Stonebreakers Yard in Kilmainham gaol and shot. One was so badly wounded he had him sit on a chair to be executed. Maxwell then ordered that a huge quicklime pit be dug in the back of Arbour Hill Prison as a mass grave. He had it dug deep enough for another hundred expected bodies. His reasoning at the time was that if he dumped the bodies in a lime pit the Irish would not have any martyrs, so it would all soon pass. Despite the impassioned public outcry of the families that their fathers be respected with a proper burial, General 'the Butcher' Maxwell ignored them. The general had unknowingly created a shrine where presidents of powerful countries would stand and bow their heads, as John F. Kennedy did. The butcher had failed. The interior of the prison at night is one eerie place.

What with the dim lighting and the sounds of an old prison, you don't need to have an overactive imagination to begin to feel the presence of things other than yourself and the prisoners. I would walk around in my socks checking on my prisoners through a small window in their doors. For the most part they were in a deep sleep, but some were not. I would hear crying at times and when I checked, they always had their faces to the wall. But there was not much I could do except make sure they did not hurt themselves during the night. I knew what crime each prisoner had committed, but it did not make it any easier.

The occupied cells took up a small part of the prison interior, so I roamed around exploring. Certain locked rooms, when I walked past them, caused my body to shiver; so did three cells. It was a cold shiver. This did not happen once, nor was it my imagination. Each time I passed by those rooms and cells, my body would shiver, night after night, and I wondered what it was. Later, when I was a homicide detective in Atlanta, then the murder capital of America, I discovered what it was: a death shiver. I would experience the same shiver when I was in a room with a murder victim, not once but many times.

There is nobody in this world who can convince me that when we die our souls just evaporate. Think about yourself as you sit reading this book. Without your soul you are just an empty vessel sitting in a chair. Our soul is a powerful force which controls our brain and our body. When the body dies, the soul has to find some place to go, because it is not a physical thing; it is just out there. I trust that I have not 'weirded you out', as they say, but I believe that our souls are powerful forces.

When my shift was over in the morning, I would walk across the street to Collins barracks and sleep until about three in the afternoon and then lie in my cot thinking about things. I know that spooky places tend to feed the imagination and hidden fears, but in the case of Collins barracks and Arbour Hill Prison, I truly believe that something or someone was with me on those long quiet nights. If it was the souls of our nation's tortured past, then I pray they find peace, for when I was there I felt no peace in them, none at all, just an unhappy coldness. I wish I could bring them peace, I truly do. They say that few people experience these chills – something to do with their sensitivity. Frankly I would rather that I had not been bestowed with that 'blessing', which is why I never attend funerals – I make everybody nervous.

After a time the prison began to press down on me a bit, and I started to look around for another assignment. As luck would have it, an opening came up at the Gormanstown Camp outside Drogheda. I jumped at the chance and was on my way. The camp was a training base for the Irish Air Corps and the reserve forces, and was right next door to Butlins holiday camp,

Ireland's premier resort at the time. All of the other military policemen were married, so I had the entire Second World War barracks to myself. Just when I thought things could not get any better, they did! The sergeant in command called me in and said that the reserves were coming in next week and that Butlins needed a plain-clothes MP for the summer. I would get an extra day off each week and Butlins would provide me with identification and access to employee meals. He assigned me to the day shift and that left me with plenty of time to change clothes and walk over to Butlins.

Although today's holiday camps tend to be more sophisticated, Butlins was way ahead of its time. They had water sports and a host of other activities. There was a bar and dancing at night. This assignment was a far cry from listening to ghosts in Arbour Hill Prison, and there were girls, lots of girls. My assignment was to keep a look out for horny FCA reservists who would sneak out of the barracks in the evening. There were two traditional routes, down by the beach and across the fields. The only problem for the 'hornies' was that I had served in the FCA and had been a reservist in the same camp, and had made a few trips myself.

It did not take long to spot a few interlopers: four single men with no wives or screaming children. When I collared them and brought them to the holiday camp office, they realised that I was an MP. All four began to blubber about losing their summer camp training bonus, which was generous. The normal procedure would be for me to call for an MP jeep and have them transported back to the barracks to face charges of AWOL and trespassing.

I did not want to see them lose their bonus, so I came up with an idea. I yelled to high heaven at them and then goose-marched them to the back fence, much to the amusement of the Butlins' patrons, who I suppose thought it was some weird event staged by the camp entertainment director. I then lined them up at the tall barbed wire fence and told them if they got over the fence in ten seconds I would not place them under arrest, and, more importantly, not file a report.

Ireland would do well if they had athletes like those four young hornies on their Olympics team. Despite yells of pain, cuts and the sound of tearing clothing, they were gone in an instant. I talked to the camp director and he said that it was a nightly problem. The hornies were after his young female staff, who were hired for their good looks. He said the girls, despite repeated warnings of dismissal, exacerbated the problem because they also were hornies, of the female variety.

I decided that if this dream assignment was going to work, I had better get a step ahead of the hornies. I borrowed a pair of dark sunglasses from the camp's lost and found. Dressed in my full MP dress uniform, with red-banded black brim hat, and wearing the dark sunglasses, I paid a visit to every FCA billet and training location. I would make a noisy entrance, glaring around like a deranged person, yelling and screaming – and I was armed. 'If I catch just one of you gurriers anywhere even near Butlins, everybody in your platoon loses their training pay,' I would shout, then depart with slammed doors, oaths and weird snarls. It took all day, and was exhausting, but it worked: not one hornie was spotted in or around Butlins for the remainder of the summer.

After a week of no resident complaints and peaceful bliss, the camp director was ready to lick my shoes clean. He foisted on me free drink vouchers, enough to put me in the gutter. The following week he gave me a key to my own chalet – 'Just in case you need to relax,' he said as he winked. He then pinned a new pink ID card on me that caused the female staff members to suddenly become overly friendly. It appeared the card meant I was in management and the word got out I had my own chalet and access to free drinks, and that made me a very attractive young man. With only married couples around and no hornies, the girls became aggressive, which was fine with me, all things considered. I exercised my constitutional rights that summer of glorious summers, never to be repeated again, sad to say.

My supervising sergeant was amazed at the lack of complaints from the Butlins camp and complimented me often. He also had a proposition.

'I understand that you are going to America when your time is up. Do you have enough money?'

I told him that I had saved every spare shilling and pound, but that I was still short. He told me to talk to Corporal Jim McEvoy, whose family lived just around the corner from our pub. A few MPs worked as labourers on a nearby farm for daily pay. Jim said it was hard work, and it was, but that was OK; it was just the way things were at the time.

On my three days off I worked on the farm picking potatoes, cleaning out cowsheds and doing just about everything that was guaranteed to give me an aching back and an odour that would gag a maggot. But I earned enough for my basic air fare to America. It would take at least an hour to scrub the smell of cow and horse shit off my body before I reported to Butlins. Even then I got a few suspicious sniffs from the girls from the west of Ireland. They were expert at sniffing out farm workers at the dances who were pretending to be doctors and accountants. It was a great summer, the best of my life, but I did not know it at the time.

Then I began the slow preparation for emigration. My earlier euphoric enthusiasm ebbed away a little at a time. The realisation that I was about to leave my family, friends and country settled in and a great sadness enveloped me. I began to reconsider my decision to leave Ireland, and I had many sleepless nights.

But there was nothing in Ireland for me then except an unemployment cheque. Our family business was dead in the water. But not even that knowledge made it easier. Those were the days when a native son emigrated, and it would be many years before he came home again, if ever. Goodbyes then were often final goodbyes. Everybody knew it, but nobody talked about it. Perhaps it is the nature of things that when a child is about to leave his family and country, those who love him withdraw; and I certainly sensed that. Maybe it was their way to make it easier for me, but it did not help at all. Even my beloved springer spaniel, Flush, began to quietly whine around me; everybody knew, and it was like a wake. It was gut-wrenching and the hardest thing I ever had to do in my life.

I began to pack and for some reason I can't remember those last few days, though I have an acute memory. There were tears and hugs and then I found myself standing in Dublin airport. The plane first flew to Shannon, but few passengers boarded there, unlike today. I was glad for the near emptiness of the plane as I strained to see the last of Ireland passing below my little window. I saw the green fields, then the grey of the sea, and then nothing: Ireland was gone, and I was gone, just like that. The stewardess was a little older than me, and left me alone in the back of the plane. She was probably used to seeing young immigrants desperately straining to see the last of Ireland. She turned off the overhead light and left me to stare out the window, and quietly cry out my anguish. I swear to almighty God that it ripped my heart apart, and my heart of hearts has never been the same again and never will be.

There can be many rewards for those who emigrate from difficult conditions, but the price you pay is severe, and you keep paying, day after day, and it never stops, ever. No matter how successful or wealthy you become in your new land, your heart always aches for home. It is one thing to move from Dublin to Cork, or Virginia to New York – you can always catch a bus or a train and go home. But when you move to the other side of the world, there is finality about it all. That was then, not now. There was no internet then, telephone calls were out of the question, and news from home came only once in a while in a letter describing events that were long past, including the death of a beloved family member.

A sense of isolation sets in and will destroy you if you let it. I did not; I stayed busy. If you allow that cold sense of isolation into your soul you will end up in Irish bars getting drunk and singing sad songs about home, glad for the company of Irishmen, but that's where you will stay. I was in a few bars in New York and came away feeling worse than when I went in. As I lay under my bridge thinking about it all, I began to get excited: my entry into the American army was but a day away; my journey was finally under way again.

# 4

# THE AMERICAN ARMY

I desperately tried to stay awake and upright as I slipped once more into the filthy grease and slop in the pit. My empty stomach retched on my bile as I collapsed into the foul smelling sewage. It had been sixteen hours since I had first been placed in the grease pit, sixteen hours out of the forty-eight hours that I had been in the American army. There is no country in the world that is more efficient at processing their cannon fodder, and for good reason. Every American generation has seen war. If somebody is not attacking America, it will go out and attack somebody.

I was processed at a dizzying speed: physicals, injections, uniform and equipment fitting, and assignment to a billet. Then things slowed down a bit as the backlog of paperwork was cleared. This was the first time that I had been exposed to the multi-cultural mix that is America, up close and personal. There were Mexicans, Puerto Ricans, farm boys from Kentucky, blacks, wise guys from New York, Italians and Europeans, and one Irishman in our billet.

We slept two to a bunk space, one up and one down. I got the top bunk and a very big scowling black recruit was down below. I attempted to introduce myself and he told me to go fornicate myself, and it never got any better. In the middle of the night he would begin to rant and rave that he had been drafted by mistake, and that it should have been his brother. They were working us hard then and we needed our sleep, but nobody wanted anything to do with this giant of a man, so we suffered in silence.

The billet sergeant, who lived in a room at the front of the barracks, stayed out late at the NCO club and usually arrived back very drunk. I guess one night he was broke and stayed in to watch television in his room. All went well until about 1 a.m. when my bunk mate started yelling. The sergeant came out of his room in his boxer shorts and he was as black and big as my bunk mate and all hell broke loose. The sergeant tried to drag the recruit out of his bed, and that was not a good idea, for me at least. My bunk mate's reaction was to kick the underside of my bed with his considerably muscular legs. I was propelled into the air and into the next bed, whose occupant also began yelling. The only light was a dim night light, so the billet soon resembled something out of a low-grade horror movie as recruits ran everywhere, and the two men commenced some serious hand-to-hand combat.

Then the peacemakers arrived, a jeep load of equally big military policemen, all seemingly thirsting to inflict pain on somebody, anybody, with their batons. Nobody thought to turn the lights on, so the MPs waded in and administered what I later learned was 'a good ol' country boy ass whipping' to anybody stupid enough to stand around. Having been an MP before, I knew exactly what to do. I went to the bathroom and locked myself in a stall and sat there listening to the mayhem outside.

When it was all over and it grew quiet, I returned to my bunk, or what was left of it. My bunk mate was gone, never to return. The bunk was destroyed so I placed my mattress on the floor and tried to sleep, thinking about it all. I came to one conclusion: these Americans were one strange breed of people and I needed to carefully study them and tread softly if I was going to survive.

All in all I had no real problems; everything was so well organised that things just clicked along. As for my first American army haircut – we stood in line then, six at a time, sat in barber chairs and were out of them in about a minute, minus our hair. They used electric shears and it was a simple matter of shearing right to the scalp, back to front. I couldn't have cared less, but many of the recruits who had carefully coiffured hairstyles acted like they had just lost a limb. At the end of it all we looked like a bunch of concentration camp prisoners. I knew what they were doing. They were breaking us down and then building us up in the military mould that was required for missions.

So far so good. They kept us busy doing odd jobs around the camp while they were getting our training assignments scheduled. I began to relax, and that was a mistake, because it became our billet's turn to perform kitchen duties in one of the many mess halls at Fort Dix. They call it kitchen police, or KP, for no earthly reason I can imagine. I believe that it should be called MS for mediaeval slavery.

As I lay on my bunk one evening, a sergeant I had never seen before kicked the metal frame and yelled 'KP!' I followed him to one of the massive dining halls and joined another batch of recruits outside it. It was there that I would experience the raw ignorance of prejudice. I was new to America and there was so much going on, and so much of the continent still unknown to me. The sergeant was in his forties and had the look of a man who had let his body sag into an unhealthy-looking paunch. (I was later to learn that these mess sergeants, once they became mess sergeants, stayed mess sergeants. They had access to free food and received kick-backs from everywhere, and did no combat duty.)

This sergeant had what appeared to be a permanent scowl on his pasty white face as he shouted the command 'Attention!' None of the recruits had any idea what was required of them, so they just shuffled about uneasily, except for me. I instinctively snapped to attention as I had done a thousand times in the Irish army. It was then that I learned the first rule in the American army, never ever draw attention to yourself.

Under the harsh outdoor lighting, in a cold drizzling rain at night, I smelled the sour bourbon breath of the sergeant in my face as his belly touched my belt – he was that close to me. I was about to be exposed to a side of America I did not know existed, venomous prejudice. 'Are you fucking with me, boy?' I shook my head. 'You think you're a fucking soldier?' I again shook my head. I was to recognise his deep southern accent later, but not then. All I knew was that I was losing ground fast.

'Where you from boy?'

'Ireland, sir.'

'Don't sir me, I work for a living.'

His eyes welled with rage as he yelled, 'You yankee fucker, we have a cure for your smart ass. Where are you from boy, Boston?'

I started to tell him that Ireland was not in North America, but decided to keep my mouth shut as I was already in enough trouble. He marched me to the back of the mess hall and pushed me inside a screen door. The noise level in the back of the mess hall was unbelievable. I had eaten there, and the noise level in the front was normal. Metal serving trays and food containers were been thrown at frantic speed, and there was yelling every-where – noise, noise and more noise.

The recruits were being marched through the front doors, pressed through the 'chow line' and then pressed out the back door. This was mass basic feeding of human beings at its most efficient, in and out, in and out. At the end of the line the metal trays were passed across metal tables to other recruits, who dumped what was left through a hole in the concrete wall into what was known as the grease pit. This was nothing more than a concrete cubicle where a recruit would try and keep the sludge moving into the sewers. There was no let-up; it was grease and sludge by the second. The sergeant stood me in front of another paunchy-looking sergeant and told him I was a wise ass. Since Fort Dix was a giant processing centre, meals were being served all the time. The hours passed and there was no respite, and I figured that at the end of eight hours another recruit would relieve me. My body became saturated in grease, then I heard whistles blowing, it was finally over. I started to yell out the hole of the grease pit when I saw a fresh batch of recruits moving around the kitchen. It seemed the louder I yelled, the more grease and sludge poured through the hole. I tried to force the door to the pit open, but it was locked from the outside. I yelled again and another sergeant started to yell at me through the hole to get a move on; so began another eight-hour shift.

Only when I collapsed did somebody open the grease-pit door, a faceless person to my blurred vision. It took me an hour to stagger my way back to the barracks. When I arrived my barracks sergeant wanted to know where I had been. I told him and he stared at me in disbelief. I must have smelled like a garbage dump because he had some recruits bring me back to the showers. They stripped me naked, turned on the hot water and washed me down with floor brushes and detergent.

The sergeant let me sleep the next day and after that just shook his head every time he saw me. He later told me what happened was wrong and he would file a complaint on my behalf. I told him no, I just wanted to get through the training and get out of the camp.

The first stage of the training was basic infantry training and firearms instruction. It was not easy, and some recruits were

weeded out for various reasons. Then it was on to advanced infantry training, and that is when it got interesting. The training
involved night patrols and live fire exercises, and a lot of plod-
ding around New Jersey's swamps. They pushed the recruits
harder and harder, and some did not make it. I don't know what
happened to them; maybe they ended up as clerks.

All in all, the sergeants who conducted the training were of
superior calibre and combat veterans. They made me a squad
leader with a temporary rank, so I was exempt from KP. One
recruit died during training after being punished for some in-
fraction. He was forced to run continuously around an oval cin-
der track, holding his rifle at high port, until he dropped, white
foam coming from his mouth; then they took him away, and
nothing more was said. Once into the advanced training, they
started to issue weekend passes.

Perhaps a million Americans have passed through Fort Dix
on their way to fight America's wars. Each and every one will
remember Wrightstown, a small clapboard army town just outside the gates. After the pressure of the camp, we had a fun time
roaming around the tacky shops. Then Tony Orlando, a New
Yorker, came up with the idea to go find a bar and cold beer, and
maybe some girls. This was not to be Tony's brightest idea. He
found a bar with a neon sign in the window that said 'cold beer'.

It was August and the heat and sun sapped our strength
and our eyesight. We were blinded as we entered the icy, almost pitch-black bar. Tony, the architect of this grand adventure,
ordered a pitcher of cold beer and four mugs. We found some
stools at the bar and strained to recover our night vision, then
we were sorry we had. Faces came into focus across the bar. We
saw hard eyes set in grizzled, gum-chewing, heavily-made-up,
smoking faces of women all well into their sixties. This was a
frightening sight for virgin Irish eyes.

All of these massive women looked capable of coming

around the bar and inflicting severe pain on our warrior bodies. If that was not bad enough, the barman, who said he was a retired sergeant, stood in front of us with a pool stick in his meaty hand. This watery-eyed person with a massive beer gut belched and said: 'You can have any of my ladies for ten minutes in the trailer in the back for twenty bucks.' Tony, who suffered from a runaway mouth, just said: 'Oh shit!' America's finest were forced into a humiliating and hasty retreat. To this day I can still hear the cackles and the curses of the ladies of Wrightstown. I have a suspicion they were on the same stools for the soldiers who stormed Normandy, Inchon and fought the Tet offensive.

It was not all grim news so far as the ladies were concerned. Each week the Army, in conjunction with religious organisations, would bus in girls for a dance at the enlisted men's club. Without exception these young girls came with the sincere intention of meeting a nice young soldier. These were nice girls, we were warned, and there was to be no hanky-panky. They were supervised by stern women with gimlet eyes.

I sometimes wonder who comes up with these hare-brained ideas. What they did not understand was that Fort Dix was populated by young men whose testosterone levels were almost out of control. Add to the mix young ladies who were the end product of a confined environment, like Catholic girls' homes, whose own sexual anticipation level was on fire. What we had were horny young men and women with no outlet. You were not even allowed to escort your dance partner off the dance floor, and tight slow dancing brought swift reprimands. I am not sure which was worse, the ladies of Wrightstown or the misery of being denied a room filled with attractive young women crying out for solace. I danced with an extremely attractive girl who held me in a death grip and breathed in my ear as if she was about to expire, then we were ushered off the floor. My first dance was my last dance.

My three years in the American army were a dizzying ride through one of the most complex societies in the world, and the army was a true mirror image of that society, especially when the military draft was in effect. It spared nobody but a privileged few.

Who were the privileged few? That's a good question. There were family hardship deferrals, college deferments and a raft of other reasons either genuine or phony. Many of the scions of the wealthy and politically powerful went ahead and served their enlistment, and I met a few.

So, at the end of the day the military draft actually took few prisoners. The sons of the poor and rich rubbed shoulders and cleansed their bodies in communal showers together. The toilets were communal also, open and close to each other. There was a row of white toilet bowls in the middle of a white-tiled room. There was no escape here for the rich or poor bigots who found themselves inches away from a black or latino naked soldier, sharing their common stinks and hating each other as they tried to look away. And those who displayed an arrogant attitude found themselves on their knees cleaning the same toilets with their toothbrushes. While they internally raged and were sickened by the indignity, nothing more was heard from their arrogant mouths.

One weekend, a soldier whom I chatted with on a regular basis invited me home for the weekend. I would be uneasy identifying him as his father was the US ambassador to a major power. I did not know that he was from a privileged family, and it really did not matter. We were picked up by a family driver and were driven to his home on Long Island, and that is where I was introduced to the side of America that controls America, though one would never know it at first glance. These people wear their money and power easily; and the richer and more powerful they are, the more laid back they are. When I later became a detective sergeant in Florida, I lived in the Palm Beaches and attended cocktail parties where I instantly recognised people from the newspapers and society pages. Yet never once in all those years did anyone ask me what I did for a living. My annual salary would not have paid their annual electricity bill. I was welcomed on their yachts and into their homes, and they did the same when my parents visited from Ireland. I am not quite sure how to describe them, but they are different. Perhaps an 'easy elegance' would fit them.

Coming from a part of the world where people with money and influence demand attention, it was quite a culture shock. That is not to say they leave their doors open to anybody; it's a closed society out of necessity and for security. I was told by one such person that they simply instinctively knew if someone was a good person or not, and if they enjoyed being around him or her, that was all there was to it.

I liked Long Island, an oasis in the shadow of New York City. There were small enclaves of wealthy homes on tree-shaded streets. My friend's home was like something out of a design magazine – pastel colours everywhere and money oozing out of every pore of that elegant house. Yet I was welcomed in as a member of the family and found them to be relaxed and enjoyable to be around. They were not catholic, yet his mother and he accompanied me to Sunday mass at a small, richly appointed chapel nearby.

The parish priest looked like he was in no need of a handout. When the collection plate was passed around I saw no money, just discreet expensive envelopes with each parishioner's name embossed on its cover. I suspect the contents were the cause of the perpetual smile on the priest's face. I am sure he was thinking it was better than being out in the mission fields. He was Irish and we shook hands on the way out as he graciously thanked all of the attendees on the steps of his beautiful little church. I had placed ten dollars in an envelope I found, and thought at the time that that amount in Ireland would have bought me forgiveness for murder from my parish priest.

So, based on my initial experiences, my status as an Irish catholic immigrant did not appear to be a problem. I ceased to be concerned, after all America was, and is, an immigrant nation. That was a big mistake on my part, a really big mistake. I was later to discover that as long as 'people' like me stayed in our boxes, all was well. It's when you excel and prosper, that's when the ugly beast called prejudice rears its loathsome head. The major problem I found was that you are never aware of the change in attitudes of those around you, including your friends. They hide it well. If you were black, you had to expect the worst, and you would probably be right to do so. However, if you look, act and talk like 'them', and stick your head out of the box you are expected to stay in, the repercussions can be severe, but well concealed.

Some readers, especially American ones, might ask: 'Who are you to talk like that about America when you are not an American?' I will answer that question. I am writing this chapter as an American. No American man or woman can question my qualifications to call myself an American. I sacrificed more for America than most natural-born Americans have ever thought of doing. I wrote these words so that, perhaps in some small way, change for the better might result.

Life at Fort Dix was becoming easier. We completed our training and were awaiting our assignments. My friend was to be off to Monterey in California to army language school to learn Russian, and I was packing to attend microwave transmission training at Fort Monmouth in New Jersey, not far away. The completion of that training and a few years' experience translated into a high-paying civilian career. Everything was fine as we said our goodbyes, drinking in the army beer garden. Times were good and I was excited. What we were not to know was that a world away – the year was 1961 – thousands of desperate East Germans had begun to stream across the open border into West Germany, as many as two thousand a day.

The East was communist and the West was democratic. The communists had slowly begun to limit personal freedoms and the East had become an increasingly harsh, oppressive state. Seeing the writing on the wall, the thousands of East Germans who commuted to work in West Germany simply did not come home at the end of the day. While the border was still open, they brought their families across, and the exodus had begun. The situation was still orderly, but the tension increased considerably as the numbers grew. Realising that East Germany was emptying, frantic East German officials ordered the border guards to harass the fleeing East Germans. If anything, that frightened the populace more, and thousands began to flow across the border in a never-ending flow. It was now a stampede of distraught people, desperate to escape communism.

Then the inevitable occurred. Moscow ordered East Germany to crack down at once and bring the chaotic situation under control. This played right into the hands of the two men who had created the situation in the first instance: East Germany's leaders, Erich Honecker and Egon Krenz. These two Hitler devotees and despots started in motion a cruel series of events that would plunge the world into a period of high tension – the Cold War.

While the entire world paid a price, America paid the highest one. The situation could have easily have been contained by West Germany, but the US Pentagon rushed to formulate plans for a massive build-up on the Russian border. I say 'easily', because nobody in that region had the stomach for a conflict since they were still recovering from the Second World War. It was a regional problem and in no way was it a threat to the United States; but the Pentagon made it one.

While we sang our songs and drank our beer, and promised we would stay in touch, we had no idea that we would be together for years to come; nobody was going anywhere but to the Russian border! We were only a day from being shipped out to our expected assignments when the bombshell dropped: we had been reassigned to the Third Infantry Division, an armoured mechanised infantry division stationed in Germany on the border with Russian-controlled Czechoslovakia. Many of the drafted soldiers were distraught, especially those with family complications who were depending on assignments close to home. I had mixed emotions; Germany was in Europe and Ireland was in Europe. Perhaps I would get to go back home sooner than I ever imagined.

Feeling much better than many of my fellow soldiers, I made preparations for this new turn in the road of my journey. I began to get excited about my new assignment, that is until we were lined up for our overseas inoculations for diseases I never knew existed. Later I was to realise that Americans were obsessed with inoculations.

When America invaded Vietnam, the needle brigades were ecstatic. Here they had every southeast Asian disease to consider. The unfortunate, already-reluctant soldiers felt like pin cushions as they were injected, pumped and stamped with every antidote then known to man. Yes, I said invaded Vietnam. It was a regional problem and no threat to America. Once again the Pentagon drew America into a disastrous, needless war. America lost that war in a shameful manner, and for what? The war cost countless Vietnamese and 50,000 American lives.

We left behind a hapless population which was brutalised by the communist regime because of our interference in their internal affairs, and America was torn apart by the war, much like it is now by the Iraq war – another Pentagon-driven war. In the 1950s America invaded Korea in exactly the same way, without provocation. This was another Pentagon-driven war. Fifty years later we still have nearly forty thousand American soldiers in South Korea on high alert.

The total cost of the Korean war came to billions of dollars, and is still climbing. At the time, North Korea was a regional problem and no threat to America. Today America is still held hostage to that war by the deranged, corrupt leader of North Korea. The Pentagon also still insists that America keeps forty thousand combat-ready troops in post-war Japan. This is over sixty years after the end of the Second World War. The accumulated cost has to be in trillions of dollars, and is still growing. It makes no sense for America to be spending all that money when Japan's economy is the second strongest in the world. A logical question would be: what are the president of the United States and all of America's senators and congressmen doing? Surely they can see what we see. America's infrastructure is crumbling, its health care systems are pathetic at best, and Americans are still living in trailers years after Hurricane Katrina struck the Gulf of Mexico. The answer is simple: politics. The quickest way to get votes is to raise the spectre of the communist flag or some Pentagon-created threat, and Americans go paranoid. Pentagon generals are paraded on television, darkly telling Americans that the Huns are coming. The Secretary of Defense backs them up, the president gets readily re-elected and another war is declared.

The unfortunate American soldiers who have to fight the Pentagon-staged war in Iraq refer to 'weapons of mass destruction' as 'weapons of mass deception'. I have American friends in Iraq and their overpowering emotion is a sense of betrayal by their leaders, especially President George Bush. They are forced to walk around using Second World War tactics fighting a guer-rilla war in the midst of a religious civil war. They are easy tar-gets, and the war cannot be won under any circumstances; yet, knowing that, the Pentagon sends American soldiers onto that butcher's block every day. And I say all this not as an anti-war radical but as a former infantry sergeant in the American army. While I am not a former general and graduate from West Point, I have enough common sense to realise that, with the exception of the Second World War, all American wars were driven by the Pentagon and their cosy kick-back friends in the multi-billion-dollar weapons industry.

It was an exciting time for me at Fort Dix as we prepared to depart. I really began to realise there was a good chance I could return home to Ireland on leave. I would think about that often – me in an American army uniform, visiting my friends in the Irish army and talking about things, so soon after I was thinking that I would never see them again. And then there were my family and friends, and a few girls I had dated – what about them? I was not sure about showing up in an American army uniform, but I had no civilian clothes. I knew I had some shirts and trousers and a pair of shoes in my bedroom, but no overcoat. Maybe I could afford to buy one in Germany before I went home. That's all I thought about: going home and making my family proud of me. I then became nervous about it all, and I don't know why to this day. Maybe it was because nobody would be expecting me home so soon.

Anyway, the two Hitlerites, Honecker and Krenz, had exact-ly what they thirsted after: a captive nation. On 15 August 1961, the two despots ordered the construction of the Berlin Wall. A monstrosity over sixty-six miles long, with forty miles of ra-zor barbed wire, and three hundred heavily armed watchtowers. These towers were manned by East German soldiers, with or-ders to kill their own people. Over the years, those soldiers murdered two hundred unarmed East German men, women and children, and badly wounded two hundred others. They would spot them in the white of the snow and turn their machine guns on them. The East German border's snow would often be spattered with red blood until the spring rains and warmth washed away the shame.

On the same day that the Berlin Wall's construction began, I boarded the USNS *Maurice Rose* at the Staten Island terminal in New York. The good ship *Rose* was built after the Pearl Harbor attack, and showed every sea mile. It was designed to carry 1,685 enlisted men and 510 officers, and it was no cruise ship, by a long haul. The *Rose* and six other similar ships ferried 21,000 troops over to the Russian border that year, via the German port of Bremerhaven. The Pentagon was ratcheting up the tension. This East and West German problem was now a dangerous international crisis fuelled by America's needless intervention.

The *Rose* has an interesting history. It was named after Major General Maurice Rose, the son of a rabbi. General Rose was referred to as the 'greatest forgotten commander' of the Second World War. He was the highest-ranking Jew in the European Command, and highly respected. Tragically, he was the only division-level general killed in action during that war. As I settled into my metal bunk, one of six stacked three to each side with only one foot separating them, deep in the bowels of the ship, I almost got an attack of claustrophobia. I was assigned the bottom bunk and that turned out to be a disaster. When lying in my bunk the space between my nose and the sagging mattress above me was a matter of inches. I thought then that I wished the ship had been named after somebody other than a general who had been killed in a muddy German ditch by a burp gun; it was a bad omen. As it turned out my sea-faring instinct was correct – the name is everything. All we could do was lie there and pray for good weather. Hurricane Betsy is recorded as having passed across the Atlantic to our stern and missed us. To this day, with my hand on a stack of bibles, I do not believe that!

After a few days at sea, all hell broke loose as the ship suddenly began to rise to great heights, pause for an agonising moment, free-fall for what seemed like an eternity, then smash into the trough of the wave with such violence that rivets could be heard popping, and that went on for days. The *Rose* was a large, three-funnel ship, but it was still thrown around like a cork in a tempest. Never mind the bad food – the soldiers, some who had never even seen the sea before, were puking all over the place. As I lay in my bunk, inches off the floor with water and vomit swirling all around me, I began to understand the motives of the *Bounty* mutineers. Seriously, it was a mess, and to make matters worse, all doors and hatches had been secured to prevent the entry of sea water. This increased the sense of claustrophobia and resulted in very poor air quality – not that it was that good to start with.

I had gained my sea legs a long time ago out on Dundalk Bay and never grew seasick, and that drew some dirty looks from my miserable shipmates. Another reason that convinces me that we were in Hurricane Betsy and that it was not behind us occurred a day later. After being tossed around, suddenly everything grew almost deathly calm and still. I could hear whispers across the quarters. Everybody started to shout and cheer that the worst was over and that the storm had passed us by. I took a chance and worked my way up metal steps to another deck and saw a porthole.

What I saw through that porthole chilled my heart and soul. It was a churning high wall of water a few miles away. The water on our side of the wall was flat as a country lake. We were inside the eye of the hurricane! My grandfather had shown me drawings that were identical to what I was witnessing. I knew that the only thing holding back that roiling wall of water was the internal pressure of the hurricane itself. I also knew our ship would eventually have to break through that wall or we would be held captive as it roared north. I returned to my quarters but did not have the heart to tell my shipmates the truth – I figured the ship's captain would do that. But he never did.

They announced over the intercom that hot food was finally available in the mess halls. Everybody lined up and we moved quickly through the line, then I saw the food – some kind of Irish stew. I don't know who the culinary brain was who thought that choice of food up for hundreds of seasick soldiers, but he should have been thrown overboard. As we drew closer to the mess hall, soldiers started to pass us going the other way, gagging and dry-puking all the way. That was enough for many in my line for they either turned back or started puking themselves.

The mess hall was like something out of a horror movie. Soldiers were sprawled across tables or leaning up against walls, dry-heaving. I have no idea what puking experience the readers of this book have had, but let me tell you that on the pain scale the dry heaves are probably akin to giving birth to a rhino.

I was very hungry and was determined to eat something. I quickly reached the serving area and immediately saw what the problem was. The four very bloated, unshaven and foul-smelling cooks were ladling onto the soldiers' metal trays something that looked suspiciously like the puke that was swilling around the floor of our quarters. Some soldiers held on and took the food away and some just lost it where they stood. There was no way in hell I was going to touch that swill, but I knew exactly what I wanted and needed: salted sea biscuits and water. I asked one cook who looked like Béla Lugosi on a binge and he pointed to a large metal box. He said take as many as you like, and I did. They had plenty of water and somebody had discarded a canteen, so I filled that up and went back to my cabin. My grandfather, who had never as much as got his toes wet in the sea, had told me about the curative powers of salted sea biscuits when it came to seasickness.

For the next day I shared the biscuits with my shipmates. They rapidly improved and that was good, but I knew what was coming. I told them a few times not to be eating candy but they only laughed at my Irish accent in a teasing manner, and ignored my advice.

I had been on many ships in the port of Dundalk and so I started to roam around. Nobody seemed to mind as the crew was busy carrying out repairs and maintenance duties. I made it down to the engine room and talked to a few of the crew. They confirmed my fears. We were in the eye of the hurricane and they feared the worst. But still nothing came from the captain or crew. They opened all of the hatches and doors and aired the ship out. The soldiers began to eat, and the food improved. I stayed with my sea biscuits and stored many in my bunk. I knew what was coming.

The five other soldiers in my cabin and I became friends and I decided to tell them about the reality of the situation. Once again they got a good laugh and told me I was a 'worry wart', whatever that was. Since I would have to put up with them puking all over our bunk space very shortly, I took drastic action. I told all five that I knew a way to an upper deck, and that the view was incredible. They eagerly followed me through a maze of hallways that eventually opened up onto a deserted deck. They just stood there and I did not have to say anything; they visibly paled when they saw the mountainous wall of water.

When we went back down below they went to the mess hall and stocked up on sea biscuits and water and that was the end of the candy and junk food. They tried to explain to some of the other soldiers what the real situation was and some listened and some did not. As for me, I prepared myself for the ship's breakthrough of the hurricane's wall. My shipmates had been noisy and talkative; now they were very quiet. They believed. Then the captain announced that we were about to encounter rough seas and the ship was battened-down, then the roaring noise began. Only those who have been in a hurricane at sea can describe the effect that noise has on a person. Standing on the deck, we had seen how insignificant our ship was in the scale of things, and the thundering noise just accentuated that fact. I sneaked up to one deck and looked out of a porthole, and there it was: a churning wall of water. Yet our ship was still quiet. Then the wind's speed increased and I ran below.

That day and the next were worse than before and then suddenly we were free of the storm. We all felt wrung out and exhausted after the experience and just lay in our bunks. My shipmates realised that I already had five years of military experience and treated me differently. We were not to know then that on our return trip I would be their supervising sergeant.

By the time we were approaching the southwest coast of Ireland the crew had the ship back in working order and everybody's spirits picked up. We rounded southern England and headed north to the Port of Bremerhaven, and Germany. For whatever reason, I was the first soldier to step off the gangplank onto German soil. An army photographer asked me to pose, then took my photograph. I forgot about the incident until about two years later when I was inquiring about the Green Berets in Bad Tolz, Germany, where they were stationed. A young clerk kept staring at me and then said: 'Sergeant, that's your photograph over there,' and it was. The caption read: 'The first US army infantry soldier to land in support of the Cold War.' I got a chuckle out of that and tried to get the clerk to give me the photograph, but he refused. He said that it was going to be included in some historical record of the Cold War. That was good for a laugh – me being a fly on the wall of history.

How can I describe the conditions on the Czech border?

Suffice to say that when we were in the field they were harsh to the extreme. The army outfitted us well. We wore large, rubberised boots that were designed to withstand the withering cold of the winters there. We called them 'Mickey Mouse' boots because that is what they looked like, but they prevented frost-bitten toes, so that was all right. We had what looked like sheep-wool-lined trousers, which we wore over our regular pants. Then there were the upper layers of insulated clothing, a thick vest, a heavy jacket and an insulated parka. This was all well and good if you were just sitting around in the snow doing nothing, which we were not. We had military objectives that had to be met, and they were not always reached by mechanised armoured carriers – we walked.

There was also the equipment we were required to carry. What with weapons and gear it weighed around fifty pounds or more. Then there was the deep snow and what it did to our legs as we slogged our way across mountains and through forests. We slept in the rough and when we were lucky and the armoured carrier came along, we slept in and on top of that. I still have photographs of those conditions, and when I look at them they give me the shudders. I wondered why America could not invade Barbados or some other tropical place.

I was promoted to team leader and then shipped out to the Third Infantry Division's non-commissioned officers academy. That raised many eyebrows as I had only been in the American army ten months. When I wrote home and gave them the news, my father, out of concern that I might get my feelings hurt, wrote back and told me not to get my expectations high as I was not an American. Six weeks later I was promoted to sergeant.

In the American army, on a day-to-day basis, the sergeants run things. The officers are there, but the rank-and-file soldier rarely has contact with them, unlike in other armies. They realised many wars ago it was the sergeant who would lead his men to battle and inspire them to climb that muddy hill and die. So, for the most part, the sergeants run the army. It is an elevated position and comes with many benefits. Free housing, free shipping of personal possessions, inexpensive food and goods at the Post Exchange and dirt-cheap liquor by the bottle, and their own NCO club.

My first visit to our club was an eye-opener because it looked more like a Las Vegas set-up. There were many slot machines, top flight entertainment, cheap mixed drinks, fine food and females all over the place. Some were employees and others were the daughters or bored wives of senior sergeants. I decided to stay away from the daughters and wives because they all probably had battle-hardened sergeants as fathers and husbands; there would be nothing more dangerous than a crazed and armed, battle-hardened father or husband on a search-and-destroy mission, with me as their objective.

I realised that I had thirty days' paid leave coming to me and my thoughts turned to home. It had been such a short time since I had left, but it seemed like years. There was a travel office on the base and I lined up the tickets. Only when I had them in my hands did it hit me that I really was going home.

I knew our pub was still experiencing hard times and that a few bottles of spirits would go a long way. I had spent much of my money on the travel tickets but still had enough left for my holiday. Each month sergeants are issued coupons for liquor and gasoline. The prices are very low because they are subsidised by the army. I pooled my fellow sergeants and collected their unwanted coupons. I went to the base liquor store and loaded up with premium brand American bourbon and Russian vodka, all at less than three dollars a bottle. My bags were so heavy that I received assistance from concerned fellow travellers who probably thought, since I was in uniform, that I was infirm.

I made it through Frankfurt, Brussels and Dublin airports and it cost me a bottle at each stop to concerned customs officials. It was only when I boarded a train at Amiens Street station bound for Dundalk that I really felt like I was at home.

It was the best of times, seeing my family and friends, then dropping by our pub to say hello to all the customers I knew so well. Even better, on the day of my return, was getting into my own bed and under the same sheets and blankets I remembered so well. As I lay in my bed, our house silent, I began to think about what I had done by emigrating, and what I had missed and would miss. My bedroom was a small room with a window that overlooked my river and mountains. I could not sleep, so I opened the small window and sat on the wide sill. I could hear the sounds of an incoming tide and the cries of curlews and mallards winging free in the wind. It was icy weather, but I felt no cold, only a little sadness as I heard a ship begin its passage in from Dundalk Bay.

It was not a bad sadness, just a person missing home. I wanted to go to my parents, who were downstairs still talking. I was exhausted and had gone to bed early, and now I could not sleep. I wanted to go downstairs and sit with them for a while and have them tell me what I had done was right. But for some reason I could not do so. I was doing well and had a good future in America, but in that small dark bedroom I was not so sure.

Later, after my parents had gone to bed, I went downstairs, careful of the creak in the middle step. I had stacked my bags in the living room and took one back to my room. It was there I started a bad habit because I opened a bottle of Jack Daniels whiskey and let the alcohol lull me to sleep. I awoke as the dark sky showed a little grey, urinated out of my small window as I had always done and fell back into a deep sleep. I dreamed of steaming jungles and machine-gun fire and that brought me awake. America was invading Vietnam and I was a Ranger-trained infantry sergeant, I knew where I was going; I didn't need a dream.

As I started to circulate I began to realise that something had changed since I had left. At first I did not know what it was, then it struck me like a hammer between the eyes: my friends were acting as if I was a stranger. There were no familiar slaps, nudges or winks, no small talk, just politeness. I cornered a friend from school and asked him what was wrong. He said: 'Look at you in your American army sergeant's uniform; it's not us that has changed, it's you,' and he appeared angry. We went to mass that Sunday and I wore my dress uniform because my mother had asked me to, and I was sorry I did. I did not take communion because I could feel the stares all over my body and they were not friendly stares. I had seen familiar faces and got back indifferent nods. The church was packed, my church where I had been an altar boy; now I felt like a stranger. I felt trapped and suffocated and wanted to get out as quickly as possible.

This was to be my first experience of the retribution even your own people can inflict on you if you get out of the box you were expected to stay in. I wish I had been more aware and smarter back then. If I had been, I would have learned a valuable lesson. If you choose to get out of the box people expect you to stay in, you had better be ready to face the consequences. They said I was smart back then, but apparently I was not, and it appears that was the case later on in my life. Maybe some smart people are slow learners, I just don't know. Somebody once said that you can't go home, and I agree.

# 5

# BEING A COP IN AMERICA

**W**hy did I not stay in the American army? That's a question that was often asked then, and even now, for I was on a fast-track promotion programme. My decision to leave came on a cold night on the Czech border and was prompted by the US army itself. My squad was assigned to patrol an area where other non-infantry units were located. I knew their positions on my map and walked over to one so that they would know we were in the area. A young lieutenant waved us through their perimeter and introduced himself.

I was puzzled by the appearance of their equipment. It was dark and I only had moonlight to see what was going on. There were a number of jeep-like vehicles with large weapons mounted on them, much like an anti-tank gun, but these were no anti-tank guns. At the end of what appeared to be a three-foot-long tube was an object with what seemed to be a large green bulb attached to it. There was much wiring and electronic equipment around the vehicle.

The lieutenant saw my surprised reaction and said: 'You do know we are a nuclear unit?' I did not know, nor had I ever heard of a front-line nuclear weapon; frankly, I was stunned. He told me it was a 'Davy Crockett' missile and we chatted for a while. He then asked me where I was from and I told him Ireland. He asked if I was a citizen and had a security clearance. He then left and used his radio. Within a few minutes my squad was replaced and I was ordered back to headquarters.

My commanding officer acted as if I had concealed the fact that I was not an American citizen. My first thought was that my army personnel file was in his office, and that he must have read the file before he recommended me for promotion to sergeant. I could not understand how he would have thought otherwise, my Irish army discharge papers were in that file. I realised I was on shaky ground as he was very upset, so I remained silent. I was transported back to base and that essentially was the end of my military career. The officers who were grooming me for officer training in America fell silent, the door was shut – no, it was slammed. I was advised I had to be a citizen to become an officer and that sounded very reasonable, but nobody had told me.

I had become friends with Winship Leadingham while we were undergoing our training at Fort Dix. He had been drafted and was to be stationed state-side as they called it. He gave me his telephone number and address and told me if I survived 'this mess' to look him up in Atlanta. I really liked him; he was a stand-in-the door kind of guy who, although well educated and from a mon-eyed background, never showed it. But I thought as we parted that we would never see each other again: I was wrong.

I left the army and headed to Atlanta. I had called Win and he had said 'come on down', and sounded excited. This was a whole new experience for me after two armies. The freedom of civilian life was almost intoxicating and it felt good. It took me a while to reach Atlanta and contact Win. He had not changed. He and his wife Susan, who was expecting their first child, insisted that I stay with them in suburban Riverdale until I got my feet on the ground. This was my first experience with real America and I loved every second. A neighbour threw a barbecue for me and I got to meet many wonderful people.

One day after arrival I started to research the *Atlanta Journal* for job possibilities, and that was some experience, for there were hundreds of jobs available. But nobody was looking for a Ranger-trained army sergeant. I was not discouraged and went on many job interviews. All gave me 'that' look, and that was that. Win saw my increasing frustration and suggested that I come to work at his family's firm, Fulton Supply Company, which was formed in 1914 and is still in business and growing. I resisted the offer for some time then finally said yes. But I did not want to take a regular job away from somebody who was planning on a career there, because I knew I was not going to stay. So I became the only white man handling the heavy steel in the lower part of the large building. The black workers knew that I came to work each day with Win and could not figure out just what I was doing in the 'black' part of the company, the sweat-shop part. I was in good shape, so it was no big deal, and I sweated right along with the black workers.

When it was time to sit down for a break, I sat with the black workers and drank out of the black water fountain, and that was a big 'no no' in the south back then. The white supervisor hauled me outside the building and began to berate me. I had just about enough of all these American 'unknown' laws and jerked him out of his shoes. His high-pitched screaming and the applause of the black workers brought the administrators from the top floor down to the loading docks. By then I had put the squealing supervisor back on the ground.

Everybody but Win just shook their heads and went back upstairs. Win and I had a talk and he said the supervisor should have been fired years ago, but nobody wanted his job. However, he said that what I had done was not right, and I agreed, but felt a lot better. We decided that it might be a good idea if that day was my last day.

Over the years we lost touch with each other. The last word I received was that he had moved out of state. Every now and then I would hear that somebody called Win was trying to contact me, but that was usually months or years later. Since I was including him in this book, I made one last effort to contact him to obtain his approval. That same week Win died in Florida. He passed away 28 June 2007. I read the comments that were made by friends and family and posted my own remembrance. Sometimes it seems life is just not fair.

In Atlanta I had moved into a cottage behind an exclusive boarding house for equally exclusive young ladies who were attending college. This was a very large red brick home on 14th Street in north Atlanta. Win's aunt owned the home and after Win assured her that I was of sterling character, his aunt rented the storybook cottage to me for a nominal rent, and that included meals. She told Win she liked the idea of having a man around the house. The first morning that I went up to the house for breakfast I nearly had a heart attack. Eighteen of the most beautiful girls I had ever seen were seated at the table.

Win's aunt made the announcement that I would be staying in the cottage and that I had extensive military experience, and they all should feel safer. If she could have read my mind at that moment she might not have made that announcement. Each girl stood and introduced herself and I smiled each time, feeling fainter by the moment. Throughout the meal, with Win's severe-looking aunt at the head seat, the girls' eyes were downcast.

As soon as she excused herself and left the room, the temperature soared. The looks I got would melt the polar cap quicker than global warming. This was a room filled with suppressed and tightly supervised young ladies.

I had assumed that when Win told me that the girls were attending college, that meant a regular college. Not so, to my joy, they were attending the Barbizon School for Modelling and Fashion Design. Only the cream of the crop need apply. There is an apt American expression that fits my situation there perfectly, 'I thought I had died and gone to heaven.'

It was not going to be as easy as it first looked to date one of the girls, and I stress, one. Anytime a girl and I made arrangements to go to a movie or go out and eat, at least three of her friends tagged along, sometimes more. Every ruse I tried failed and it was not because the other girls were deliberately intruding, they were just bored to tears.

There was a pizza bar around the corner on Piedmont Road which ran specials for mugs of beer and large pizzas and that became our hangout. So I would trudge down to the bar with four or five beautiful girls on my arms just about every evening. By the time we all pitched in and shared the tab, it was very inexpensive. Afterwards we would all go for a stroll in Piedmont Park which was across the street. While the majority of customers tended to be of college age, other customers would usually drop by at 'happy hour' when the cold beer was cheap. There was some construction going on nearby and six workers started to come by every evening at about six. All six were large, tanned and muscular, and exhibited the body language and noise of a group of lowland gorillas. I say that with apologies to the gorillas. All of them, at one time or another, came by our booth and tried to get something going with the girls. I could sense tension building as each one was rejected, then he would go back to the bar and make loud remarks about the 'faggot with the girls'. I ignored them and thought that was that.

Then one evening they arrived at about 7.30 p.m., obviously drunk. My first reaction was to get the girls ready to leave, but it was not me they were interested in, it was the owner. She apparently had been reprimanding them on a constant basis and had barred them from her pub the previous evening, after we had left. We had just had our pizza delivered along with a large mug of cold beer. I implored the girls to leave and beat a hasty retreat. I don't know what it is about American women but they love to see men fight, more so if it is over them. The next thing I knew one of the workers smashed a beer bottle into the bar's back-drop, engraved mirror, the owner's pride and joy, then his friends followed suit. The owner, who weighed in at a stocky two to three hundred pounds, swung at them with a pool cue she had concealed under the counter.

The kitchen staff started to scream and somebody called the police. We could not escape because the drunks were between us and the door. The girls all looked at me expectantly. I assumed that meant they wanted me to get involved with the primitives at the bar. Their beautiful eyes were wide with excitement but mine were wide with trying to find a way out of there. I would rather have volunteered for a frontal lobotomy than get involved. Then the front door opened and a young Atlanta police officer stepped inside. He took one look at the fighting and went back outside. I wondered what that was all about. Then he returned and yelled for peace and quiet.

The primitives immediately stopped and sullenly stood there, heads down. I figured that was that, but the owner decided otherwise. She took a swing at the biggest primitive and he went down as if he had been poleaxed, and it started all over again. I saw one of the workers pick up a large, full mug of beer and begin to creep up behind the policeman, who was trying to break up the fight. That changed everything: I rose up and took our mug of beer with me. I stood behind the primitive until he swung the mug at the back of the policeman's head. Mine hit first and he started to stagger around like a chicken with his head cut off.

Just when I thought it could not get worse, the front door burst open and about five young policemen charged through, swinging their night-sticks. Naturally I looked like a combatant and suffered a few healthy whacks on my back and arms. It was only when the policeman I had rescued yelled for them to stop that the barrage ended. The girls were ecstatic and gave me lots of hugs and kisses as a reward for my bravery, which did not help my personal situation of privation very much. The police were very apologetic and began appraising my companions. They thanked me for stepping in and saving the young policeman from serious injury. They asked for my name, address and telephone number and assured me I did not have to come to court to testify. I was not to know that their real motive, as six single police officers, was to get close to the girls.

A few days later I received a call from the officer I had rescued from a serious head injury and he thanked me profusely. He invited me to a get-together he was having at his house with some other officers. That sounded great because I was getting 'crazy in the head', as they say, squiring around the girls. Then, as we were about to end the conversation, he asked if I could bring the girls along. Too late I realised I had been snookered, but I said yes. I told Win's aunt that I was taking the girls to a recital at Emory University and she seemed fine with that.

The day of the party arrived and the word had got out that ten girls were going to the party. The logistics of transporting them there was solved by my new policeman friend. On the evening of the party they met us one street over in four cars. I had a feeling of impending disaster that had in the past proved accurate.

The party was really enjoyable and I made many new friends. They had all assumed that I was gay. When they discovered my background and lack of employment, they brought me into a back bedroom and recruited me for the Atlanta police department. Unfortunately the girls also had an enjoyable time and also made new friends. When it was time to leave and make the boarding house curfew, I found myself alone. I was assured by my new policeman friends that they would get the girls home on time, so I took a bus back to the cottage. The next morning I awoke rejuvenated and excited about becoming an American police officer. I strolled up to the house and sat down at a table which was missing ten girls. Win's aunt glared at me and told me to move out right away.

What appeared to be a disaster turned out to be a blessing in disguise. One of the girls told me there was a very nice apartment just around the corner and the rent was reasonable. I had never noticed it before and had walked by there many times. I looked at a nice, one-bedroom furnished apartment and moved in that same morning Just sitting on the couch gave me a feeling of freedom. For the first time in my life I realised that I had privacy. The apartment had a nice kitchen and, while the TV was black and white, it was crystal clear.

I took a shower then lay down on the bed and relaxed. I was beginning to drift off when somebody began knocking on my door. Pulling on a pair of blue jeans, I opened the door. All of the girls were out in the hallway smiling with wide-eyed expectancy. They moved in and began cleaning and generally making themselves at home. I was stunned but what could I do? They informed me that my apartment could be reached through a lane directly behind the cottage I had just been evicted from. My new home was but fifty yards from my old home.

The girls kept coming and going that evening and soon I had a stereo and records, and my refrigerator was full of things that made me prefer to starve rather than eat them. Within a week I became a neutered male. My apartment became their hangout and a place to do their laundry and sleep over. When I would go to take a shower I had to wade through wet panties and bras, and many nights I had difficulty sleeping because I had to share my bed with two or more scantily clad girls. They used my phone but paid for the calls. I became their confidant and big brother. Then I started to cull the herd; enough was enough. I told them the management had complained and they all had to go.

The girls were sad because my apartment was an escape from their guarded boarding house. I made sure that I gave my telephone number to the ones who had been casting extra lusty eyes in my direction. It was then that the apartment truly turned into a blessing.

But my money was running low and it was time to get a job. I contacted my police friends and a week later I was investigated, examined and tested for entry into the Atlanta police department. As luck would have it, a new academy class was starting the following week. I was impressed by the professionalism of the academy staff, all senior officers, many with rank. I did well for a recent immigrant as I graduated eighteenth out of thirty. I could have done better but I was concentrating on the cultural differences as much as I was on the complex instruction.

The academy was primarily academic and surprisingly light on firearms and physical training. Sad to say, this was to change with the advent of Hollywood-inspired 'super cops' and Rambo-like detectives, with everybody pumping iron and carrying high-tech weapons. What was lost was the human touch.

After graduation I was assigned to the day watch. I expected to be given a walking beat in some remote area or to be driving one of the paddy wagons that transferred arrested prisoners to the city jail. I wondered about the name 'paddy wagon'; it sounded suspiciously Irish, and it was.

Captain Mullins, whose family emigrated from the west of Ireland, explained to me that when cities like New York and Boston were creating their police departments, they sent recruiters to Ireland. His version was that they signed up big country lads and arranged all of their travel documents. In many instances the new recruit was sworn in as a New York police officer while they were still in Ireland. How true all that is, I just don't know. However, the fact remains that even today all of those police departments still have a deep Irish culture ingrained in their organisations. They have Emerald societies and their bagpipe bands play Irish laments at policemen's funerals.

The first day I reported for actual duty was exciting. The relieving shift assembled in the large basement of police headquarters. There they were briefed and given assignments, if they did not already have one – and most veteran officers did. Many officers worked the same beat for years, but always coveting the back-up car. This car had the freedom to roam over much of the city, and its purpose was to back up regular beat cars on difficult or dangerous calls like armed robbery. It was a bit of a lone-ranger type of assignment and often led to promotion to detective and the gold shield.

Captain Mullins and Lieutenant Shephard, the day-watch commanders, rattled off the beat assignments, even for those officers who had patrolled their beat for years. Then Captain Mullins raised his hand and announced that the officer who normally drove the back-up car had been promoted to detective, after fifteen years of service. That caused a stir in the ranks of the veteran officers, and some congratulated a senior officer who was the expected heir to the back-up car. Then Mullins made a stunning announcement: 'Car B30 is being permanently assigned to Officer Mac Manus.' For a few moments I did not understand why everybody was looking at me in bewilderment. Then I realised that B30 was the back-up car. I was in a daze as we walked outside and up the stairs to meet the midnight shift coming in for replacement officers. I stood in the hot southern sun and listened to the muted comments of my fellow officers.

Nobody could understand what was going on. They could see my consternation so it was confusion all around.

The procedure was that the midnight shift patrol cars would come through the tunnel behind the jail, and then drive to the front of police headquarters where the day shift officers would take over the cars. It was a fast operation; it had to be. Atlanta was a high-crime city racked with racial unrest, and there was no time for idle talk. The replacement officer needed to get to his assigned beat as quickly as possible. Today, police training includes extensive driving skills, including pursuit driving, but back then it didn't. Nobody had ever asked me if I knew how to drive or even had a driver's licence; if they had, the answer would have been 'no'.

Everybody in America drives, but I had never driven a car. I had navigated an armoured personnel carrier at night using night vision and two lateral controls. That was not even close to driving a high-powered car on busy American streets. Now I had to contend with B30. It was a mammoth Chevrolet Impala, an eight-cylinder throbbing beast that growled. I jumped in and frantically scanned the dashboard, and on the steering column I saw D and R and other letters. I pulled the shift handle down to D and 'stomped' on the gas pedal, as they say down south; a big mistake.

The Impala lurched out of the driveway propelled by a big Irish foot and a powerful engine and straight towards a terrified officer who had been assigned to stop the traffic on Decatur Street and wave the police cars out onto the road so that they could get to their beats. To this day I can remember the look on that police officer's face as I swerved around him and narrowly missed hitting a sandwich shop and two drunks who had just been released from City jail. It was reported back to me that Captain Mullins said: 'He is raring to go.'

The city survived my first eight-hour shift because I did not hit anybody or anything. Getting around a major metropolitan city was no problem. They had supplied me with a map and a street guide. So when I received a call for assistance, it was easy to find the street – reading a map is what army sergeants did. Whether it's mountains, jungles, woods or streets, it's all the same on a map: coordinates.

My first call was a knife-fight at the notorious Duke Hotel on Piedmont Road. This was a hot-pillow joint, where rooms could be rented by the hour, day, week or whatever. Its residents had long given up trying to make a meaningful contribution to society and and instead had become public nuisances. The regular beat officer was tied up on another call, so other outlying patrol cars were dispatched to back me up.

The reason I remember this call in such vivid detail is that it was my first. I parked in front of the building, put on my hat, slipped my nightstick into its holder on my belt, rearranged my holster and gun, and stepped into the world of the Duke Hotel. All this rearranging is a psychologically reassuring ritual all police officers do prior to entering a dangerous situation. I am not sure what I was expecting to see on that scorching day in Atlanta, but whatever it was, it was not what I saw. The lobby smelled of urine and God only knows what else, and it was stifling hot. A bovine-faced clerk, safely ensconced behind a wire cage, said: 'Upstairs on the fourth floor, a knife fight.'

There were no elevators in this four-floor building. As I worked my way upstairs the yelling and shouting and the smells increased in variety and density; this was no place for a honeymoon. This chaos did not seem to bother the junkies, drunks or prostitutes who, as I made my way upstairs, kept yelling out: 'It's the fucking man!' I was thinking how proud my parents would be of me now that I had an official job title in America. Doors were slamming everywhere and the noise on the fourth floor increased. I finally reached it, and there they were, my future clients in my new profession.

Four men were entwined in a violent bloody struggle over what I later learned was a dollar bill. They were not just wrestling, but really trying to hurt each other, and apparently had done so. Then I saw a big knife in one of their hands and that changed everything. Knives kill just as effectively as guns. I yelled: 'Freeze, police.' That had an immediate effect on three of the men who broke loose and charged down the stairs, but not the man with the knife. His crazed, bloodshot eyes told me I had a big problem. He went into a crouch and moved towards me slashing with the knife. I ducked a slash and flipped him over the wooden stair rail and he plunged four floors down to the cracked marble floor beneath.

Shortly afterwards I heard other policemen coming through the lobby door. I yelled down: 'Call an ambulance for the one on the floor, and secure his knife.' As I started down the stairs a police officer met me halfway. 'About that guy, Mac...' I dreaded this moment. 'Is he dead?' The officer shrugged: 'What guy?'

When I reached the lobby I saw no sign of the knife-wielding man. He should have been dead, his body splattered all over the floor, but there was nothing, not even a sign of blood. The clerk said he had jumped up and ran out the door just before the other policemen had arrived.

To this day I have no idea how he survived that fall; it was an incredible case of survival and, I might add, escape. In retrospect I was glad he had made it out alive. All I needed on my first day on the job was to kill a man by throwing him off the fourth floor of a fleabag hotel.

A month later I was checking a pool hall on Hunter Street and there he was right in my face, red-eyed and grinning at me. I remembered the knife incident and moved towards him. He literally jumped over a full-sized pool table and was out on the street running in a matter of seconds. He was obviously none the worse for his four-storey fall.

We would see each other on a regular basis, but I guess we must have mutually agreed mentally to just ignore each other; better that way. He and I both knew his life was on a short string, and it was. All of these discarded street children seemed to have gained a death wish as they got older – on the streets with nowhere to go, not much to eat, no family or love in their lives, victims of sexual predators and society in general, and hopeless in the richest country in the world; just thrown away like garbage. There they were, perhaps with red eyes and a knife, knowing some cop or somebody else might shoot them someday; but what else was there for them?

I was to get to know many street children, young and old, just riding out their life's clock until they became a statistic, dead or alive. There were as many lost white children as there were black ones, and I saw little difference; same story, just a different skin colour. There was one difference, however: the white kids would hurt a cop quicker than a black kid, and that's a fact. Anybody who would dispute that has never worked an inner-city, high-crime zone as a beat cop. The really anguishing thing about these lost street children is that in Atlanta some of them were to become victims of what became known as the Atlanta Child Murders.

I have been asked many times what it was like being a police officer in America. To this day I truly believe I have not ever given a satisfactory answer. It is difficult to explain the complex nature of the beast on paper. I have rewritten these pages over and over again, and this is the best I can do. It's an emotional issue with every cop, especially street cops.

Cops are people who risk their lives every time they strap

on their guns to protect society, and society treats them like unwanted step-children. While this may appear to be somewhat melodramatic, that's what street cops believe; I know, I was one for years. My personal police experiences range from a high-crime city like Atlanta to the sultry wealth of Palm Beach County in Florida. A quarter of a century of law enforcement in high-crime street patrol, as a detective in vice, homicide, undercover narcotics, labour union riots, executive protection and all else that comes with the badge have given me a reasonably clear perspective of what it is to be a cop in America. Then why have I had a hard time defining that on paper? Maybe it was because I was hesitant to hurt some people's feelings, those of street cops I have known; or maybe it was because I was not being honest with my own self. As I said, it's a complex beast.

I was a training officer in Atlanta and Florida and conducted national conferences. I also addressed numerous national and international meetings. The reason I am going into such detail is that some of the things you will be reading about in this chapter require that you feel comfortable with my qualifications. Movies and television feast on police drama, and very little of it is close to reality. Major best-selling novels and movies delve into police work but never seem to grasp what it is all about. While entertaining, they paint a false picture of what it is really like inside our close-knit brotherhood, and what we do inside that brotherhood, legal and illegal. It might be objected that I am no longer a cop. But I am, because once a cop, always a cop. It's like your skin; you can never shake it off, and society won't let you.

Even when I achieved a high-executive management position with a corporation ranked on America's Fortune 500 list of top companies, I was still considered to be a cop. Fellow executives, friends and family never let it go, always asking me questions about what it was like being a cop. When I started my own corporation and ran it successfully for ten years, I was still a cop. People have this morbid fascination with cops, more so now because of the novels, movies and television programmes that either demonise or glorify them.

I wonder how those Hollywood script writers and the crime novelists would react on a hot night in a vomit-filled patrol car. Or how they would react to the gut-wrenching odour of a green, fly-covered corpse in the trunk of a car. Or if they were forced to walk around in a stifling hot room where a murder just occurred, smelling the sickly sweet smell of freshly-spilled blood. There is no other smell like it, but the creators of police fiction stay away. They stay away from the reality of it all. It is probably is better that they do because the truth would not sell, so they create this Hollywood version of a cop's life. People believe that version and many young cops fall into the trap of trying to become something they shouldn't be, and then everybody gets into trouble.

So the real truth about police officers and police work stays where it probably belongs, hidden deep inside the closed brotherhood. Why call it a 'closed brotherhood'? Because it is and that is a rock-hard solid fact. The police have fraternal orders, societies, and an endless variety of closed groups, but at the end of the day, they are all one big brotherhood of police officers. And what causes this polarisation between the police and the citizens they are sworn to protect is difficult to say. A startling metamorphosis occurs when civilians cross that threshold and become police officers. If they are married, the vast majority end up divorced within a year. If they do not drink, they start during the first year. If they were never unfaithful to their partners, they will be in that first year, which will be the most dramatic, life-changing experience they will ever encounter.

If they are big-city cops, they can experience more life-threatening experiences and trauma in one shift than their entire neighbourhood at home will have in a lifetime. And then they are expected to be just like their neighbours when the sun comes up. Sex will always be in their face, free and unfettered, offered by men and women who find the dangerous attraction of a uniformed cop irresistible. It has always been that way, but more so today. Temptation is everywhere: money, drugs, favours and everything the underbelly of life has to offer, and which was unavailable before. Some resist the temptation, many do not.

A few years alone at night in a patrol car in a high-crime area starts the rot. Cops see fellow officers shot, assaulted and killed. One police officer is murdered every forty-nine hours in America, and thousands are wounded and hurt, and the numbers keep growing. Then the rot spreads to the worst place of all – where you live. That group of neighbours who used to invite you to barbecues and block parties stop calling, and you wonder why. Old friends drift away and a sense of isolation sets in. It's not that people suddenly stopped liking you, they just don't understand who you have become, and they are uncomfortable. That easy-going guy they used to know is now harder around the edges, touchy about being a cop, so they let go, leaving the cop out there alone, resentful. The cop risks his or her life every day to keep the barbarians away from their safe neighbourhoods, and it seems nobody understands that, especially their neighbours; they take it for granted.

Then the worst thing of all happens – cops turn to people who understand them and offer a close relationship and trust: other cops. That's the first and last step into the brotherhood of police officers. It is at this point that the edges really harden; it's cops against 'them', and I don't mean the criminals, but the citizens they are sworn to protect. I have known officers where I could almost hear the mental steel gate slam shut in their minds, never to be opened again.

There are thousands of police officers in America who will dispute these facts because they just don't know; because there is no reason for them to know. There are many medium to small police departments in America where an officer has never fired his or her weapon in the line of duty. There are police departments in towns where the homes cost more than their entire annual police budget.

I know many police officers who risked their lives constantly to protect the citizens they knew did not give a damn about them, then turn around and commit acts of corruption, over and over again. Some of the most corrupt cops I ever knew were the best cops I ever knew. So, what is an American cop? Having been one for decades, all I can come up with is that we are an enigma. The end product of a corrupt system of justice. An inevitability then, now and in the future.

# 6

# THE BLACK REVOLUTION IN AMERICA

The tear gas burned my eyes and lungs and the noise was deafening as the crowd surged towards us one sweltering hot day in Atlanta. We knew it was coming but had hoped it would not happen. Atlanta's black population rose up and attacked the most visible symbol of the white city government – the police department; and I was a detective, one of the first officers to arrive on the scene at the beginning of the riot.

The black civil rights movement had turned violent, and anarchy descended on America. The sins of slavery were about to be atoned in fire and brimstone. All across America blacks rose up and went to war against their own country. Many had just returned from Vietnam, battle-hardened and bitter, a deadly combination. The stage was set for Armageddon and this was the time for America to pay for the horror of keeping slaves in mental and physical torture. It was the blacks' turn now, and they did not let go until they had gutted the city of its racist soul; Atlanta would never be the same again.

The slave trade was and is a terrible stain on the British. Their slave traders raided villages on the African west coast and ripped native families and villages apart. They selected fit males and breeding females and slaughtered the rest. These slaves were transported to England and then were shipped from Liverpool and Bristol harbours to America. They were then sold on public auction blocks much like livestock were sold. This lucrative trade flourished and fortunes were made, on both sides of the Atlantic.

Then there is worse, there is an Irish connection, a Scots–Irish connection. The initial wave of immigrants from Europe included large numbers of Scottish farmers that the British had moved into Northern Ireland to establish a pro-protestant voting base and as landlords over the impoverished Irish tenant farmers.

These Scottish landlords learned well the techniques of domination of a race, the Irish race, and held them in abject submission. These same harsh men, with pockets full and Ireland rising up in rebellion, fled to America and bought large farms. The only problem was that there were no labourers to work their farms. They let it be known in England that there was a ready market for African slaves, and so the horror of slavery began. The British have acknowledged their participation in the slave trade, but never addressed their apology to African Americans. They fear law suits for compensation.

Recently a slave ship was discovered in southern waters with the leg irons secured to the hold bottom by iron chains. The storm that sank the ship also drowned the unfortunate slaves in the hold. They could not escape.

There are Irish parallels here. The British 'coffin ships' that transported Ireland's dispossessed masses to America would batten down the holds in a storm. These Irish immigrants died by the thousands in those holds either by drowning or from inhumane filthy conditions which caused disease. The only difference between what the British did to the Irish and to the African slaves was the degree of extreme cruelty and enslavement techniques.

White Americans still do not understand the festering black rage that nearly destroyed America when the race riots began. I did, and hated facing those angry black faces as an Atlanta police officer. We had to contain the riots otherwise the rage would have spilled across Atlanta and burned it to the ground; and then afterwards everybody would have suffered, the blacks more than the whites. It had to be contained.

Those slavery wounds were festering and probably will never heal, at least not in our lifetimes. People questioned why the slavery issue was still a problem after all that time. But back then there were still surviving relatives of slaves, and they had talked to their children about slavery; they in turn had talked to their children, and the wounds stayed unhealed and open. Compound this with no voting rights, separate dining facilities for blacks and substandard living and working conditions, and it seemed nothing much had changed.

My colleague and I, both detectives, were driving down Eastwood Avenue. Suddenly the radio transmissions grew tense. We were not to know then that the black revolution had begun, and we were on ground zero, on that beautiful clear blue southern afternoon. Car theft detective R. H. Kerr had an arrest warrant for a convicted car thief known only as Prater. Kerr requested the assistance of Officer R. Harris, a traffic court warrant officer, who had arrested Prater before, knew where he lived and what he looked like. It should have been a routine arrest, but, tragically, it was not. We were close by and drove in that direction, listening as the drama unfolded on our police radio.

Kerr and Harris drove towards 39 Ormond Street, where Prater lived. At the corner of Capitol Avenue and Ormond Street, Prater pulled alongside Officer Harris' car. Harris told Prater that he had a warrant for his arrest but Prater jumped from the car and ran behind a small clapboard grocery store, then east on Ormond towards his home. Harris began yelling at Prater to halt, over and over, and when Prater continued running, Harris shot him in the side, and then in the hip. Prater staggered to the porch of his home and collapsed. An angry crowd started to gather around the two officers, who called for assistance.

This is probably where I need to step back from this tragedy and tell you I knew Harris and Kerr well, and probably knew Prater as a teenager, because he was a habitual offender. To this day I do not know why Harris shot that young trouble-maker because he could have been arrested anytime. I have made countless arrests of people like Prater without even a thought of drawing my service weapon; there was just no need. I would get them while they were asleep, hanging out or just being plain stupid, but shooting them never crossed my mind, ever.

Officer Harris was legally within his rights to shoot a fleeing felon, but why did he do so? Harris and Kerr desperately called for immediate assistance. Then another hoarse radio call from C. O. Hestley and B. L. Barron, fellow detectives in my unit, who had wrecked their car on Capitol Avenue on the way to assist Harris and Kerr. After that, everything went into virtual melt-down. What had been high-crime radio reports now turned to mayhem; the black revolution had begun.

I stood amid it all and saw we were pathetically outnumbered. Black rage was everywhere; there were flying bricks and bottles and people screaming. This was to become the worst riot in the south's history. The federal government was later to rate it as a scale-one riot, the most violent possible, and we were not prepared for it, not by a long shot. On this day, 6 September 1966, the city of Atlanta and its police department were woefully under-equipped and undermanned. This was due to the leadership of Ivan Allen, the wealthy white patrician mayor of Atlanta.

Allen arrived on the scene and began to shout orders at the police and the black rioters. I was on the street next to him and was stunned by what he was doing. His imperious manner further infuriated the crowd, and then he did something that was mind-bogglingly stupid: he began to march up and down the street ordering the rioters to march up and down the street with him. Whereas before they were a disorganised mass of angry people, now they became an organised mob, and Allen did not seem to notice the consequences of his actions. He then jumped up on top of a car and began shouting for the angry crowd to disperse and go home, but it was too late. Bottles and rocks rained down on him. A Coca-Cola bottle came arching over the crowd directly towards his head. A black patrolman swung his baton and the bottle exploded harmlessly just before it was to hit the mayor. We surrounded the car and tried to keep the crowd, who were yelling 'white devil, white devil', from pulling him off the top of it.

Allen seemed to realise that the situation he had helped create was now out of control. He jumped off the car and beat a hasty retreat. Allen in essence had taken control of the streets away from the police and provided the catalyst for a riot by organising the mob. His old, southern, imperious manner had only infuriated the angry people further, and we had to pay for his actions in the violent days and nights that were to follow. While we were under-equipped and undermanned, we knew the people and could have contained the situation – of that I am convinced. But Allen prevented that with his arrogant ignorance of his own citizens. Allen was later to be recognised for his leadership of the city during those turbulent days that followed, and even the president placed him on a fact-finding commission. But we never saw him again once he left the scene.

Now totally out of control and fired up with the knowledge that they had literally run the mayor of Atlanta away from the scene, the rioters escalated the violence and what followed was a week of mayhem. As for me personally, during this initial outbreak of violence, I squatted behind a burning news car and wondered just what the hell I was doing there. It seemed like it was just yesterday that I was squatting on the bottom of the jetty in Dundalk dreaming about America. Well, I was there now, and who in Dundalk would have believed me if I'd told them about those terrible days; so I never did. I was not to know there were worse days ahead.

It was chaotic and dangerous and we had no riot equipment, tear gas or shotguns. Gunshots were ringing out, some from the rioters and some from the police. We were badly outnumbered and the rioters grew in number and rage. We were attempting to maintain a holding action until reinforcements arrived. All off-duty officers were called in and that helped a little. However, our department itself was under strength. This was due to Mayor Allen's refusal to maintain a strong enough force in spite of rumblings of approaching civil unrest. He had had ample warning. We were in sight of the gold dome of the state capitol and the massive government complex. There was no doubt that if we did not contain the situation the mob would surge toward the capitol, which was a symbol of black repression. So an alarmed Governor Sanders mobilised a hundred state troopers and stationed them inside the Atlanta baseball stadium.

Our police chief, Herbert Jenkins, a carbon copy of Allen, never once showed his face. The uniformed commanders tried to round up equipment and some shotguns were sent to the scene. Then came a major error in judgment. An antiquated, Keystone-Cops type of armoured car arrived spluttering and filled with senior officers. We had just begun to gain some semblance of control when this comedy of errors occurred. Just what purpose it was supposed to serve was beyond everybody's comprehension, it just looked ridiculous and totally out of place.

Then suddenly there was a loud noise from inside the armoured car: a large canister of tear gas had exploded and a number of officers had to be rushed to hospital. If this had occurred under any other circumstances it would have been hilarious; but it was not what we needed that day, eyeball to eyeball as we were with a mob of rioters. We desperately needed riot helmets. The physical damage a jagged rock can do to one's head can be severe, even life-threatening. Later that afternoon, boxes of construction helmets were distributed; they were baby blue in colour and nearly as bad for our morale as the old armoured car – but they had to do.

Initially the majority of officers were detectives in suits like me, and we were hardly a stirring sight with our baby-blue designer helmets, dodging rocks and bottles. The mob clearly realised that they had the upper hand and grew more violent. In order to attempt to disperse them, we were ordered to discharge our shotguns and pistols simultaneously in the air. The barrage of shots momentarily stopped the rioters. Then, emboldened by the fact we were only shooting in the air, they attacked us again, this time with more violence, and the bedlam of arrests began.

One thing I learned that day was to never draw your weapon unless you intend to use it and not just shoot in the air. It is the implied threat that is the real deterrent and we had just lost that deterrent. We then began to receive reports that other pockets of Atlanta's black population were growing restless. If those heavily populated areas had rioted that day, we would have lost control of Atlanta's streets and Atlanta itself. Sensing this, Governor Sanders offered the assistance of a hundred heavily armed state troopers.

Once again Ivan Allen stepped in and refused the offer of assistance, demonstrating his total lack of understanding of the severity of the situation. There is no doubt that a show of force would have stopped the riot and allowed the rioters to cool down. Then their black leaders could have taken control and worked with the city authorities to resolve their grievances, for that is all they wanted in the first place. But Allen was adamant; there was no way he was about to admit to the white voters of Atlanta that he had mismanaged and neglected the Atlanta police department and could not control the streets.

We only had seven hundred and fifty sworn police officers, and we needed twice that number even under normal circumstances. So there it was: the police angry and resentful that the city had not provided them with adequate equipment to do their job; and the angry black rioters with their own set of grievances. All of this was fuel for violence. The black clergy did their best to calm things down, but to no avail; nobody was listening to anybody any more. They wanted to vent their anger on the streets. The one man who could have instantly quelled the riot just by his presence inexplicably did not respond to calls for his help. This was Martin Luther King Jr, who instead boarded a plane for Chicago.

I have never understood that, for it was he who had fanned the flames; yet he stood back as Atlanta burned. He was a great civil rights leader; it's just that I will never understand the reason why, when his community desperately needed him, he was not there for them. All of this is not supposed to be taken in a negative way: I admired, and still admire, him; but it just doesn't make any sense to me.

King was to die at 6.01 p.m. on 4 April 1968, allegedly at the hands of James Earl Ray, on the balcony of the Lorraine Hotel in Memphis, Tennessee. I say 'allegedly' because the facts scream out otherwise, and the King family to this day do not believe that Ray killed Dr King; nor do I and many others.

Ray was a hopeless drunk with a diminished level of intelligence. He was also a petty criminal whose most serious crime was robbing a taxi driver for a few dollars. The US army threw him out for being a drunk and a general all-round nuisance. This breed of southern street drunk is all too common, and I have arrested hundreds of them from under bridges, behind buildings and in every rat hole in and around Atlanta. They all act and smell the same, never give you any trouble and are glad to go to jail, especially on a cold night, for a warm meal and a clean bed. Over the years I have never met one of these hopeless men who had the ability to string one coherent thought after another, not one; the alcohol had all but destroyed their motor functions. They had enough willpower to get around and look for alcohol, but that's about it.

These people did not drink normal distillery alcohol, but their own lethal brand of home brew. I remember well on many occasions responding to complaints that suspicious men were seen congregating under bridges or in abandoned houses, and knew right away what I would find: homeless drunks. Often as not, they would have a little apparatus set up to make their home brew. It was simple, but the end result was lethal. They would find a discarded woman's pantyhose in the garbage, go behind a supermarket and then scavenge or 'Dempsey dumpster dive', as they called it. This is what happened. One of them would be hoisted up and into those large, green garbage containers that are put out behind all supermarkets. They would root around for spoiled fruit and anything else of value. The last ingredient was something to cause the fruit to ferment. Sometimes they got lucky and found some torn sacks of sugar, which was a plus for fermentation. However, the liquid that would activate the fermentation process was what killed the brain cells. Appropriate liquids included cans of paint remover, solvent, or anything similar that caused fermentation.

They would then stuff the spoiled fruit into the legs of the pantyhose and suspend them from a tree limb. After placing tin cans under each panty leg, they would carefully start pouring the fermentation liquid over the fruit, and then wait. It might take an hour or more, but slowly a potent brew of alcohol would start dripping out of the toes of the pantyhose into the tin cans. They at least had the sense not to drink the brew straight, which would have sent them down in a heartbeat. That was no problem as the supermarket dumpsters had an ample supply of badly dented cans of discarded fruit juice, still good but unfit for sale.

After many heated debates as to who had earned the seniority for the first drink, the drinking would begin. Gradually they would fall into a drunken stupor and sleep where they sat for many hours. Then came the scramble for the fermented fruit, which was even more lethal than the liquid. I once came upon one of these unimaginable fights, with drunken filthy men rolling all around the bushes clawing at the pantyhose and stuffing the fruit down their throats. Many vomited, but they would soon start in again, desperate for the alcohol. When I see those mega-expensive liquor ads on television and in sophisticated magazines, I wonder how a scene such as the one I just described would go down on the next TV commercial or the next page of the magazine.

I digress from Martin Luther King and James Earl Ray for a very good reason. I want the reader to imagine the sort of life that Ray had and to consider just what he was accused of doing. Then it might be possible to make a decision as to whether he had the potential and ability to commit what was arguably the most sophisticated assassination in history.

The night King was murdered, over sixty American cities erupted into violent race riots. America was again on fire and Atlanta was no exception. A frantic race to identify the killer or killers was launched by the FBI and every federal agency. A killer had to be quickly apprehended, otherwise America would burn to the ground. As an experienced homicide detective in Atlanta and a former street cop, I will present the details of

King's murder so that readers can make up their own minds as to his guilt or innocence.

The night before the murder of King, Ray paid for a cheap room at Bessie Brewer's boarding house in Memphis. This was an abject, sordid flop house where you could buy a bed for a few dollars, and which catered to alcoholics and losers like Ray; he had been there before. The FBI alleges Ray placed King's room – which was in the Lorraine Hotel, just across an alley – under surveillance with expensive binoculars.

When King came out on the balcony with others, Ray, who the FBI said was perched on a bathtub, shot him in the throat with a single bullet, with pinpoint accuracy. The FBI further stated that Ray had used an expensive Winchester 30-06 rifle with a sniper scope. While those details may cause eyes to widen, considering the calibre of the man Ray was, what follows insults the intelligence. According to the FBI, Ray then ran from the boarding house with a bag which he dumped on the sidewalk in front of the store next door. Incredibly, the rifle was sticking out of the bag, and quickly discovered by responding Memphis police officers. Neatly, the murder weapon had been secured: step one in any successful murder investigation.

From there, Ray was alleged to have driven eleven hours to Atlanta and to have abandoned his get-away vehicle, a sporty white Mustang, in the city. That is where I come into the picture. It was around midnight and I was driving around Capitol Homes, a public housing project close to the state capitol. I had heard look-outs all evening for the white Mustang. We were advised that if we located the car we should just report its location. We were to stay away from the scene, but keep the Mustang under surveillance.

Then I saw the car, down a side street under a dim street light. I radioed it in and was told the FBI were on the way. A few minutes later I was told to leave the area. The car was parked a few hundred yards from the governor's office. Like the murder weapon, it was easy to find, and the homicide investigation was moving efficiently along. Now all the FBI needed to do was identify the suspect.

The FBI alleged that after abandoning the Mustang, Ray checked into a pre-paid room at Garner's boarding house, and then picked up clean clothes and laundry at Piedmont cleaners. They then claimed that he boarded a flight for Canada with a forged passport. Ray became an international fugitive for two months, moving around Europe, and then was accidentally arrested at Heathrow airport in London after his passport raised suspicions. Incredibly, Ray was in possession of yet another forged passport.

James Earl Ray went from being a documented pathetic loser with no visible form of intelligence other than that of a primitive man, to being an international assassin in a James Bond movie with unlimited funds. I am convinced that Ray was indeed in Bessie Brewer's boarding house that fateful day, but somebody else pulled the trigger of the Winchester that killed King. I am also convinced that somebody other than Ray dumped the Mustang in Capitol Homes. I am equally convinced that somebody was with him all the way on his travels from the US to Canada and Europe. I am also convinced that Ray would have been killed for what he knew if that careful immigration officer at Heathrow airport had not detected his forged passport, and that was the last thing his handlers needed or expected. I suspect that since then they have regretted not killing Ray sooner.

I say 'handlers' because people like Ray are incapable of doing what he was alleged to have done. At the end of the day, he was nothing but a fall guy, as they say in America. Dexter King, Martin Luther's son, even visited Ray in prison and pleaded with him to reveal who was behind the murder of his father, but

Ray refused to reveal who had used him. It was not because he was afraid, it was because he was one happy camper. There was no way he was going to leave his private room, good food and living conditions with many privileges in his federal high-tech prison, a far cry from the old days. Plus he was a celebrity prisoner among his peers in jail. There was nothing outside prison for him. This was the reason I went into such excruciating detail to describe the lifestyle of the James Earl Rays of the world. What did Dexter King have to offer Ray? Nothing at all.

If Dexter King had offered Ray a guaranteed place to live for life, a pay cheque for life and an unlimited supply of booze, we would now know who really murdered Martin Luther King. To place things in an even clearer perspective, somebody took a miserable derelict from the gutter, dressed him up and gave him the best two months of his life. He was squired from Canada to Europe and in all probability lived well. He became an instant celebrity whereas before he was gutter fodder. Those who are supposed to know just don't understand how the mind of a James Earl Ray works. But I do, and so does every beat cop who has worked the underbelly of American society. They might as well have checked Ray into the Ritz Carlton when they put him in jail.

If not the convicted James Earl Ray, then who killed Martin Luther King? After his murder a flurry of investigations flourished, as did books and movies about him. Ray, playing the game, first recanted his confession and claimed a mysterious 'Raoul' was behind the murder. The FBI went into full gear and that was what Ray wanted, attention and special privileges. I suspect they did not look very hard for Raoul; they already knew the name of the assassin, and it was not Raoul. Then the favourite theory of all bloomed. An unknown southern businessman had put up $50,000 for the hit. I thought that was far-fetched. While a wealthy businessman would have access to

The author as a military policeman in the Irish Army, 1960.

As fire team leader taking a break on the Russian border, 1962.

In the US Army as a Sergeant. Russian border, 1963.

As a homicide detective with the Atlanta Police Department, 1967.

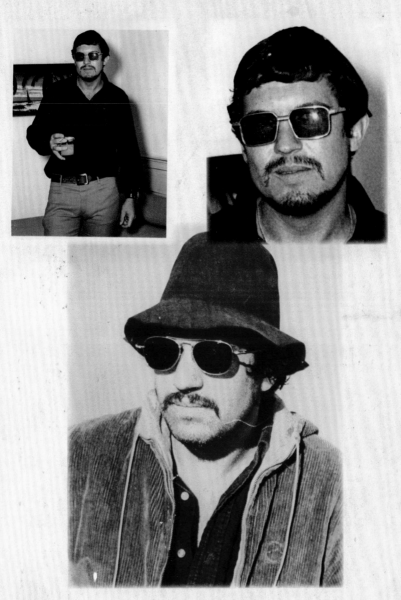

**In undercover mode in the 70s.**

The author, undercover again, in the 1970s.

As a Detective Sergeant in the south Florida swamps,
hunting drug smugglers in the 1970s.

Atlanta Police Chief George Napper presenting the author
with an award for heroism, 1980.

**Receiving another award – the Meritorious Medal
for Heroism, 1980.**

## ATLANTA
## CRIMINAL INFORMATION
## NETWORK

MAYNARD JACKSON, MAYOR

**BUREAU OF POLICE SERVICES**
175 DECATUR ST., S.E.
ATLANTA, GEORGIA 30303

Vol. 2 No. 1                                    January 1981

## missing children

JEFFERY LAMAR MATHIS
4'8", 71 lbs., DOB 6/13/69
Last seen wearing grey jogging
pants with a blue stripe up one
leg, white long sleeved thermal
shirt, green short sleeved tee
shirt, brown tennis shoes, on
South Gordon Road in Southwest
Atlanta 3/11/80.

DARRON GLASS
4'9", 75 lbs., DOB 5/23/70
Last seen wearing a yellow
shirt, brown khaki pants
and white tennis shoes, in
the Memorial Drive area of
Southeast Atlanta 9/14/80.

LUBIE "CHUCK" GETER
5'1, 125 lbs., DOB 6/30/66
Last seen wearing a purple
coat, green shirt, blue
jeans, brown loafers in the
Stewart-Lakewood Shopping
Center 1/3/81.

A $100,000 REWARD IS BEING OFFERED FOR INFORMATION LEADING TO THE
ARREST AND CONVICTION OF THE PERSON OR PERSONS RESPONSIBLE FOR THE
DEATHS OF THIRTEEN ATLANTA CHILDREN, AND THE DISAPPEARANCE OF THREE
OTHERS. ANY AND ALL INFORMATION SHOULD BE FORWARDED TO THE SPECIAL
TASK FORCE ON MISSING CHILDREN AT 404-658-6818, 6824, 7469, 7477,
7478 OR AT 175 DECATUR ST., S.E., ATLANTA, GEORGIA 30335.

**A flyer on the latest murdered and
missing Atlanta children. The author was
the network coordinator in 1981.**

The author in his role as Managing Director of ADT
Ireland, September 1988.

The author's wife Eva with their Jungle hammer, as they nick-named it, in the Philippines, 2001.

The author and his wife Eva.

forged passports and money, there is no way they would have been able to navigate the myriad local police agencies from Memphis to Atlanta to 'plant' the rifle and the Mustang. It definitely was not an elaborate civilian hit job with local law enforcement involvement because it had to go much higher in the American government.

My rationale is simple and based on a lifetime around the law enforcement community. The murder of Martin Luther King was a complex and convoluted conspiracy that could not have been executed by any person or group other than the government of the United States. They had the motive, which is central to any murder investigation: fear. The United States government believed at the time that Martin Luther King presented a clear and present danger to the security of America. This was based on the ongoing black civil unrest across the country, and the FBI believed King was the catalyst for this unrest. They falsely claimed that he had met with communist agents and sought to stir up all of the deep-seated fears of the American people.

As head of the FBI there was no more qualified man to organise the conspiracy than J. Edgar Hoover. This dogmatic man was convinced King was a communist and assigned agents to track his every move, including monitoring King's telephone without a legal warrant. Hoover was the creator of the FBI, and both deserve volumes to be written about them, but for all the wrong reasons. Hoover held all politicians in contempt. To protect himself and his organisation he ordered his agents to place all powerful politicians under close surveillance, including the president and the vice president. He amassed a vast array of damaging information on these politicians and by doing so assured himself of a lifetime of job security and immense power. Should a politician resist his many budget increase requests, Hoover would show up on that politician's doorstep with the politician's dirty laundry packaged in an FBI file.

A confirmed bachelor, Hoover lived with his very close friend Clyde Tolson in a trendy townhouse. He had appointed Tolson deputy director of the FBI. The constant gossip of Hoover's penchant for dressing in women's clothing and hosting wild cross-dressing parties at his townhouse persisted until his death. I was later to become friends with – of all people – his postman, whose friend was an employee of Hoover in his townhouse. We used to get a laugh out of what really went on in that house, and it was not gossip. To this day, the FBI remains the most incompetent and corrupt law enforcement agency in America. It is also not trusted by any other American or foreign law enforcement agency in the world. This reputation is well-deserved.

The average FBI agent acts as if he is stitched as tight as a Virginia ham. I personally have worked with agents on cases ranging from bank robbery to terrorism. They will 'screw the hell' out of local police officers, and work feverishly to imprison any officer they suspect of wrongdoing, yet the FBI itself has a long history of rampant corruption. They desperately require an oversight agency to monitor their activities. However, the problem is who is going to investigate them, as they are the leading law enforcement agency in America – Hoover made sure of that. To get on the internet and type 'arrested FBI agents' is to experience a rude awakening so far as the agency's clean image is concerned.

The FBI has a long history of serious ingrained corruption. A good example is veteran FBI agent Paul Rico. He makes Al Capone look like an altar boy. Rico was regarded by his Mafia associates as a drunken slob with a serious gambling problem. Agent Rico had knowledge of the direst murders and of organised crime activities and did nothing.

Then there was Agent Robert Philip Hanssen, a veteran senior counter-intelligence agent, one of the most sensitive positions in the American intelligence community. The only problem was that Hanssen was also in the employment of the Russian KBG. Over a number of years he delivered to the KBG over sixty packages of highly classified documents in exchange for over $600,000 and envelopes filled with diamonds. His illegal activities went on for over a decade. He was finally arrested, but the damage he inflicted on America's intelligence community was severe.

FBI Agent John Connolly, who was a cocky, well-dressed agent in the Boston office, was worse than the organised crime figures he was charged with monitoring. One of his so-called informants was the notorious murderer James 'Whitey' Bulger. He would throw lavish parties at his home and Connolly was his master of ceremonies at the dinner. Also in attendance would be other FBI agents, the president of the Massachusetts state senate, who was Whitey's brother, and also there was none other than gangster Stephen 'the rifleman' Flemmi. These were no casual mob dinners: they plotted how to take over all criminal enterprises from the Italian Mafia, which they eventually did, but with the assistance of the Boston FBI office. This was not a case of Connolly's superiors not knowing about this criminal collusion between his office and the mob – John Morris, the Boston office's Organised Crime Squad supervisor, was sitting at the table with Bulger and the rest of his agents. While Agent Connolly was 'supervising' Bulger, the mobster committed eleven more murders, and Connolly was aware of the details. With the assistance and protection of the Boston FBI office, Whitey Bulger ruled Boston's underworld with an iron fist.

The FBI in Washington finally cleaned out their Boston Office and Whitey left the country with ease; he had been warned well beforehand. The FBI vowed to track him down, and that was cause for a few laughs from local cops. He was the last person the FBI wanted to see. Then came a bombshell: in

September 2007 an American tourist provided a photograph of Whitey Bulger in southern Italy with his long-time girlfriend. In spite of having FBI agents in Europe, Washington sent an agent from America, allowing Whitey ample time to make his escape. As I said before, Whitey is the last person the FBI wants to see. If captured, he would sing like a canary for a deal to keep him out of prison. In spite of a million-dollar federal bounty on his head, Whitey lives the good life, protected by the secrets he carries in his head. There is not one ambitious, politically fine-tuned federal prosecutor who would not give him a free ride in exchange for the names of all those government agents he had and still has on his payroll.

Whitey Bulger deposited millions overseas in anticipation of the day he would have to flee. He was careful to stash the money in many banks under many names. He was coached by his FBI friends on how to hide money, and he learned well. There is no way Whitey Bulger can strut around Europe, dine at the best restaurants and be photographed knowingly by tourists without protection from the highest places.

However, the most grievous failing on the part of the FBI was that they had prior warning of the impending 9/11 attack, including names. Coleen Crowley, an FBI attorney, desperately tried to get FBI director Robert Mueller to concentrate on the terrorist Zacarias Moussaoui. She was ignored.

So it was that we found ourselves in direct confrontation with the black citizens of Atlanta. They felt like they had nowhere to go with their grievances. The federal agency they should have been able to approach was the FBI. Blacks in America still have a deep distrust for the FBI. It was even worse then. So they took to the streets and we had to attempt to control the situation.

The Atlanta police department did not have a history of

black suppression, and it showed during the riots. The officers were reluctant to shoot anybody, even when provoked or justified. I saw no excessive use of force, and the tragic part of all this is that I believe that we, the police, and the black rioters wished we were someplace else. The rioters were attacking the wrong people – the police – whereas they wanted to attack the people with real power in Atlanta. But they were nowhere to be found. So we battled it out on the streets, accomplishing nothing. We finally grew tired and the rioters saw the futility of it all. They would probably be calling these same officers for assistance the next day.

As the night wore on, the frantic radio transmissions gradually slowed. We hoped it was coming to an end. We parked on a dark side street and turned the radio down, but still listened to the transmissions. The tempo of the calls would tell us the mood of the rioters and on what street there was trouble. Before, we could see figures darting between buildings; now there were just a few. It seemed they had all left and we assumed they had gone home; we were horribly wrong. Other forces were at work that night, outside forces who poured gasoline on the smouldering fires of the dying riot, and it exploded again, with a vengeance.

We were not to know that the angry young rioters had not gone home but to a meeting. Two avowed black revolutionaries, Stokely Carmichael and Rap Brown, flew into Atlanta and called a meeting of the rioters. Carmichael fired up the angry young black men and the city went to hell.

We were sitting in our police cars when suddenly our radio transmissions grew in pitch and tempo, and we knew it had started again. This time it was just the young blacks who were out on the streets because their parents had gone home. Now it was more dangerous because nobody was watching them.

While we attempted to control the rioters in the Capitol

Avenue area, firebombs began to explode around the city. Sexton Brothers tyre company on Ashby Street was burned to the ground and over two hundred black employees lost their jobs. That company paid a good wage and was a decent employer; it made no sense. Then Boulevard Avenue erupted. This riot was very dangerous, with all the gunfire and firebombs.

I remember crouching behind a fire truck, armed with a military carbine, the glow of the fires illuminating the violence of the night and thinking about the insanity of Americans fighting Americans. Surely there had to be a better way. Here I was, holding a military carbine in an American city, prepared to shoot an American.

The city finally calmed down and went about repairing the damage that had been inflicted on the people and property. The first time I reported to duty after the riots, I knew Atlanta would never be the same again, for better or for worse. The sense of trust was gone between neighbourhood policemen and the residents they were supposed to protect. The policemen remembered the violence that had been inflicted on them by these same people and were bitter, and stayed away.

What about the two black revolutionaries who tried to burn Atlanta to the ground? The month following the riots he had helped to incite, Rap Brown became a founding member of the Black Panthers in California and Stokely Carmichael became their prime minister.

As an aside on Rap Brown, I was once attending a reception in Washington and ended up having a drink with Edwin Meese, President Reagan's attorney general. While we were chatting I remembered that Meese had once been a professor and Rap Brown had been one of his students. Brown, it seems, had been a surly student with a budding afro.

Brown was at heart a dangerous and violent man. Stokely Carmichael would incite violence and literally run away, but not

Brown; he revelled in violence. At the Los Angeles sports arena in 1968, Brown emotionally called on all African Americans to kill police officers and burn American cities. In prison he converted to the Nation of Islam and became a Muslim, and changed his name to Jamil Abdullah Al-Amin. However, Brown was not to be a peaceful Muslim, but a dangerous radical one.

I remember once stopping in my detective car at a small grocery store on southside Atlanta. A man was sitting on a bench outside and he told me to get what I needed and leave the money on the counter. I did that and came outside and looked at the owner. He was dressed in traditional Muslim garb and appeared relaxed, so I joined him on the bench. It was a cool, sunny day and it felt good to just sit there and relax. We talked about the weather and sports and then I realised I was sitting with Rap Brown. I later learned that he had bought the grocery store and from all reports had settled down. His afro had some grey, but he looked fit and well. He obviously knew I was a policeman but I figured his fire had gone out. I figured wrong.

In 2002 his true nature came out when two black deputy sheriffs came by his store to serve him an arrest warrant. Brown was not there but the deputies were told he was on his way back. According to all reports the deputies were two laid-back individuals who were serving a routine warrant. All Brown had to do was post bond and go free until the court date. Brown drove up, stepped out of his car and immediately shot and killed one deputy and badly injured the other, all without provocation as neither deputy had even unholstered his weapon.

Brown is now serving life in prison. Stokely Carmichael, who was born in Port of Spain in Trinidad, died of colon cancer, and that was that for both revolutionaries. What did I take away from all that violence? Nothing at all, because when it was over, all I felt was numbness.

# 7

# THE GOOD AND THE BAD TIMES

I was really beginning to enjoy America and had rented a nice apartment in an old Victorian home from a returned Vietnam veteran. He and his wife had lived there but moved out when she became pregnant. The stairs were very steep and the house was just too big, so they bought a nice cottage a few doors down. He then divided the house into four self-contained units. That worked out well for them: one unit paid for their monthly mortgage payment and the rest were for preparing for their baby.

When he saw I was home he would call and then drop by for a beer. He knew that I was a military veteran and told me he had been an infantry lieutenant in the jungles of Vietnam for eighteen months. I enjoyed his company until one day he began to cry. I was taken aback and feared there was something wrong with their pregnancy, but it was not that: it was Vietnam. He looked up at me teary-eyed and said: 'Sarge, they keep coming at me every night and it's getting worse; my wife is very worried, what can I do?' We talked far into the night after he had called his wife and told her he was talking to me about 'that thing', and he said she was glad. I listened and listened and cried right along with him until he had cried himself out and went to sleep on my couch. I went to work and left a note and told him I would call his wife and not to worry. I wish I could remember what I told him that long night because his wife later told me had changed, and had no more nightmares.

On 15 June 1215, extremely unworthy King John of England was given no choice but to sign into law the Magna Carta, which today is recognised as the single most powerful legal document ever enacted. This set of laws even subjected kings to the full force and majesty of the law, awesome powers at the time. The Magna Carta became the legal foundation for all British law. When the founding fathers of America sat down to write the constitution of the United States, they based it on the Magna Carta. Today every British and American citizen's day-to-day life is governed by that single-paged document in some way or the other.

On 31 October 1965, somewhat unworthy Irish citizen, Atlanta police officer Gerard Mac Manus, was advised to proceed to the Atlanta High Museum of Art. It was a mild sunny day when I parked my patrol car in front of the museum. I assumed that it was some kind of minor call. Lieutenant Shephard was standing outside and was visibly upset about something. He shook his head and said: 'We got hell on the streets and they pull an officer off to guard a piece of fucking paper.' I was introduced to a museum official who explained that I would be guarding the Magna Carta, and that its commercial value was in the high millions. Then he went to great lengths to explain the historic value of the document and its history.

The British had sent over their precious document to remind Americans just where their own Constitution had sprung from. I guess they were still a little touchy about a bunch of American farmers who whipped the cream of their army and sent them packing in the War of Independence. That said, it is a magnificent document.

The document was being displayed inside a glass case, a very small and light and fragile case. I was supposed to stand next to it and prevent its theft or vandalism. Since the exhibition had still not opened, I examined the document. It lay flat and was a beautiful piece of work. I asked a museum official if the case was wired for an alarm; it was not. I tentatively lifted the case and it was not heavy. The bottom line was that if I was disarmed, all somebody had to do was simply pick up the case and walk out the door. Then I tried the lid, and it opened easily. Now all somebody had to do was disarm me, roll up the Magna Carta and stroll out the door. That's all I needed: an Irish cop losing the Magna Carta.

I promptly returned the comfortable chair they had provided me and stood next to the case. I read the information sheet on the Magna Carta in case somebody asked me a question. This was a remote possibility as I was wearing an Atlanta police department uniform with the Atlanta police patch on the sleeves. Nobody would mistake me for a British bobby or a beefeater. I was wrong.

As the seemingly endless line of the curious filed by, each and every one of them had a question. Was I an English policeman? Did I travel with the exhibit? Where in England was I from? Was I in Scotland Yard? On that day I realised why eyewitness accounts of a crime are the weakest form of evidence.

Around lunchtime the staff began to flutter around and the word went out that the British ambassador to America was about to make an appearance. The local media began to arrive and even one of them asked me if I was a British policeman. Soon afterwards a covey of tall, well-dressed, plum-faced men strode through the front doors of the museum.

After the museum staff and local politicians had paid their

humble respects, and the media got what they needed, the group moved to the exhibit and me. I was hoping that one of them would ask me if I was a British policeman, but they didn't. For whatever reason, the crowd stood back a respectable distance and that just left me and the British dignitaries. I believe that British Ambassador to the US Sir David Ormsby-Gore and Sir Patrick Dean were present, along with a group of official-looking embassy staffers. I assumed that the rat-faced, shifty-eyed guy was British security, at least I hoped he was. I kept an eye on him anyway. I remember the smiles and polite behaviour as they gathered around the exhibit and me. They all had the smarmy smiles of professional politicians and lots of small talk to place me at ease, to show that they had the common touch, I am sure.

Then a tall, rose-water-smelling gentleman said to me: 'Ah, I see we have a descendant of the mother country here, a Scotsman, Mac Manus.' A voice inside my head shouted at me to keep my mouth shut, but there would never ever be a moment like this again, so it just came out, in my thickest Irish accent: 'No sir, Irish, from Dundalk.' That stopped his little routine dead in his tracks. He appeared confused. 'You mean your ancestors…' and his voice trailed off. Again that voice was telling me not to say anything. But it came out: 'No sir, I was born and raised in Dundalk.'

Apparently Dundalk's reputation was well known in British diplomatic circles because his face began to turn a deeper shade of purple, his lips pursed and his eyes were squeezed into pinpoints. Then, in a whoosh of English rose water, the dignitaries swept out of the museum. Thirty minutes later I was back in my patrol car fighting heathens. I met Captain Mullins and Lieutenant Shephard in a parking lot and they asked me what happened. They seemed to think it was funny and told me they got a call from the mayor's office that the British ambassador wanted somebody 'more suitable' guarding their precious

Magna Carta. I will give the British this much, they sure have got a way with words.

I had no idea when I first started writing this book that it would turn into the most difficult thing I have ever done. The book opened doors into places where I did not want to go any more. I wrote draft after draft and ended up throwing them all away. Some of those pages left me sweat-drenched at night after I wrote them. Other nights I would lie in my bed looking at the ceiling and the worst in me would roil my heart and soul. Then there was the sadness for those whom I had lost, and I would lie awake until the welcome grey of dawn came. Then I began to waken far from dawn with no sleep possible, but I was reluctant to leave our bed.

Then one night, my wife Eva reached for me and held me and told me she loved me and that I should just write at night. I did that and she made sure nobody bothered me during the day while I slept, and I slept well because there was no darkness, which used to be my friend. I sent a few rough drafts to friends who had either served in the military, police or in corporate. They came back and some took the easy way out – by saying it was a great book. The ones who were with me in the military and the police replied last and they were not kind: 'All the hell we have been through – where is it in this bullshit book?'

And then there was sensitive Mike: 'Sorry it took so long, it was just boring crap. At last count you got about twenty-seven holes, cuts and fractures in your body, and a screwed-up mind, and all you can write about is that philosophical crap.'

I tore up that draft and tried again, but I found it a worse nightmare to write about the mud and the endless senseless violence of it all. I tried describing life on the streets and it was worse – like writing about violence for violence's sake. I emailed one revised chapter to my two harshest critics and both basically said I was in denial. But they had been there, through it all with me, and I valued their opinion. Or maybe they were right. So I wrote again and again about the violence that had been so much part of my life, and they stopped replying.

It is a fact that people who are exposed to long-term violence and danger come away with severe emotional baggage. While in the past, if somebody was diagnosed as having Post-Traumatic Stress Disorder, or PTSD, your career was shot and everybody thought you were a nutcase, in our more enlightened world it is treated as a normal result of certain causes. But that was not always the case and we lost many good men because of that ignorance.

Writing about violence is repugnant to me, for I believe that I can write this book without blood running off every page. Besides I truly believe that there is a more severe form of violence than bombs and bullets; it's the misery of the victims of violence. While the memories of the bombs and the bullets eventually fade away in the minds, hearts and souls of people like me, what keeps veteran soldiers and cops awake at night are the memories of the haunted eyes of the victims of violence; always the eyes.

Those eyes will never go away, and we see them when we least expect them, and we hold our loved ones closer, because we of all people know life is precious and a fleeting thing. We have witnessed the abrupt and cruel end of innocent lives and had to try and explain to the victims' friends and families what had happened and how sorry we were, and we truly were. Their sad, desperate eyes haunt cops, who become victims too, forever. And the survivors want you to stay a while and comfort them. But you can't because you know there are more bodies and survivors just waiting for you when you break free.

Even when you jail the perpetrator, you know that the hell

the victim's family is going through will never end. The murderer is of little consequence to them, because nobody can bring back their father, mother, sister, brother or child. I cannot remember even one criminal's or murderer's face, but I can vividly recall the victims and their tortured eyes. Soon you begin to assume guilt because we did not protect those victims; and that was our job, was it not? Many survivors of crimes accused us to our face of failing them, and they lashed out, sometimes flailing at our chests, because they had to find some release from their torment, and we understood. But we take away the memory of it and it all accumulates inside us and soon it eats us alive, if we allow it to.

We failed to protect them from the dark angels that murdered their loved ones, and that sense of helplessness is devastating, and at the end of the day we become victims also. But we keep it bottled up inside us until it leaches out and poisons our own relationships and our lives as we try to act like normal people, which we are not any more. Once we cross over into the world of the dark angels, it's the end of us.

There are moments in time that are so fraught with danger and violence that you can pull them back up in your mind years later in freeze frame. Even the smells come back, especially the smell of the fresh blood of the dying person who had tried to kill you. I want to share with you a few instances of what a street cop experiences in a major American high-crime city. Perhaps then I will have told the truth instead of skirting around the issue, like my friends accused me of doing.

**D**etective Julian Spence and I checked in at the vice squad office before hitting the streets. Other detectives were coming and going, everybody knew what we had to do and where we had to go: the underbelly of Atlanta. Detective Bobby Peppers, who worked narcotics on the day watch, had left a search warrant that had to be served at night. The suspect had a serious and violent criminal record in Louisiana, including burglary, narcotics and resisting arrest. Peppers had given us a brief write-up and it told us that the suspect's wife had apparently put up with his lifestyle until he and his friend, who also lived with them, began to sexually abuse their nine-year-old daughter, and involve her in his narcotic addiction. Then she called the police for help. People are like that; they wait until a situation becomes so bad that they need police intervention, and by then the damage is done, and people have been hurt, like her little girl.

Spence and I read the report and he said, 'Shit,' and it never got any better than that. We would normally have had to conduct a surveillance of the target address, but Spence had grown up in the neighbourhood and I knew it well. It was an older, middle-class area with well-cared-for, three-bedroom homes with nice mature trees and flowers. The houses were very close to each other, about fifteen feet apart. Lighting was basically from the street lights. Most of the homes would burn a small light in the living room at night to let people know somebody was home.

It was a very quiet neighbourhood and everybody knew everybody, except at the house on Oak Hill Avenue. The suspect's wife had said that on the night of the raid she would signal us that her husband was injecting himself with narcotics by turning on the porch lights.

We parked down the street and knocked on the door of the house next door to the suspect's house. We quietly explained that we were the police and had to serve a warrant on the house next door. They were elderly but seemed relieved that somebody was doing something about 'that mess next door'. They invited us in and told us we could use their living room window to observe what was going on over the fence. We could observe some movement at the rear of the house and somebody was moving around in the living room.

The plan was that Spence would take the back, and I would go in the front door. Then the porch light went on. Spence sprinted to the rear and I moved to the front door. Almost immediately Spence rejoined me. The suspect's wife had failed to mention that her husband owned a large, ferocious, mean-tempered German Shepherd which had attempted to relieve Spence of his private parts. Now the situation was ratcheted up a level as the suspect had been alerted by his barking dog; he knew somebody was inside his fence.

We could not just pull back and wait for another day because a child was in danger. This was no longer a narcotics-violation situation; it was a rescue mission. We had to get that young girl out of that house, one way or the other, no matter what the cost to us was going to be personally. We had no other moral choice. We knew there were four people in that house: the suspect Ryan, his friend Herman Edwards, the suspect's wife and the child.

Spence opened the screen door on the front porch and a man stepped out with a gun in his hand; it was Edwards. We disarmed him and moved through the house. Virginia Ryan was crouching in the dark living room, pointing towards the kitchen door. Spence already had caught a glimpse of Ryan boiling down paregoric on the stove to make an opium base which he would inject in his system. Then everything seemed to go into slow motion as Spence pushed open the kitchen door, and the nightmare began. Ryan was standing there with a hypodermic needle which he was in the act of handing to his daughter. Next to him was a gun.

The little girl looked up at us with watery, fearful eyes as her father grabbed the gun and started to shoot at us. It was a very small kitchen and one bullet struck the right, side-door jamb next to us. Spence shot him under the left eye with his

.357 Magnum. The powerful bullet exited through the back of his head, spewing blood and brain matter all over the kitchen. Then it was very quiet except for the girl's crying. When the ambulance, homicide cops and the medical examiner had left, and we had given our statements at headquarters, I had to go back to the house. The original purpose of the search warrant was for narcotics, and I had to gather the evidence for the follow-up death investigation. This was no place for Spence, he had gone home. The girl had been turned over to family services, who, after an investigation, removed her from her mother's custody and placed her in a nice, loving home. I know, because I followed her case.

It was about four in the morning when I parked in front of the house. The building and the neighbourhood appeared the same as they had earlier in the day. The elderly couple appeared to have gone to bed and the only sounds that could be heard on that warm night were the crickets talking to each other. It was as if nothing had ever happened. The house was still open and, from the street, appeared peaceful and quiet. I walked back to the kitchen and the sweet smells of blood and boiled paregoric assailed my senses. The brains and the blood of the girl's father were still all over the floor and kitchen and the acrid smell of gunpowder still hung in the air. The girl had seen it all and smelled the same smells I had smelled, and, when they took her away, the blood of her father was on her dress.

Her watery, tortured eyes still haunt my long nights, even after all those years, and won't go away. I pray that she survived that night, because I haven't. Her father was the scion of a wealthy South Carolina supreme court justice. My only hope is that he reached out in some way to his grand-daughter. I sent an unsigned letter to his local newspaper with news clippings of the shooting. Maybe he read them – I just don't know, and that's the hard part.

We knew when it happened that we had been used by the suspect's wife to kill her husband. She had been asked earlier if there were any dogs on the property and she had replied no. She had been asked if there were any guns in the house and she had said no. I can still see her crouching behind that couch in the living room, knowing that there would be shooting once we opened the kitchen door. She could have warned us, but she manipulated the situation and got what she wanted: her husband killed. The only real victims in this nightmare were the young girl and us.

One Saturday night it was hot as hell and I had been as-signed to work a patrol car in the Stewart Avenue sector on the evening shift. This area and population is the same size as many small countries, but more violent. There were nude bars, biker bars and dives of every description from end to end, almost running the length of Atlanta's south side. To describe the denizens of this hellish area as barbarous heathens would be to do a disservice to heathens.

From my radio came a continuous stream of calls telling me of every kind of crime, and I was working alone. It was insanity to assign a single officer to this beat. But the city had imposed a freeze on hiring police officers and was caught up in racial discrimination suits, all at the same time. I was already at least four calls behind when I received one for a disturbance on a side street off Stewart Avenue. I happened to be on that street and pulled into the address. It was a large, dirt parking lot with a trailer on the left side. There were bright overhead lights and I assumed that somebody sold used cars there during the day, Stewart Avenue being the used-car Mecca of the south.

Adjusting to the glare of the lights, I focused on a bearded, pot-bellied man with crazed, red eyes and a snarling mouth. Then I saw them. First, a bedraggled-looking, small young woman in a tattered dress who was holding a baby; then a young boy holding a rifle, which was pointing at me. I requested another officer as back-up, but nobody was available. I approached the man and he appeared to be comatose even though he was standing. I had deliberately ignored the boy with the rifle. I have learned that if you give somebody with a gun pointing at you centre stage they are liable to act out what they thought they were going to do.

I walked over to the woman and child, my back to the boy, then I heard the father say: 'Shoot him, son.' I kept on walking because I did not want to kill what looked like a thirteen-year-old boy. My back felt a mile wide. The mother and child's appearance was shocking. Both had been beaten black and blue. They looked sub-human. Their eyes begged me to help them and my heart was torn apart. I placed an emergency call for an ambulance, a paddy wagon and family services, all of which were at least thirty minutes away.

I glanced at the boy and he also had been severely beaten and was crying; but he kept aiming the rifle directly at me. I asked his mother what his name was and it was Ryan. I gently called his name and he fell apart, and dropped the gun. I went over and gave him a hug and he fell to the ground in a pre-natal position. I had turned down the volume on my radio during the confrontation so as not to escalate the tension level, if that was possible. The radio dispatcher was frantic when he inquired if I was all right because, as he reported, an officer on Stewart Avenue had had his gun taken away from him and was surrounded by bikers. He desperately needed help. So I left right then and that decision has haunted me ever since. I returned in thirty minutes, and they were gone. I put out a look-out on the old, battered, pick-up truck I had seen on the lot, and which was now gone, but it was useless. What few officers were out there were concentrating on keeping the lid on the violence in their sector. The last thing they needed was another sector's problems. I stood in the parking lot and the ambulance and paddy wagon pulled in. They said nothing when I told them I did not need them any more. I knew them, and they later said they thought I had been crying. It goes with the job. But the hell of it all is that you just can't do anything about it, because all you can do is let it eat into you, and then stay there.

I still live with the faces of the mother, her baby and the boy. But, more so, I live with their sad, sunken, desperate eyes, pleading with me to help them, and I did not help them, and that's the worst part. Psychologists say that the trauma of war and urban combat stays with you; its imprint stays in your mind, heart and soul until you die. I had intended to write many pages for this chapter, but I just can't continue. And I am sorry because I said I would. I feel like I have aged a hundred years since I began this book, and that's not fair on those who love me and keep me safe, except from the night; nobody can do that.

# 8

# GOING HOME AGAIN, AGAIN AND AGAIN

It was a warm sunny day and my mother was asleep in the front sun-room, her head down, surrounded by the Sunday papers. I was sitting in the living room thinking about things, absorbing the sense of being home again. The familiar smells of our Sunday dinner, the same I had smelled as a child, comforted me. But was I really home? I had been gone for nearly twenty years. While everything familiar was still there, my father was gone. He left a great big empty void in our lives when he died, and Sundays would never be the same again.

This was the one day that our father could come home and relax, and he loved Sunday dinner. My mother would make sure that the pork crackling was not touched because that was his favourite. Then he was gone, just like that. My siblings Marna, Canice and Terry were getting on with their lives, and doing well. It was just my mother left in our home now, a home filled with memories.

Outside, the street where I used to play with other children was now quiet and deserted. It used to be filled with the excitement and noise of children playing every Sunday. As I sat in the orange evening sunlight, I thought of my home in America, and then I thought about the room I was sitting in. This was my third attempt to return home permanently, and it was failing, just like the other two times.

Once when I was on a plane heading to Ireland a fellow passenger asked where I was going and I replied 'home'. Then on my return to America another passenger asked where I was going, and I replied 'home'; and there was the truth over the middle of the Atlantic Ocean. I didn't know where I belonged any more.

My father, sensing my frustration on one of his visits to me in America, told me a story he had heard from a returning emigrant many years before. An Irish fiddler emigrated to America and settled in the deep south. He found work in some of the honky-tonk bars where he learned to play hillbilly music. He prospered and became famous. His audiences would stomp their feet and whoop and holler as he reeled off the country music. American southerners love fiddle-playing musicians, and this Irishman was the best they had ever heard. Then something strange began to happen. He would be in the middle of a foot-stomping country song and all of a sudden his fingers took on a life of their own and he began to play Irish fiddle music. His audience fell silent, unsure of what they were hearing, then he regained control and off he went again with the country music.

In the beginning it only happened once in a while, then it was almost every night, until somebody yelled out: 'Play what your heart tells you, Irishman'; so he did. His performance brought the house down and soon the husbands brought their wives and started what is now known as square dancing. Nobody realised that all they were doing was responding to their Irish blood. The deep south was heavily populated by early Irish immigrants, not as much as in the north, but enough that if you listen carefully to today's country and western music, you will hear the strains of Irish fiddle music.

I have lived in the deep south for many years and often find my own feet tapping to the music, but in my head I am tapping to a Galway reel. It's strange to think of an Irishman tapping to country music, and country boys tapping to Irish music. So there it is, I am caught betwixt and between; half my heart's in Ireland and half in America. And there is no cure, is there? In the light of my God, and deep within my heart of hearts, I wish that I was not caught.

The detective bureau was located on the third floor and was a very busy place, twenty-four hours a day. Alongside one wall was a row of offices containing all of the various squads, starting with vice. Then there was robbery, car theft, larceny, burglary and so on, ending up with the office where the most experienced detectives of all worked: homicide. It would take years of experience and grey hair to even be considered for that squad.

I reported for work one evening to the vice squad and was told I had been transferred to the homicide squad. I thought there had been a mistake or it was a joke, but it wasn't. I will never forget when I first opened the door to the homicide office the looks on the faces of the grizzled detectives. I was very young-looking to start with, and every detective in there looked old enough to be my father. I got a few 'Can we help you?' comments, but all I did was shrug. What could I say?

Lieutenant Helms was the squad commander and I was told to sit in front of his desk. He was a very large man, his midriff had settled into a comfortable bulge and he had a shock of white hair. He had a bemused expression on his face as he told me I would be working the evening shift, the squad's busiest. Atlanta was then the murder capital of America. He obviously had been told I had been transferred to his squad, but he had not advised the squad of this. He later told me he wanted to see how I would handle the situation, and he said he fought my transfer to his squad.

The other homicide squad members, both day and evening shifts, suddenly realised what was going on, and, stunned, they did not say anything. Helms looked around the room and said: 'Who wants to work with Mac?' I knew there was no need for that question because he had the authority to assign a detective to work with me. Later he told me that he was just 'busting my chops'. Nobody moved and nobody said anything and there was a pregnant silence in the small room. Then detective Henshaw, one of the older detectives, said: 'I will work with him.' Helms just gave that little smile of his and that was that, I was a homicide detective.

Henshaw nodded for me to leave the room and follow him down to the interrogation rooms. A serial rapist was loose in southwest Atlanta and a young man had been apprehended by a uniform car while jumping over a fence close to a rape scene. What made the rapist different was that he was attacking elderly women only: very elderly, black, frail and sometimes sickly grandmothers. The neighbourhoods in the area of the rapes were in an uproar, and the media was smelling blood in the water.

Apparently, Henshaw and other detectives had been interviewing this suspect for hours, and were beginning to believe that he was the wrong man. This was the man's last interview; if Henshaw was not successful, he was going to release him. He went inside the interrogation room and told me to stand outside the door. I could hear the murmur of voices from inside the room; both voices were calm. After about an hour Henshaw emerged shaking his head and told me to stay outside the door while he got the suspect's release papers signed.

After about five minutes I heard a light tapping on the door of the interrogation room. I opened the door and a young black man smiled at me and said he really needed to go to the bathroom, which was two doors down. I was not concerned as I had used the interrogation rooms many times, and besides, he was about to be released. I walked him down to the bathroom and stood behind him while he urinated. He had a stocky build and was about five foot ten and had a light complexion, all of which matched the description the victims had given the police. He also had a very soft voice which all of the victims had commented on; a very soft voice.

I brought him back to the interrogation room and entered with him, and he appeared surprised. 'I am supposed to be getting out of here – what are you doing here?' His voice was honey-smooth and soft, and right then I knew I was in the same room as the rapist. I smiled at him and he smiled back. He was very calm and self assured, like he had the situation under control. I sensed I was in the room with a clever, conniving, dangerous man. I told him that the other detective was just getting the paperwork and to relax.

If there was one thing I had learned while working black neighbourhoods, it was that the vast majority of black males are raised by their grandmothers. The reason was simple: the fathers refuse to be responsible for their out-of-wedlock children, even today. There is even a name for those unfortunate children, 'outside children', whereas children born in wedlock are called 'inside children'.

The room was as small as the average bathroom and we were inches apart. I knew then why he was savagely raping old black women. He was an outside child and probably had been mistreated by his grandmother. I placed my hand gently on his arm and said: 'You are an outside child, aren't you?' It was if he had received an electric shock and his eyes widened and dilated. I felt his arm tense under my hand, and I knew I was right. 'She beat you all the time?' He started to nod his head violently, tears streaming down his face. 'You raped all those old women because they reminded you of your grandmother, isn't that right?' His head slumped down onto the table and he began to cry: 'Yes I did, yes I did.' I locked the interrogation room and went back to now smoke-filled, homicide squad room. The chief of detectives, Clint Chafin, was talking to the two shifts of detectives, and it was not a happy meeting. They were getting ready to release the only suspect they had and the media was breathing down his back, as was the mayor's office. Henshaw handed me some papers and told me to 'cut him loose' and drive him home. I said: 'He will give you a confession now.'

You would have thought a bomb had gone off in the room. Just like before, nobody said anything as Henshaw hurried from the room. He was back in about a minute. 'I need a uniformed guard on the door, a tape recorder and a stenographer; this fuck has been doing this since he was fourteen.' One thing I can say about homicide detectives is that they don't say much. Helms gave that little smile of his and shook his head ruefully. I guess that he was admitting to himself that he had been wrong to fight my transfer to his squad. Chafin smiled because it had been his idea. He went out into the lobby to give the press the news that a suspect had confessed to the rapes. Many of his previous rapes had not been reported because the victims had been too ashamed. Nobody said a word to me, not that I expected much from that taciturn bunch.

The next day when I reported to work Henshaw handed me the car keys and told me to go handle a death on the south side. He was going to be tied up for a week wrapping up the witness statements on the rapist and preparing them for presentation to the state prosecutor's office. I wondered why all that was necessary since all the suspect wanted to do was to plead guilty and go to jail for the rest of his miserable life. It was then that I was introduced to the world of politics and ego, as found in law enforcement, where everybody wanted a piece of the action.

I went to a service station on Cleveland Avenue and saw just how senseless death can be sometimes. A shaken young mechanic was standing by a uniformed cop, and a dead young man lay on the floor of the grease pit. They had been playing Russian roulette and when it came to his friend's turn, the bullet had torn half his head off. They had heard that when you put a single bullet in a revolver's cylinder and rotated the cylinder, the weight of the bullet automatically would carry the bullet to the lower position, well away from the firing pin. That's all very well unless you are using an old rusty revolver that has forgotten the law of gravity. I booked him into jail on a manslaughter charge, something I had to do because it was up to the courts to decide his fate.

The next morning the judge turned him loose after yelling at him for a few minutes. Over the next few months I was to learn that people killed people for the most inane reasons. 'You burned my pork chops.' 'The TV is too loud.' 'You farted in my face in bed.' 'I can't hear the TV.' 'I think you are fooling around' (and she was in her mid-sixties and almost infirm). 'Turn down the stereo.' 'Did you take that five dollars I had in my shoe?'

Perhaps a classic was when I was called to a home on Capitol Avenue, close to the stadium. The young uniformed officer was wide-eyed when he pointed at a very dead person lying on the street, his chest torn apart. 'The shots came out through that screen door,' he said, pointing up at a clapboard house up a steep incline. Then he added: 'I wouldn't go up there if I was you, he's crazy.' I walked up the steps to the lit screen door and looked inside. An elderly black man sat in a rocking chair holding a double-barrelled shotgun on his lap, rocking back and forth. 'Mr Jefferson, may I come in?' I had been told his name by the uniformed officer, who had found it out from a neighbour. The latter had also said that the old man was fanatical about Braves baseball games, one of which was in progress at the stadium a few hundred yards away.

The old man was supposed to have once played baseball in the old Negro league and had stayed eternally angry because his name could not be found anywhere in the record books. Apparently his wife would go and visit family when a game was on, and the neighbours maintained a fearful and respectful silence while he watched the game on his old black-and-white television. He always kept the front and back doors open for the cross breeze, and the screen doors kept out the insects, and people.

Why in the world would fate take an unfortunate man up those steps to ask directions because he saw a light in an open door when the Atlanta Braves were at the bottom of the ninth in a tied game? Since the old man was hard of hearing and the television was very loud, the stranger had yelled at him to ask if he knew where a certain family lived. The old man responded by picking up his shotgun and firing two barrels through the screen door. The force of the twin blasts blew the poor man off the porch and out into the heavy traffic on Capitol Avenue. If he was not dead by then, the four cars that ran over him finished the job.

'Mr Jefferson, open the door, we need to talk; I am a policeman.' You tend to remember conversations like the one I had. 'I know who you are, boy. Relax and I will be out shortly.' His eyes never left the television as he rocked back and forth with his shotgun still on his lap. Since there were two empty shotgun shells on the floor beside his rocking chair, I assumed he had reloaded. I went back outside and sat on a chair on the porch and listened to the roars of the crowd at the nearby stadium. More uniformed officers arrived and secured the gory scene on the street. When I told them I had to wait until the game was over before we could proceed with processing the crime scene, I got a few strange looks.

However, one of the perks of being a homicide detective in charge of a murder crime scene was that you outranked everybody in the department, including the chief. Nobody wanted to become involved in the chain of evidence because that might mean they would be sitting in Superior Court for days on end.

The game finally ended and he set the gun down and opened the door. I charged him with manslaughter, and the look Judge Little gave me the next day would have withered a strong oak tree. He bound him over to state court and that is the last I heard of it. I am guessing the state prosecutor negotiated some kind of deal and the old man walked free; maybe they were Braves fans, who knows.

That is not to say every homicide was a 'smoking gun' type of murder; some were not. I remember, for example, the Mary Little case well. She had gone shopping at Lenox Square mall and was never seen again. Her credit card was used farther north and there was blood on the lime-green front seat of her car. This case, concerning a young housewife, was worked on exhaustively, but was never solved. And there were others. I think about them, even now.

I knew I was burned out and I needed to get away. I could not see myself processing bodies through the system for years to come. The myth of being a murder detective is just that – a myth. It is a nasty dangerous job filled with corpses and people who just don't care, often not even the victim's blood relatives. Many times we cared more for the murder victims than their relatives did. The lot of a homicide detective is an endless procession of human misery and that's about all I can say about it.

The only thing in my life I was certain about was that I had to get away from the Atlanta police department because it was

eating me alive. I got to the point that I inquired about returning to the army with my former rank as sergeant. It was so bad
that muck and war was better than where I was in Atlanta.

Then a deputy sheriff from Florida passed through the detective bureau one day on an extradition warrant. He had flown
up to bring back to Florida a prisoner who was wanted for
murder. Since I had never seen a deputy sheriff before, I had a
chat with him. The first thing I noticed about him was that he
was very relaxed and tanned. He told me that the Palm Beach
County sheriff's department was recruiting experienced detectives and that they paid a lot more than I was being paid.

I wrote down the information and told him I would probably give him a call. All I knew about Florida was what I had
seen in movies and on television. White beaches, blue water
and beautiful girls – a far cry from the city morgue. I called him
the next day. They told me I could have a job as an agent in the
intelligence unit and sent a letter of confirmation.

With the stink of the morgue, tear gas and the ghetto still
in my head, I walked into the chief's office and handed in my
coveted gold homicide detective shield. No other officer in the
long history of the department had earned that shield as fast
or at such an early age; it was a bitter-sweet moment. I said my
goodbyes and felt bad about leaving those who had mentored
me, I truly did. Their eyes told me they thought that I had
betrayed them, but I had to get away. It was a long walk to the
parking lot, and I felt accusing eyes everywhere.

I was not to know that the corruption and violence I was
trying to escape in Atlanta were nothing compared to violent,
drug-ridden southeast Florida. Staying in Atlanta or going to
war would have been better choices – far better, for I was on my
way to a pit of venomous snakes.

I had researched Palm Beach County and was impressed.
A little over a million people lived there then, and the sher-

iff's department had a huge geographical area to cover – 2,386 square miles, with an ever-expanding thirty-seven cities that were in its jurisdiction. The county is the largest one east of the Mississippi River, and that is a lot of land in anybody's book, especially mine since I had come from tiny Ireland.

If ever there is a diverse county in America it is Palm Beach County. To the west, all of the sugar that was formerly grown in Cuba is grown there, and it is the vegetable garden of America as it produces vast amounts for the kitchens and restaurants of the nation. I once flew in a helicopter over the Glades, as the western section is called. As far as the eye could see were sugar and vegetable fields. Not fields as I knew them, but vast plantings stretching on and on.

Coming from Ireland with our little, stone-wall-marked, fraction-of-an-acre holdings, I found that the sight of a totally flat, agriculturally landscaped horizon took my breath away. I saw massive combines, sometimes ten in a straight row, moving across the vegetable fields. As the vegetables, like celery, were sucked into the giant machine, they were being ejected out the rear end onto a waiting flat-bed truck. Not just ejected, but washed and clear-plastic wrapped and labelled for immediate delivery to America's supermarkets.

The flat-bed truck, when full, drove back to the warehouses and the packaged vegetables were loaded on refrigerated tractor trailers which then hit the road once. I estimated that the total time from picking the vegetables until the trucks were out on the highway was less than an hour. To somebody who in recent times had picked potatoes by hand, this operation was mind-boggling. As I sat in the helicopter with other deputies, I decided to keep my mouth shut; they wouldn't understand anyway.

The eastern part of the county was in sharp contrast, what with all the billionaires and their mansions. It is a far cry from the squalor of the homes of the migrant workers, who harvested the sugar cane to the west. The rich may have seen the vast fields from their private Lear Jets, but that is as close as any of them would ever get; not that they wanted to get any closer.

In short, Palm Beach County is a place of stark socio-economic contrasts, wealth and poverty sharing the same day's sun. While some people were luxuriating in it for a fashionable tan by their pools, others suffered under its relentless scorching heat as they laboured for a pittance.

I had rented an apartment in Juno Beach and was gradually settling into my new life. After Atlanta, it was a welcome relief for me and I found it an exciting place to live. I grew a beard and worked undercover assignments for four years. Everything seemed open and above board, and my fellow deputies all appeared friendly and relaxed. In retrospect, I now believe that I wanted my new job and life to work out so badly that I was blind to anything but the positive.

There were warning signs of corruption, but I ignored them, to my regret. Unlike Atlanta, there was not the daily tension of street combat, and that was a welcome change. My personal lifestyle was almost like a vacation. My place in Juno Beach had the ocean and a white beach only steps away. I was born almost in the sea in Ireland, grew up around the sea, and it was in my blood. Even today, if I am away from the sea for any length of time I feel despondent. A quick trip to the beach and I am in top gear again.

The east coast of the county stretched from Jupiter Island to the north to Boca Raton to the south, a vast coastline for a single county, and it was a hop, skip and a jump from the Bahamas. There was a huge amount of marijuana and narcotics pouring into America through and across counties like Palm Beach with little or no interference. The smugglers would land their cargo on the many deserted beaches there, off-load onto trucks and from there it was smooth sailing. A safer and quicker method was to simply fly it in from the Bahamas to an airfield in the Glades area, which is dotted with small landing strips that are used by the many crop dusters in the area. As vast as that agricultural area is, not much goes on there that the locals don't know about, and the sheriff's department maintains a fully staffed and manned office there.

I was sometimes involved in surveillance in the area – not involving drug smugglers – and I would hear small aircraft fly overhead with no lights showing. I asked the local deputies what that was all about and they would just shrug. I had been a big-city cop and the wherefores of this vast agricultural land were as alien to me as Mars would have been. I later realised that they were drug smugglers who were instrument-flying at night. When they got close to the target landing strip they would radio ahead and at the last moment somebody on the ground would turn on some rudimentary landing lights to guide the plane to the landing strip. It was risky business but the immense amount of money involved made the risks worthwhile.

After the Vietnam war ended, there were thousands of flight-trained men who found themselves back home without a job and not much going on in their lives. The grapevine caught up with them and the next thing they knew they were making more money in one night than they had made in a year in the military. While it was a risky business, it was tame compared to being shot at on a daily basis by the Viet Cong. Many stashed the money away and when they had enough to do whatever it was they wanted to do, they simply disappeared. Many stayed with the business and set up their own smuggling operations. Others just became so involved that they started to rub elbows with very bad people and they too disappeared, but for the wrong reasons.

I had some tough assignments. I infiltrated a group that was planning to blow up the Navy Seal base in Key West. That almost ended up with me staying down in the Florida Keys with a severe case of rigor mortis. By and large I did what most 'Narcs' do: arrest drug dealers. My work was dangerous and I began to wonder what life would be like if I didn't have to worry about some low-life getting lucky and stamping my card, permanently.

So I began to take classes at night, and while my scummy appearance gave some of my professors a problem, I kept a low profile and did reasonably well. But more importantly, I was really enjoying myself; I liked being in a classroom environment. There were other benefits, too, as tanned, blonde-haired, beautiful Florida girls were in abundance. However, my long hair, beard and wretched appearance kept them at a distance – except one, Cindy, the most beautiful of them all. Whenever we took our evening break to go out and get something to eat, we would go to a nearby pizza parlour. We dated for a month or so, then she asked me if I could attend a party her parents were throwing at their home in Boca Raton. I said yes, and you can rack that mistake up with the other mistakes I have made in my life.

Her parents' home was on the water in Boca Raton and had a boat tied up behind it that looked like the Queen Mary. The other guests' cars were parked in front of the house – which looked like a luxury car sales display room – and many of them contained uniformed chauffeurs. I parked my old, dingy, white Ford van and after taking a deep breath entered the world of serious money. When I was introduced by their daughter, her parents' faces began to transform into grotesque horror masks. Her father, dressed in pink and lavender, the uniform of the wealthy in Florida, called me into his office and closed the door. He went to his desk and produced a German Luger which he then stuck under my chin. I can't remember exactly what he said to me because of the gun under my chin. But I did find myself driving back north on US Route 1, alone, and in very short order.

Cindy did not return to class and that was that. I later heard that her parents had shipped her north to some exclusive girls' school which she had refused to attend before; maybe he used the Luger to convince her.

One aspect of undercover police work which gave me a startling insight into the psyches of beautiful women is that they are attracted to scummy-looking, dangerous men. I never told any of these beautiful women I dated what I really did for a living. It seemed the more outrageous the story I told them, the more attracted to me they became. To one I was a Mafia hit man, and to others I was a drug dealer, a burglar and a bank robber. It just did not matter, and these girls came from up-market families.

It seemed that one of the benefits they saw in dating a scumbag like me was that they could do whatever they wanted with me, which was all right with me. They would tell me they hated dating 'regular' guys, who made them feel constricted.

I well remember a beautiful young lady who moved out of my life and married an extremely wealthy son of a building tycoon. I saw her wedding announcement in the paper and it read like a run-down on anybody and everybody who was rich and famous. I remembered reflecting on her weird bedroom tastes. I hope she did not try them out on her innocent, bliss-ful-looking young husband. And – like all the rest of them – after a few months my phone would ring and she would want a quick and private engagement. And, like all the rest of them, I declined; even pseudo-scumbags have their own set of moral standards, most of the time.

I loved the streets, from Atlanta to the Palm Beaches. But – and I don't know when it happened, but it did – I suddenly wanted to get off the streets. I wanted a normal life, or as normal a life as a cop can have. I had paid my dues on the streets, and then some. I wanted inside and as close to a normal life as I could achieve and still carry a badge. I asked and was reassigned to work in the Special Investigations Section, or SIS. This section handled sensitive and confidential investigations. But first I had to get a haircut and clean up my act so far as clothing went. I went to a mall and got a shave and a haircut and the barber charged me double.

It was a strange feeling walking back through the mall looking like a regular person. There was no more of the disgusted looks I used to get or people moving away when I approached or women holding their purses closer. It was as if I had suddenly become invisible, and that felt good. I had no problem with the clothes because I still had my suits from when I was working in homicide in Atlanta. I had everything dry-cleaned and, apart from updating my ties, I was ready to go.

My SIS partner was Bob Menahan and he was good to work with. Very settled and calm, and he stayed that way. I was asked to write some articles for the International Narcotics Enforcement Officers' monthly publication. Through that journal I made many vital and interesting contacts around America and the world. I was also asked to speak at national and international conferences; my world was changing and I liked where it was going.

Russ Jessup, the regional training director for the Federal Drug Enforcement Agency, or DEA, asked me to speak at some of his seminars. I then attended and graduated from the full DEA course and afterwards Jessup approached me with an offer. He wanted me to coordinate and teach a DEA course utilising the Law Enforcement Training Academy in Palm Beach County. I was taken aback as I was still a detective sergeant with the Palm Beach sheriff's department, and not a federal agent. Jessup said I was qualified and that was that. He had box-loads of training material shipped to the academy, and, stranger still, blank DEA certificates for the successful graduates.

The classes went well and were heavily attended, and I enjoyed the experience. I was then appointed the county training officer and moved into a nice office adjacent to the county training academy. It appeared that my days as a street cop were over.

My ambition always had been to become a federal agent with the DEA, and all indications were that that would be no problem as I was well known to them. Then something totally unexpected happened: organised crime once more raised its head in my law enforcement career. And, like before, it was wearing a badge, a deputy sheriff's badge this time around.

I had been in the process of creating some form of communication among the almost countless law enforcement agencies in southeastern Florida, which was the hot-bed of drug smuggling in the United States. Federal, state and local law enforcement agencies rarely communicated with each other, if ever. It was an insane scenario in the out-of-control, multi-billion-dollar narcotics supermarket in south Florida. The drug barons loved the situation as they had free rein all over the region and every law enforcement agency refused to share intelligence information with any other agency, either knowingly or through sheer ignorance. Incredibly, it is the same today.

I formed the Florida Narcotic Enforcement Officers Association, or FNEOA, with some powerful backing. Florida governor Rubin Askew signed a state declaration of support and the membership response was very strong. We finally had a means of communication that could circumvent the politics and corruption of every law enforcement agency in Florida. We printed a monthly bulletin containing articles and information that was otherwise unavailable to the rank-and-file narcotics enforcement officers. But what was more important was that the bulletin contained the names, agencies and contact numbers of narcotics officers across the state.

Then the phones began to ring. This was the last thing that the corrupt police officers and the drug barons needed and they moved to destroy the FNEOA, and me in the process. I was not to know this as I went about building the FNEOA. It had been a loose, fledgling organisation; now that we had the backing of the powerful governor of Florida, everything had changed. We became targets.

Cops make peanuts compared to the billion-dollar profits raked in by the drug barons. It is a simple matter of economics versus morality. In south Florida, money has won out over police morality. Certainly there are pockets of honesty – not all cops are dishonest. However, those honest cops who protest my contentions in this book are naïve and, I guarantee you, ineffective. They do not understand the big picture because they are just pawns and are used to making a few 'big' phony busts to satisfy the media and the unaware public. The drug barons feed their handlers in the police department what they call 'loss leaders'. These are drug dealers who work for the barons, who are suspected of stealing from their operation, or of working for a competitor. For the barons, there is no loss, and in essence the police end up doing their dirty work for them, knowingly or unknowingly.

Sometimes the drug barons even throw in a few kilos of heavily cut cocaine just to make the police look good. Then you get headlines like 'Biggest Cocaine Bust in Years', and everybody is happy. For the drug barons it's a cheap price for keeping the politicians and the public placated. It's all in the cost of doing business, as a drug dealer once explained to me. Honest cops are the drug barons' greatest asset because they use them like pawns in a chess game. And crooked cops, working on the inside, guide things along nicely, keeping everybody happy.

It was around that time that one of the best things that ever happened to me in America occurred: I met Duke and Elaine Short, who were to become life-long friends. As I mentioned earlier, Duke was the chief executive for the powerful US Senate Judiciary Committee. He was a quiet, powerful man who wielded his considerable influence with quiet humility.

Over the years we grew closer and Sydney, his daughter, stayed with me in Atlanta for a while when she was in college. They also hosted my mother and father in their Virginia home when they visited from Ireland. Duke arranged for them a tour of the White House and the US Senate, which he personally conducted. It was mind-boggling because everywhere Duke went, doors were thrown open for him and my parents. I am not sure if they ever realised just what a privileged tour they had, for Duke brought them to private restricted areas that few American ever see – he was that kind of person, good to the core.

In the meantime, people in dark places began to rip and tear at the FNEOA, and at me personally. I never saw where the attacks were coming from, but they were law-enforcement inspired. There was too much power behind the attacks for them not to be. What took years of hard work to create, took only months to tear down. Then rumours began to circulate that I was abusing drugs, and that was the end. There was no defence against faceless people or organisations. My lifetime of public service was being systematically shredded and I was helpless to prevent that happening.

I resigned from the sheriff's department and went back home to Ireland for a holiday and to recharge my batteries. I had the luxury of time and being able to afford a break. Duke suggested that I go ahead and apply for a position with the

DEA. I returned to Washington and submitted my application. Neither he nor I was worried about the drug abuse rumours as I had already volunteered to take a comprehensive lie detector test. I waited while my application was being processed and enjoyed Washington; it is a fascinating city. Then the phone rang one morning and it was all over: 'I'm sorry, Jerry, you've been rejected.'

I was stunned, as I had been an instructor for the DEA and had worked cases with many of their agents. Duke obtained a copy of my background investigation but parts had been deleted and we could not understand why; later we would. I read the report and there were no references to drug or alcohol abuse or dishonesty, but deeply personal insults from people whose names had been blacked out by the FBI, the investigating agency. I felt sick to my stomach; who were these people?

I read and re-read the report and soon I began to realise that the negative comments had originated from within the Palm Beach County sheriff's department. I found myself basically with nowhere to go, so I picked up the phone and called Eldrin Bell in Atlanta. Eldrin was my friend and a high-ranking officer in the Atlanta police department. He simply said 'come back' and that was that; no need for explanations. I was a police officer, pure and simple; that's what I did best. What I had accomplished in Florida was gone, and I had to start again, down in the ghetto. But that was all right; at least there I understood the rules.

# 9

# THE TRUE LION OF ISRAEL

My years in the Palm Beaches exposed me to exciting experiences that could never have occurred in Atlanta – they were two different worlds. Before going back to Atlanta, I want to tell you about some of those experiences.

While with the Special Investigations Squad of the sheriff's department, I was assigned to the protection detail for Yitzhak Rabin, the Israeli ambassador to the United States. He was on a trip to raise money to buy fighter aircraft for the Israeli air force. With his wartime record and fierce reputation, Rabin had to be the most sought-after target for every anti-Israeli country in the world, and there were many, as there are now. It promised to be a relaxed assignment for me though. I figured that there would be many federal and state agents assigned to his security detail. My role would probably end up being that of the local back-up, keeping an eye out for any unfriendly faces.

The hotel in Palm Beach where they were staying is on a quiet street and is still stately but beginning to show its age. When I arrived there, I drove to the rear parking lot expecting to see a large number of security detail automobiles; there were none. I checked the front and the side parking lots; still nothing. I parked and went inside the hotel to check. I asked the desk clerk if the Israeli ambassador was a guest at the hotel. 'Yes sir, room 302.' I was taken aback because I had assumed that he would have given an evasive reply because of security concerns. I identified myself and asked the clerk if anybody had requested that no staff member should reveal that Rabin was staying at the hotel, and he said no.

I asked to speak to the manager. When I had briefed him he immediately hurried off to inform his staff to keep their mouths shut. I then asked him how many rooms had been reserved for federal and state agents, and he told me none. About that time I began to experience a sinking feeling in my gut, a feeling I always got when I knew I was in deep trouble. Rabin was a walking assassination target, and I was guarding him with a single police revolver.

With a growing sense of urgency I called my director and voiced my concerns. He told me that Rabin had specifically requested that there would be no security because he had his own. The director did not sound concerned but I sure as hell was. Rabin was a lightning rod for attracting dangerous situations and I was ground zero in this one.

Rabin's background makes him sound like a one-man war machine, and he had made numerous enemies in the Muslim world. When he was still a teenager in high school, he was one of the deadlier operatives in Moshe Dayan's feared Palmach, a highly effective, underground organisation sworn to driving the British occupying forces out of Palestine. Like others in the Palmach, Rabin was branded a terrorist, but he and other teenagers succeeded in their goal.

There was a lesson to be learned there, but nobody noticed or cared enough to reflect on military history. Traditional military forces have never won a conflict against a guerrilla army; it can't be done. Examples abound: the British against the IRA; the Americans against the pyjama-clad Viet Cong; and, today, the Americans against the invisible armies in Iraq and Afghanistan – both futile wars fought at a great human cost.

With his reputation established in the Palmach, Rabin was eventually appointed commander of the feared Israeli Harel brigades, charged with defending Jerusalem during Israel's war of independence. Rabin ordered his men to actually break the bones of Palestinians if they resisted expulsion from Palestine, and then they expelled fifty thousand men, women and children. Hence the conflict today. Yes, he was deeply hated by many people.

Later on, Rabin was appointed chief of staff of all Israeli forces. He then went on to conceive and execute the most brilliant military victory in the history of warfare: the Six Day War. His American-equipped forces routed the combined military forces of Syria, Egypt and Jordan in just 144 hours – an unbelievable military feat and one that embarrassed the Muslim world. To this day, a smouldering hatred exists in those countries for Israel, and Rabin in particular. They had Yitzhak Rabin in their crosshairs, and were determined to kill him, one way or the other. When it came time for the warrior to hang up his sword, Israel rewarded him with the plum job of the ambassadorship to the United States. He was to remain there for five years, and it was that posting that brought him into my life.

The hotel manager then approached me and told me the suite next to Rabin had been reserved for his security detail, which was good news. I raced upstairs, relieved that Rabin did indeed have a security detail. I knocked on the door and expected to see a room full of Israel's Mossad members. However, when the door opened, a slightly built, timid-looking man peered out at me over his reading glasses. I identified myself and asked if the ambassador was in the room next door and he nodded. I looked over his shoulder expecting to see heavily armed men, but the room appeared empty. I then asked him where the security detail was located. He blinked a few times and said: 'I am security.' He looked like Woody Allen.

That familiar sinking feeling came back in my gut, this time with a vengeance. I went to Rabin's room and knocked on the door. An elderly version of the man next door asked how he could help me. I identified myself and told him I needed to talk to the ambassador. He turned and spoke to somebody in the room and then stepped aside to allow me to enter. I did, and then the smoke hit me. I was accustomed to smoke-filled rooms, having worked in our family pub, but this room was more like the inside of a chimney – all four occupants of the room were furiously smoking. Rabin was sitting in a chair beside a small round table and papers were strewn all about the room. The other three men were reading and talking quietly to each other. Rabin asked me what I wanted and after I had voiced my concerns he just scowled at me. I was later to realise that was the way he looked all the time. He lit another cigarette although there was another one half smoked still smouldering in his ashtray. It looked like the room was filled with patients from a nicotine addiction clinic.

As I stood in that hotel room with the almost overpowering smell of cigarette smoke heavy in my nostrils, eyes and lungs, I sensed I was in the presence of an extremely dangerous man. I had worked the streets of Atlanta as a cop and had experienced four years of undercover work, and my instincts were honed sharp as a razor. They had to be to survive around those feral criminals whose instinct for survival was equally sharp. But their eyes always gave them away, just like an animals. Rabin was different. His were not like the hoodlum's eyes, which always generated suspicion and rage. This man looked at you in an almost casual way, a chillingly dangerous way. This man knew and understood his fellow man and was afraid of none of them. That fact bled through his cold, blue eyes as he sized me up and then said, 'I will call you if I need you,' and then lit a third cigarette. While others claimed the title, Yitzhak Rabin was the true Lion of Israel. But I sensed his vulnerability and my concern increased. The window in his room looked out at another hotel, and the curtains had been pulled back. Even a mediocre sniper could easily have shot Rabin from any of the opposite rooms. His enemies had always wanted an opportunity to kill Yitzhak Rabin and they lost one that day, an easy opportunity.

I went to the room next door and the door was ajar, with a small man sitting on the bed, security obviously far from his mind. He had his back to the door and was reading what appeared to be a Bible, seemingly oblivious to my presence. I went inside and tried to make myself comfortable. If I was to protect Rabin it would appear I would be in this hotel room until his departure, and I had no change of clothes – or anything else for that matter. I stared at the back of the praying man and thought that perhaps it might be a good time for me to say a few prayers; the situation I found myself in was bleak.

I studied the man and knew enough about the Jewish religion to know that he was probably reading the Talmud. He was wearing a plain black yarmulke on his head and a prayer shawl. I sat on one of the two beds and read a free travel magazine. A full two hours later he finished and went through a short ritual and then turned around and saw me on the other bed. He jumped as if a dog had bitten him on his rear end; he obviously did not even know I had been in the room. This was no Jewish James Bond. By then I had had enough and asked him: 'What weapons do you have?' He sighed and opened a suitcase next to his bed. After rummaging around for a minute he produced a familiar, blue Smith & Wesson box. He gingerly opened the box and carefully unwrapped the brown wax paper and produced a snub-nosed .38-calibre revolver. He handed me the gun by holding its barrel with two fingers as if it were going to bite him. Things were going from bad to worse, fast.

Then I had a thought and asked him if he had any ammunition. Another big sigh and a return visit to the suitcase. After a few more minutes of rummaging, he shook his head: 'I must have forgotten it.' Why was I not surprised? Just when I thought the situation could not get any worse, it did. 'I am studying to be a rabbi; I have never fired a gun and have no desire to ever do so – I trust you understand.'

I understood all right. I was up the proverbial creek without a paddle. If somebody killed Yitzhak Rabin before he died of lung cancer next door, it would be my fault. Who else were they going to blame? Not fervent, timid Woody Allen, that was for sure.

It promised to be a long, agonising day. I made some phone calls requesting assistance or weapons. I might as well have called the Vatican for somebody to deliver me a pizza. There were a number of crises out in the Glades with the migrant Jamaican sugar cane workers and some other vague problems in the eastern part of the county. However, I was sincerely promised that as soon as one deputy was freed up he would be dispatched immediately to my location. I have learned that it is not a good idea to hold your breath on sincere promises.

So there I sat with a very nice Jewish rabbi-to-be and his empty gun, charged with the protection of the most hated man in the Middle East. I watched TV with the sound turned off as my companion had returned to praying. At least I had one thing to be thankful for: Rabin had stayed in his room. There I had some chance of protecting him once he closed the curtains after dark. Then the phone rang. The rabbi-to-be answered the phone and calmly said 'yes' a few times and then hung up, and went back to meditating. As I lay on my bed I began to develop a familiar sense of unease. It was an acutely uncomfortable feeling, and the longer I lay there, the more intense it became.

I got off the bed and asked him what the call was about. Another big sigh and then: 'Nothing really, the ambassador and his party are going out to eat. He said we are to stay in the room.' Now it was my time to jump off the bed. I grabbed my suit coat as I rushed out the door. I was almost too late, as Rabin and his party were already standing by the elevator. I was about to have what promised to be a most interesting conversation with one of the most controversial men in the world. He walked up to me, a scowl on his face, and in his trademark deep voice said: 'I left instructions that there would be no security, now go away.' He was angry and was obviously not used to anybody disobeying his orders.

If I allowed Rabin to go downstairs and he then had his brains blown all over Palm Beach, I was the one who would pay. So I stood my ground. He stood there, right in my face, trying to stare me down with those cold blue eyes, a cigarette in his mouth. This was a battle-hardened warrior; being nice would not work. 'Sir, I am a veteran of two armies and years of tough times on the streets as a cop. If you get whacked, it's my fucking ass. So I am tagging along with you whether you like it or not.'

I said this low enough so the others could not hear – better to keep it man to man rather than have Rabin's pride pushed to the wall by a public display. His stern face slowly dissolved into a bemused look, but he stood firm. 'I do not need security.' It was unseasonably chilly in Palm Beach that night and Rabin was wearing a full-length black overcoat, and it looked like cashmere. As he turned to walk away I noticed the unmistakable bulge of a weapon on his left side; Rabin was armed. 'Sir, I am from Ireland. Surely that makes a difference, does it not?' He stopped short and slowly turned around. The Jews, when fighting the British, were given sanctuary in Ireland and I knew he had to know that. What probably was his attempt at a smile crossed his face: 'Irishman, you can tag along, whatever that means.' Yitzhak Rabin, the true Lion of Israel, winner of the Nobel Prize in 1994, had backed down in front of his party, all because I was Irish.

At the end of an evening during which Rabin assiduously ignored me, we reached our floor on the elevator. I could not just let it go and said, while all the time staring at the bulge under his overcoat, 'Sir, I really would appreciate it if you could send me one of your Uzis.' He gave me another one of his bemused looks and said: 'I will see what I can do.'

I watched him depart in the morning with his party driving a small rental car – no limousine. I guess that no assassin would ever suspect that the most wanted man in the Middle East would be driving a cheap rental car.

Rabin, in my humble opinion, was ill served by his own instincts for survival. The world had changed but he had not. It was a more frightening and dangerous world, and he was a marked man. Whether he liked it or not, he desperately needed to shed his tough guerrilla persona and avail himself of tight security. However, he had dodged so many bullets and death itself that he probably thought nothing would ever happen to him. Here was a man with many enemies, yet, he felt so empowered and invulnerable that he scorned protection, and that is what eventually killed him. I remember watching him board a commercial flight at the airport and thinking that I was watching a dead man walking, and I was. On the evening of 4 November 1995, Yitzhak Rabin was gunned down in Tel Aviv, shot in the back – the one place security agents would have been.

# 10

# STRANGE RELATIONSHIPS

**P**oliticians are attracted to the Palm Beaches like bears to honey. While working executive assignments there, I saw everybody from former and present kings, rulers of countries, industrialists, millionaires and billionaires, old- and new-money people, movie stars: all had one thing in common – money. And what I have never understood is why these wealthy people would just give their money to rising and powerful politicians, because they did not need them, on a business, political or social level.

I once had a slightly drunk established and powerful politician try to explain why he had been 'kissing that prick's ass' all night at a reception hosted by a Palm Beach old-money type. 'They collect fucks like me,' he said, 'so that they can show the power of their money. I don't care as long as their cheque clears the bank.' Maybe he was right, I just don't know. What I do know is that American presidents and presidential pretenders, senators and congressmen gather for their nectar on a regular basis, cup in hand for contributions. There is no shame when one is on a quest for power.

I found the political executive protection assignments very interesting. If you stayed with the politicians for a few days, you heard the same speech over and over again, and saw the same ingratiating smiles, the same hand-shaking, back-slapping and endless media interviews. What I found interesting was some of the conversations I would overhear while the candidates were in the smoky rooms with their advisors and spin-doctors. After a short time, the people you protect cease to see you, and I would just blend in with the wallpaper – I would be like a fly on the wall, there but not there. I would listen to their 'sweet deals' and who they should glad-hand for a contribution to their campaign coffers; and I'd see them sneak off to hotel rooms for illicit liaisons with staffers and political groupies, conveniently forgetting their spouses.

While the secret service is charged with the protection of principal political figures, they have to rely on local law enforcement for back-up assignments. That said, once they gained confidence in some 'locals', as they called us, we tended to fit right in with the secret service details. That caused some hilarious moments.

I was once assigned to support the secret service when Vice President Hubert Humphrey visited Atlanta. Agents were supplied with discreet pins of different colours that were attached to the lapels of our suits. Somehow somebody stuck a secret service pin on my lapel and I found myself driving the secret service car directly behind Humphrey. This car contained three heavily armed agents who, in the event of an emergency, would rush forward to protect Humphrey.

Following a speech at the Marriott Hotel on Piedmont Avenue, the vice president was to be driven to the north side to attend a cocktail party at the palatial home of a wealthy contributor. These parties are designed to show all of the contributor's friends just how powerful they really are: the vice president of the United States comes to their cocktail parties, and everybody gets their photograph taken with the man of the moment. Needless to say, many rush to fill out generous contributions to the war chest after being promised special treatment at the White House.

After the speech, I was ordered to drive a pale blue Ford Custom with three agents and fall in behind the vice president's armoured black limo. All exits and intersections were blocked by Atlanta traffic cops and we swung smoothly into the expressway north. I had no idea what driving techniques the secret service used in these situations, so I fell in directly behind the limo. The three agents began to yell at me and told me to get in the middle of the expressway and prevent any traffic from passing the limo. That inner city expressway includes the merging lanes from I-85 and I-95 and is full of giant speeding trucks, vacationers going home from Florida, plenty of drunk drivers – traffic which has one of the highest counts of cars in America. And they wanted me to pull in front of these speeding vehicles in a nondescript blue Ford? I politely told them where to go and they then went ballistic: 'You are with our Atlanta office, right?' one of them screamed, as trucks and recreational vehicles stormed past the limo, just inches from it. 'No,' I retorted, 'I am with the Atlanta police department.' You would have thought I had said I was Bin Laden by their reaction. Everybody blamed everybody else as we hurled along trying to just stay alive in this manic traffic. I asked them why they had not used quiet residential streets for the trip to the cocktail party, and that just brought more finger-pointing from the three.

We finally reached our destination and some senior secret service type started to yell at me about my driving until a red-faced agent informed him that I was a local cop. He looked like he was going to have a heart attack. The red-faced agent pleaded: 'Well, he looks like one of us.' I wondered what that meant. I am sure the erring agent found himself in Nome, Alaska, the next day, guarding sled dogs.

In the interest of job security, they rushed me behind the big house and told me to guard the swimming pool and find my own way back to police headquarters after the event. Then one of the agents grabbed the pin in my lapel and gave me a look as dirty as a cesspool.

The secret service have a mission objective that is critical to America because they protect its leaders and its currency. Yet there is no way I would ever want that sort of assignment. Some assignments are exciting and high profile, like protecting sitting presidents; most are not. Many agents protect former presidents and their wives. A friend in the service told me about an agent who was assigned to sit in the darkened living room of deceased president Harry Truman's home, guarding his wife Margaret who was upstairs. He would sit there in the dark, listening to a small radio at low volume, on the lonely plains of Missouri. I would have needed the mental tranquillity of a Tibetan monk, which I don't have, to survive for a week.

It's just not just the secret service who have mind-numbing assignments; the FBI has its share of Gulag-style situations. A long-time friend of mine, a retired agent, told me of his nightmare in New York City where he was assigned to keep an eye on suspected Russian KBG agents' activities. He was assigned to the midnight shift and his mission was to ensure that should any KGB agents sneak out at night and do whatever sneaky KBG agents do, he would monitor their movements. The only problem was that nothing ever stirred at the Russian embassy at night. So he would sit out there in his car alone, every lonely night, staring at nothing.

My friend grew so frustrated with his assignment that he began to do some very strange things in the dead of night, like squirting instant glue into the door locks of known KBG cars, and doing some other unsanitary things to the offending vehicles. He told me about another team of agents who sat in twenty-four-hour shifts photographing everybody coming and going from a travel agency. Each person was then investigated at great cost and a lot of agent time was expended. It was only after two long years that it was discovered that somebody had made a mistake – it was the wrong address.

There are so many other examples that I would need to write another book. I was assigned to provide back-up security at the Palm Beach International Airport for the arrival of President Richard Millhouse Nixon. He would be forced to resign in disgrace over the Watergate scandal on 9 August 1974, the only American president to be forced out of office. It was common knowledge that Nixon was an intense, humourless man, with no male friends; that is, until Bebe Rebozo came into his life. And it was at that airport that I nearly killed Bebe Rebozo.

Early on in his political career Nixon felt the constant strain of Washington politics. He asked Florida congressman George Smathers if he knew anywhere in Florida where he could relax in the sun. In December 1951 Smathers arranged for Nixon to go on a fishing trip with his friend, Charles Rebozo, who liked to be called 'Bebe', as he was the youngest son of a Cuban immigrant family and was always called the baby. I am convinced that the fishing trip was the beginning of the downfall of the thirty-seventh president of the United States and ushered in an era of American and world insecurity. Because of Nixon, the most powerful and respected country in the world shamefully lost its way, never to be the same again.

Much has been written and said about the Nixon debacle and Watergate, but few have attempted to shed light on the origin of the rot that brought down an American president. I maintain that it was that single fishing trip.

Weak men are easily corrupted, and Nixon proved to be the weakest of us all. Rebozo reportedly did not enjoy Nixon's dour company on that fishing trip. He said Nixon did not like women, booze or cigars and was dull and boring. However, as Nixon's political career blossomed, so did Rebozo's affection for the potential president to be. Bebe began to work feverishly to raise funds for Nixon's run for the White House. He had close contacts with billionaire Howard Hughes and obtained generous contributions from him for Nixon. However, Rebozo apparently had sticky fingers and not all of Howard Hughes' contributions made it to Nixon's campaign coffers. During the Watergate investigation, Rebozo had a tough time trying to explain why $100,000 of Howard Hughes' political contribution to Nixon was discovered in his, Rebozo's, bank's safe deposit box.

When Dwight Eisenhower chose Nixon to be his vice president in 1953, both Nixon's and Rebozo's fortunes soared, and these now-inseparable men were on their way. To understand that unlikely relationship, one has to take a close look at Rebozo's background and how Nixon ended up his close friend.

Bebe Rebozo came up the hard way. He epitomised the American dream for Cuban Americans. He worked hard and saved and borrowed enough money to buy a service station. There was a war going on and he sensed a business opportunity – the severe shortage of automobile tyres. The troops were the first priority for tyre manufacturers, leaving hapless nervous civilians driving around on onion-skin-thin tyres. I had a resident of the Florida Keys tell me that during the Second World War, if you even ran over a crab you had an instant flat tyre.

So Bebe went into the lucrative tyre-retread business and hit the nail on the head. He opened a car-supply shop and began to invest in self-service laundromats. In 1964 he opened the Key Biscayne Bank. His friend Nixon was on hand for the opening ceremonies and opened the bank's first savings account. By then Rebozo had delved in a big way into Florida real estate and had bought just at the right time when property was cheap. Shortly afterwards, the Florida land boom exploded and Bebe's acute business sense paid off. Not content to sit on his laurels, he then opened a shopping centre for Cuban refugees fleeing from Castro's communism. This endeared him further within the Miami Cuban community.

While Bebe's business life was a runaway success, his personal life was an unmitigated disaster, especially when it involved women. In 1931 he married Clair Gunn, but they divorced two years later. According to Gunn, Rebozo was unable to consummate their marriage. Then he married Jane Lucke, and upon his death on the 8 May 1998, left her a childless widow.

Gossip swirled that both wives had been 'beards', a term used when a man marries a woman for appearances while his real interests lie far from his marriage bed. Gossip like that can be motivated by jealousy and any number of reasons, but Bebe did not help the situation by being observed frequenting gay bars.

Once Nixon became president, his relationship with Rebozo intensified. He went to the extreme of having a private telephone line installed in the White House for Rebozo and provided him with his own personal telephone. Rebozo roamed at will around the White House as if he lived there, and he practically did. Anthony Summers wrote a book on Nixon and estimated that Rebozo was literally at Nixon's side one day in ten during his presidency.

Apart from the president's wife, such free and constant access to a sitting president was unprecedented in the history of the White House. Even while flying with Nixon on Air Force One, Rebozo wore his own presidential flying jacket, complete with the presidential patch. This situation placed the FBI and the secret service in an extremely uncomfortable position for Bebe was no longer that hard-working Cuban immigrant; they suspected he had serious Mafia connections. For example, Rebozo was involved in real estate deals with Richard Fincher, who was an associate of Meyer Lansky, the money man for the

Mafia in the United States. Rebozo was also connected with Carlos Marcello, the ruthless New Orleans Mafia boss. He was connected, too, with mobsters Santa Trafficanta and Vincent Teresa, all targets of every organised crime law enforcement agency in America. But what could they do? Their boss was the president of the United States.

Worse yet, the heads of both the CIA and FBI had been appointed by Nixon, and they were nothing but political hacks whose very jobs depended on him. Both agencies were, and are, saturated in politics. If they are not, as they claim, let them explain the failure of both of them to protect the office of the presidency of the United States – not Richard Nixon, but the office itself, which is a sacred trust. The Nixon–Reboza scandal was a clear case of both agencies being incapacitated by their fear of political retribution from Nixon himself.

Going back to my brush with Rebozo: my assignment at the airport should have been a routine matter. President Nixon would fly into the airport on Marine One helicopter, backed up by Marine Two. I would be assigned to the perimeter to cover an old hanger. This massive tin structure, with large open bay doors on both sides, was located directly in front of the landing area where the two presidential helicopters would land.

On the tarmac a band struck up to warm up a large crowd of Nixon supporters, many of whom were waving red, white and blue posters and banners. The media were testing their strobe lights and the excitement level was rising. The president was due to arrive shortly. The hanger I had been assigned to was closer to the tarmac than I had remembered, and it was pitch-dark inside. I checked the back of the hanger and found it deserted. The bay door facing the tarmac where the president was due to arrive perfectly framed the spot where the presidential helicopter would land. The tarmac was brightly illuminated with spotlights and fixed media lighting.

A growing sense of unease began to envelop me. Why were there no secret agents in the dark hanger? A single marksman could easily pick him off as soon as the chopper doors opened and he stepped out and gave his familiar two-hand victory salute. It just did not make sense. The secret service would never have allowed a local law-enforcement officer to protect the president at such a vulnerable location.

Then I heard the faint but powerful noise of the two giant helicopters as they approached the airport. The band struck up again with patriotic music and somebody had handed out small American flags for the crowd to wave. The tarmac was lit-up as if it was a floodlit football game, and the noise level increased dramatically as the two helicopters began their slow descent to the tarmac. Then I saw a shadow move to the right of the bay door and slip away. It was not just my imagination. I had too much military experience in night combat and years of working the streets as a cop to be mistaken; there was somebody else in the hanger. I tensed, desperately trying to adjust my night vision to the contrast of the darkness in the hangar and the bright lights outside. The noise level grew thunderous and there was pandemonium out on the tarmac.

Then I saw another slight movement to the right of the door and my every sense screamed at me that somebody was trying to conceal themselves in the darkness. All this as the president of the United States was about to stand in the doorway of the Marine helicopter. My radio was useless because of the noise. I drew my weapon and slowly approached the dark shape, both of us in the darkness. My night vision was useless after the bright lights. As I drew nearer the shape began to raise his arms from his sides. From behind it was identical to somebody raising a rifle. I was calm because I knew what I had to do.

The door to the helicopter opened and the president stepped out. I was now directly behind the black shape, now identifi-

able as a man. I held my cocked gun behind his head with my
right hand and tapped him on the shoulder with my left. If he
had as much as flinched he was a dead man – I had made that
decision. He turned his head slightly and smiled: it was Bebe
Rebozo! 'I am just waiting for the president and stretching a
bit,' he said. He never saw my gun as he turned and walked to
the back of the hanger. The presidential limo drove around the
back of the hanger and its rear door swung open to the smiling face of Richard Nixon. Rebozo entered and then they were
gone, just like that.

The entire surreal incident happened so fast that that I
stood in the hanger for a long time after the music had stopped
and everybody had gone home. I was in a daze because I knew
I had nearly killed the president's best friend. I thought about
the president, who was so ashamed to be seen with his friend
that he had been reduced to meeting him in the dark.

I eventually left and drove back to my home on Juno Beach. I
changed into an old pair of cut-off jeans and a faded denim shirt
and walked to the beach. It was a clear, calm night with a full
tide. I have a message for the now-departed President Nixon and
his intimate friend Bebe, wherever you are, and I suspect I know
where you are: both of you owe me big time. If a deputy sheriff
other than me had been in that hanger, Reboza's brains would
have been all over it. Why did I say any other deputy sheriff?
Few if any would have had the experience you get from having
been in two armies and spending years as a policeman in a major
city. Until this moment, as I type this chapter into my computer,
I have never mentioned the incident to anybody.

The sheriff of Palm Beach County was William Heidtman,
a powerful elected Republican, and he would have had my
badge the next day. And if I had killed Rebozo, he would have
had me charged with manslaughter, of that there is no doubt.

That night I sat on the beach and sought the comfort of the

water as it gently lapped at my bare feet. I looked across the moon-lit sea and thought about the same sea touching the jetty behind my home in Dundalk, and sipped Jack Daniels.

I like people around me when I drink, that's the Irish pub in me, but that night I just wanted to be alone. I sat on the beach until the horizon started to lighten and thought about Bebe Rebozo and President Richard Millhouse Nixon. I thought about what I had almost done, killed Bebe Reboza, the President's best friend.

# 11

# JUMPING JACK FLASH

**V**ery young, nubile, female breasts, buttocks and private parts were exposed all over the hotel suite. The only problem was that their owners were comatose as were their hosts, and there was enough evidence to suggest they were in possession of drugs. The large suite looked like a training aid for teaching cops how to handle a mass investigation of state and local law violations. It was 1969 and I had a decision to make: arrest everybody on what had the potential for serious jail time, or walk away.

The West Palm Beach rock festival was one of the first big rock festivals, and it turned into an orgy of sex, drugs and nudity in the midst of mud and rain, but nobody cared, because everybody was high as a kite. Sodom and Gomorrah had nothing on that festival, nothing at all. It attracted every singer and group that dominated the rock scene at that time and in some cases for years to come, like the Stones and Tina Turner.

I and two other narcotics agents had been assigned to live within the festival grounds in an undercover van and make buys from heavy dealers of heroin, opium and acid. Since I looked like a white Jimmy Hendrix and had been working undercover for years, it promised to be a relatively easy assignment. My two partners were Cuban Americans, who, with facial hair and sunglasses, looked like who they pretended to be: Cuban drug dealers.

We had converted an old Ford delivery van into a hippy van that could sleep three if everybody knew each other very well and body odour was not a problem. In the event of a 'buy', we would radio from inside the van and a 'grab' team of deputies would swoop down, arrest the suspect and be out of the festival grounds before a crowd could gather. Back in the van I would record in detail the transaction and be provided with a case number for court by radio.

Undercover officers would photograph the transaction in the open, and the photograph would follow the suspect all the way to state court. Many heavy dealers know that by the time their case finally reaches a judge or jury, they will have shaved, got a haircut and be wearing a conservative suit and an angelic smile. They will plead their innocence and swear they were in, say, the Congo on the day of their arrest. I used to smile inside when they did that, because I knew their ambulance-chasing, shyster lawyer had not told them that he was well aware that a photograph existed of the drug sale. The lawyer wanted the clock to keep running to drive up his fee. The jury always looked like they sympathised with the innocent-looking defendant during their tearful testimony when he described how he was the victim of brutal police entrapment and now he could not become a medical missionary.

Then the state prosecutor would introduce the eight-by-ten enlargement of the defendant clearly handing me drugs and accepting money. Apart from the defendant's sudden pallor, there is nothing like the fury of a deceived jury. A woman scorned has nothing on a bunch of highly pissed-off jurors. The defence lawyer, still running the clock, would then jump dramatically to his feet and start yelling about how there was no way the scummy person in the photograph was his saintly client.

The only problem with that defence is that a scumbag is a scumbag no matter how he tries to disguise himself, and after viewing the picture, the jaws of the jurors would begin to protrude into a predatory profile, and the defendant usually slumped in the witness chair.

The happiest person in the courtroom is the shyster lawyer, as he yells for an appeal, a very expensive appeal. However, a shyster lawyer has many faces, and, after his client has been sentenced to the maximum prison term, his outraged sad face appears. As he embraces the dejected drug dealer he whispers in his ear that an appeal is a piece of cake and that he will be free soon.

At every appeal I have had experience of, the defendant has been lucky not to have been sentenced to have his gonads cut off. Those appeal court judges are a conservative bunch. However, the shyster lawyer's bank account swells and he is one happy man, while his deceived client languishes in prison.

There was one particular lawyer who represented many of the dealers I arrested. He looked like an inflated, sweating, rapacious pig in a very expensive retrofitted Ralph Lauren suit. After each guilty verdict, when his client had been led away in chains, he would always glance at me in the courtroom and give me a sly smile and raise his eyebrows slightly. He knew I knew and, if he could, he would have performed unspeakable things on my body in the privacy of the courthouse men's room to show his gratitude. Drug dealers pay cash up front, and I had brought him manna from heaven, a lawyer's dream. Lawyers who specialise in defending drug dealers tend to be a scummy bunch of people who have always given me the creeps. I shook hands with this man once and it was like being clasped by a limp, oily, warm, sticky blob of flesh. I made it a habit to keep my hands in my pockets when I was around him after that revolting experience.

When you attend these long-term rock festivals, the key is to get in early and stake out a spot for your van. It is critical that you choose wisely because that is where your van is going to stay for almost a week. There is no way anything is going to be able to move in or out of that intertwined mass of humanity and their vehicles.

We arrived early and parked our van close to the stage and down by a small river that ran through the property, which was nothing more than a country auto-racing speedway. As a former Ranger-trained army sergeant, I figured that clear-running water might come in handy later on, and my instincts did not fail me.

Nobody paid any attention to our scruffy van or its occupants – an equally scruffy Irishman and two bearded Cubans. All around us were vans crammed in bumper to bumper. Prior to the festival nobody had any idea just how many people would attend. Even wild guesses were wrong. Some even said a few thousand, but everybody was wrong, very wrong.

There were no cell phones back then, no internet, and no prior television or radio coverage; it was all word of mouth. Yet people arrived at the festival from all over America and the world. They hitch-hiked from California and just about all of the American States, and found their way from Europe and many other countries. They came only because 'they had heard' that every major rock musician in the world was going to come together in a massive celebration of the glory of rock music. Even though it was only a rumour, that was enough, and their pilgrimages began.

This vast conglomeration of humanity – bedraggled hippies, young and not so young, bikers, students, boys and girls from next door who had run away from home, pseudo-hippies, lawyers, dentists and doctors – staked out their muddy little piece of earth around the elevated stage and prepared to pay homage to rock's best. At least that's how it appeared on the surface.

But there was something else at play here, something deeper than just the love of rock music: the promise of moral freedom. These people who trekked to that rainy mud-soaked rock festival were the children of a straight-laced generation. The festival promised freedom to do whatever they wanted, anything, or so they had heard.

This vast community, which was estimated to be close to 100,000, was ill-prepared for living in an almost communal style amidst rain, mud and lack of sanitary services. When they did finally settle in, the scene resembled a refugee camp from a third-world country in the midst of war. Yet everybody seemed happy. There was no parental supervision and no visible authority figures. Drugs were being openly sold and used, and there was nudity, sex and music, so everybody forgot their inhibitions and basically did what they had always wanted to do.

We were not there to enforce the law as it was normally enforced. We were there to protect the festival goers from the criminal predators that are attracted to mass gatherings of out-of-control naïve young people, who were easy pickings. We saw those predators almost as soon as we arrived. One thing any streetwise cop learns early on is to spot the craven, calculating eyes of criminal predators. Even when they wear sunglasses, their body language gives them away.

We were there not to arrest anybody for using drugs, being naked, fornicating in public or selling a little pot. We were there to arrest the heavy dealers of heroin, cocaine and opium. But our overriding concern was the safety of the blissful young concert-goers as they walked around stoned and naked, believing that all the world was filled with love, flowers, music and that everybody loved everybody. Meanwhile, the predators circulated in their midst like sharks on a crowded beach. We knew them for what they were, and we circulated just like they did, but with different intentions.

One source of concern was that there was so much cash around because credit cards would not work there. So many people had passed out from booze and drugs that the predators had a field day going through their pockets and stealing their purses, jewellery, drugs and wallets. They also took advantage of passed-out young girls. They ransacked hundreds of vans while their occupants were enjoying the music. In some instances I waited until the predators returned to their own vans and then radioed in their location and their descriptions. A grab team would swoop in and bundle them out of the festival along with a stack of stolen property, which was later reclaimed by very relieved, penniless festival-goers.

The rain continued to pour down and the festival-goers began to resemble zonked-out, mud-caked zombies, a very surreal sight. Not that we were doing any better, and our van looked like it was growing out of the mud; and it smelled to high heaven. We made buys from some heavy-hitting dealers, but no marijuana buys. If we had had every marijuana dealer arrested it would have taken an army of police officers to arrest and process them.

Now is a good time to tell you about our festival neighbours, who we nicknamed the 'van people'. After a few days they all began to exhibit signs that they were there to stay. One van's occupants strung up a clothes line, washed clothes in the river and then hoped for sun. Another van's occupants began a little garden beside their van and, when I asked one of them what he was so industriously planting, he groggily said it was marijuana.

Four young couples in another van exhibited the sexual traits of lusty rabbits as they kept their van bouncing up and down for a week, only occasionally coming up for air. Their van had a Utah state licence plate and I wondered if their parents knew where their children were, and what they were doing.

Another van was occupied by two industrious marijuana dealers who gave me a small bag of marijuana to guard their van and their 'stash' when they went up to the stage area to listen to the performers. After three days they passed out from smoking too much of their own merchandise.

Let me now share with you an experience where I wished I had had a video camera. On the second day I heard over the loudspeaker system that there were public bathrooms on the west side of the festival, but people were to bring their own toilet paper. This I did, and waded through the mud and rain towards the bathrooms. The promoters had driven a bulldozer out to an empty field and dug a ten-foot-deep trench twenty yards long for 100,000 zonked-out festival-goers. It would have taken fifty trenches just to keep the human waste situation under control, because diarrhoea had reached epidemic proportions.

The first clue I had as I approached the filthy, foul-smelling toilet that this was not a good idea was when I saw it was deserted. Bleary-eyed hippies were all over the field relieving themselves in the primitive squat position. Florida's famous and eager flies and mosquitoes braved the now-receding rain and turned out by the millions for the grand event. It was truly a sight to see: the food chain in its most revolting and primitive state.

I decided that if the toilets were empty I would go inside the makeshift hut-like fixture and see what was going on; surely it could not be that bad, I reasoned. There was a long row of holes cut into planks laid over the trench. I cleaned off around one of the holes and settled down for a blissful evacuation. I was halfway through reading a magazine on marijuana growing that my neighbours had loaned me, when I heard a plaintive male voice: 'Hey man, ease up.' Since I was alone I assumed that after two days living in this insane asylum, I was beginning to hear voices and continued what I was doing. Then I heard: 'Hey man,' and a voice began singing. This time I realised the voice was coming up from the trench, right under me and between my legs. I jumped up and looked down into the hole. A shit-covered man was sitting in about three foot of human waste trying to re-light his soggy marijuana joint, with no success. I yelled at him that I would pull him out, but he shook his head violently: 'No man, I live here.' Then he gave me an address in Alabama which he claimed was the toilet's address.

The sun came out on 30 November, a glorious day I will always remember because we were saturated in rain and mud and did not have the benefit of mind- and body-numbing drugs. I headed for the river with my towel and discovered naked America. Thousands of the great unwashed were cavorting and doing things that would be good for severe penance from any parish priest in Ireland, if not excommunication.

I did my best to curtail my frolicking, washed and returned to my two now-dour Cuban companions. They had decided to trek out of the grounds every night and go home. I had to stay there. I was the 'Narc'; they were the back-up team. All that changed when the open side-panel of our van was graced by Samantha 'the snake' Tutcheroni.

'Sam' was my room-mate and long-time friend from Coconut Grove in Miami. To put it mildly, God had his mind on his job when he created this most beautiful of women. She was a cross between Beyoncé, Halle Berry and every *Sports Illustrated* model ever photographed. I assure you that this is no exaggeration. Sam was in her early twenties and knew she was uniquely beautiful in a quiet, sultry, sensuous way, and that drove men crazy. She was tall and self-assured in a way that even put women at ease, and that is no easy feat for a beautiful woman. She had Italian and a little Indian blood in her and had no temper; she just got even.

I had met Sam years ago at a Coconut Grove poolside party on Tigertail Avenue, the place where, if you were married, you were hunted down and killed: this was singles country. Seriously, Tigertail Avenue was the hunting ground for both sexes who only had sexual gratification in mind. I was the guest of Jim Cooper, a long-time friend, who was the manager of the Playboy Club and hotel on Miami Beach, an exalted position, all things considered, at that time.

We were sitting poolside when I spotted Sam. She was the centre of attention for a rabid horde of muscular, tanned jocks who clustered around her pool recliner like dogs around a bitch in heat. Jim noticed my interest and said: 'Do you want to meet Sam?' I most certainly did, so he casually waved and she walked over to our cabana. That was some spectacular walk and she left behind many disgruntled hunks who gave us dirty looks. 'She is a family friend, but let me warn you that she just does not date. She is one picky woman, so good luck.'

That is where it all began and we agreed to see each other when I was in Miami. Jim just sat there with a bemused expression on his face and said, 'Well, I'll be damned; Sam likes Irishmen.' She wanted nothing from me; she was her own woman. She had two degrees and was interesting to talk to as long as you could keep your mind on what in the hell you were talking about. Her family operated a fleet of fishing boats in the lower Keys, and was solid as a rock. They also had a thriving lobster business and that is where the big money was. I love lobster, so this was a relationship made in heaven.

Sam lived in Coconut Grove with her grandmother, who was also an independent soul. She looked me over on my first visit and said, 'He's a keeper,' and that was nice. The only problem with dating Sam was that we had no privacy. We would go to a restaurant for a meal and everybody wanted to take a peek. That created a big problem for me as an undercover agent because my very life depended on anonymity.

The day after our meeting by the pool, Sam called me at Jim's suite at the Playboy Plaza. She wanted me to drive her down to the lower Keys to pick up some lobster from an uncle. She had many uncles, who had many lobsters, and I was one happy camper. We stayed overnight in a shack her uncle owned that was on stilts over water so clear you could see the fish swimming around the pilings, which contrasted with the white sand underneath.

We went to a small market nearby and bought the makings of a salad and some other stuff Sam industriously selected. I discovered Sam could cook and really enjoyed preparing the meal. She had chosen a nice, chilled white wine and we had a glass as she prepared the lobster. She cleaned each lobster and covered it in garlic butter then wrapped all four in tinfoil. In the meantime I had started the charcoal grill and, when the coals were glowing white, Sam placed the foil-wrapped lobsters on the grill and replaced the cover. I don't know about you but everybody has their price. This was mine.

We feasted out on the deck with a tropical island sunset soothing our souls and our bodies. The lobster was succulent and I have never eaten a more magnificent meal before or since. I do have a confession to make. I qualified for excommunication that long and sensuous night enjoying Sam's delights. Sam accepted that I was Jim's friend and that I was an artist. Jim knew what I did and called it 'insane'. She trusted Jim and that was that.

After our night in the Keys I began to suspect that perhaps Sam was in 'nesting' mode and was looking for a husband. I was very mistaken because Sam never at any time over the years indicated she was even remotely interested in marriage. I proposed to her and she kissed me and told me that she loved me and if she ever felt the desire to get married I would be the first man she would call. Sam never called.

We drifted into a relationship where Sam stayed close to me and those were magic times. She turned out to have her own money and when her grandmother died she inherited the family home and in excess of a million dollars in cash. Nobody could understand why she was involved with a scumbag like me. Sam never pried and I did not tell her what my true occupation was as there was just no pressure to do so. Even when I was gone for weeks on undercover assignments, she said nothing and never asked me personal questions.

It's not that I did not trust Sam; I trusted almost nobody. Jim had known me for many years even before I was involved in undercover investigations, and I trusted him. It's not easy to morph from being a laid-back writer to an undercover agent whose gonads are on the chopping block all the time. The company you keep has nothing to lose and everything to gain by killing you if they discover you are a police officer. An officer with no back-up and no witnesses is certain to be killed if discovered. There is a degree of paranoia that creeps in and that can't be avoided; it's just a matter of keeping it under control, and that's not easy. The problem is that there is so much money out there as well as crooked cops, that a little paranoia can save your life. I have always nurtured my paranoia and I am still here.

Sam and I cohabited, fished and basically just hung out and enjoyed ourselves – two young people making the most of life. Then there was that evening when we were watching the sunset in her uncle's shack down in the Keys. 'Jerry, you are not who you say you are; you are a very dangerous person. You are either a criminal or a cop. I sense you are a cop.' Sam knew, and I was glad.

As to my assignment at the rock festival, I would have paid my department to put me there because I love music, all music. Strauss' 'Nuns' Chorus' swells my heart as I listen to the soaring, rich tones of the chorus, and I can experience the same emotions listening to a recording of the late Pavarotti or the

Three Irish Tenors. A sip of Jack Daniels, an open road and Willie Nelson singing 'Georgia on My Mind' will fulfil my country soul's desires. That said, a riff by Jimmy Hendricks or full bore with the Stones will do it for me too. That rock festival brought the best rock musicians on earth to that stage. The Rolling Stones, the Chambers Brothers, Ike and Tina Turner, Iron Butterfly, Rotary Connection, Janis Joplin, Jefferson Airplane, Sweetwater, Johnny Winters, Pacific Gas and Electric, Grand Funk Railroad, King Crimson, Country Joe and the Fish, and Covington Tower, who brought the house down with songs like 'California Dreaming' and 'Brown Eyed Girl'. The very earth reverberated with rock music and strobe lights were everywhere, illuminating the helicopters which were delivering and plucking the performers to and from the elevated stage.

Sam came back to the van and told me to come with her to the back of the stage. She was wearing a stage pass and handed me one. Sam had a habit of being able to go anywhere, be it an up-market social affair or a rock festival. Janice Joplin was guzzling a bottle of Jim Beam before she went on stage to belt out 'Ball and Chain', 'Foolish Woman Blues', 'Lewd Conduct' and, my favourite, 'Southern Comfort'.

Johnny Winters, the southern guitar-playing master, freaked out a lot of already freaked-out people when he came on stage for his night show wearing a long black coat. What with his pale white skin, long white hair and psychedelic lighting, he looked like an albino undertaker. He brought his brother Edgar on stage and they burned the house down.

Then Uncle John and Jimmy Shannon jumped on stage and the audience went crazy. Tina Turner and her husband Ike rocked the festival too. I am convinced that no other singer in the world gives their audiences 'bang for their bucks' like Tina Turner. She literally had steam rising off her sensual body at the end of her performance – I was that close. For a change of pace, Janice Joplin and Johnny Winters stood alone and blasted out the purest Texas Blues I have ever heard sung. They dug down deep into their guts and I can hear the echoes of that music today.

Then we heard that the helicopter service had not been paid and the Stones still had not performed. We got the word over the police radio, but the crowd was not aware there was a problem. We knew that if the Rolling Stones did not perform as promised, things would turn ugly, very ugly, and very fast. We did not have anywhere near enough police officers in the county to control a crowd of that size. We had a choice: stay or get out. The Stones had this bad habit of hiring Hells Angel head bangers as security guards. The bikers had this bad habit of meting out brutal beatings to anybody they thought was posing a threat to the band.

Then, at the last minute, the helicopter service was paid, and we all gave a deep sigh of relief. The Stones ripped the concert apart as no other rock group can do, even today. 'Satisfaction' and 'Jumping Jack Flash' swept through the massive crowd like a wave of hysteria. They, too, were steaming hot by the time the helicopter landed on the stage. Sam and I went back to our van and she said she'd heard that a Miami dealer was selling high-grade opium. I was surprised that she would tell me this as she tended to mind her own business. She told me darkly that a cousin had become addicted to opium and had died on the streets.

Opium was not commonly found for sale on the streets, but it was beginning to surface in certain cities. Opium was the sticky fluid that farmers scraped off the opium poppy and was the initial ingredient in the production of heroin. The reason that it was beginning to appear as a street drug was that American soldiers were either shipping it home from Vietnam or bringing it home themselves. One of the most gruesome means of smuggling was discovered when it was found that army morgue workers in Saigon were stuffing the bodies of dead soldiers with narcotics. Upon arrival in America, confederates would retrieve the plastic bags filled with drugs and sell them to major drug dealers.

Sam said that the dealer at the festival was the same one who had got her cousin addicted. She told me to wait a few minutes and she would bring him to our van. She said to get a lot of money because she wanted him arrested selling a large amount of opium; she wanted him in jail for a long time. She was visibly angry and I hoped that was all she was going to do to the dealer, but, true to her word, she was back in a few minutes with the man.

After the dealer got inside the van he opened his army parka and displayed a stash of illegal drugs, including hashish. He said his brother was in the army and he was lining things up to establish a major drug ring in south Florida. I had already alerted the grab team and an undercover photographer. I made the buys and within minutes the grab team had him bundled out of the festival being photographed all the way. Sam told me she followed the grab team and the protesting drug dealer all the way to the prison van. She then went back to my home and called her mother with the news of the dealer's arrest.

The drug dealer did not know it but his life was going to get even more complicated, very dangerously complicated. Do you remember Sam's uncles in the lower Keys? Well, they were all first-generation Sicilian-Americans, and the dealer had murdered their niece. One of the things Sicilians have in common is their family blood vendettas. It does not matter how long it takes to avenge an injury to one's own family. The vendetta is passed from generation to generation, and one thing is for certain: the offender will die. The dealer was now identified and his address, mug shot, and just about everything else about him was a matter of public record. He was doomed.

Four of Sam's uncles showed up for the dealer's short trial and guilty verdict, their eyes burning with the desire to rip him asunder. As the dealer was led away to begin his sentence, one of the uncles said, just loud enough for him to hear: 'We will get you inside.'

Later on that day at the festival, after the dealer had been arrested, Sam and I took a shower that lasted about an hour until we had scrubbed the grime of the festival off my body. She had bought a bottle of chilled Asti Spumante and we were looking forward to relaxing on the beach at sunset. My mind and body were aching with fatigue, but then the phone rang. Sam told me not to answer it but I did; a mistake. It was the director of law enforcement, Bill Bennet, who said: 'There are some problems at the Colonnades on Singer Island.' I knew this is where the festival bands were staying. I protested to no avail because he wanted the situation handled with kid gloves.

The hotel was owned by John D. MacArthur, one of the richest men in America at that time. My mood turned dark as I bade goodbye to Sam. She told me to hurry up and said she would prepare dinner and keep the Asti Spumanti chilled, but her body hot. That was Sam; she could put a positive spin on a mass suicide.

Singer Island then was a sliver of beach whose only claim to fame was the Colonnades and the TV show *Treasure Island*, which was filmed there. The hotel was a fading beauty, sadly neglected by MacArthur. This man was born in poverty, the son of an itinerant preacher, yet went on to become a self-made millionaire. He managed to buy Banker's Life and Trust in 1935 for a paltry $2,500. Today it's worth six billion dollars. This enterprise yielded big cash dividends for him, and he promptly invested every penny in Florida real estate. He purchased vast tracts of dirt cheap waterfront property. Today, that same property sells for millions per square foot.

Incredibly far sighted, MacArthur amassed 100,000 acres of prime property in the Palm Beaches alone. To place a value on that property today is beyond my financial capabilities; it certainly has to be in the trillion dollar range. I have often thought that perhaps his name should have been changed to Midas.

From the outside, the hotel appeared calm as I drove up and parked. Inside was a different story. Rockers never rest, they just keep on rocking one way or the other. A thin, nervous-looking man in a suit said he was the manager. I asked him what his name was and he mumbled something. I asked him for a business card, but he had none. He acted like a man who was about to have a nervous breakdown – jitters everywhere, and nervous tics and frantic head turning. I decided to try the front desk and that was worse: there were at least ten paparazzi demanding to know what floor the Stones were on.

The clerks all looked like they were close relatives of the manager, so I decided to see what all the excitement was about. I soon found out. Old people were yelling and pointing all over the place, and I wondered where they were all coming from. The Chamber's Brothers, highly aggravated at the grossly inflated price of everything, had apparently done something awful to the fruit salad buffet, so I left that situation in a hurry.

There was a lot of finger-pointing towards the sauna area, so I investigated. I was passed on the way by very elderly white-faced men wrapped in towels, being dragged by angry old women. The men all had their mouths open, drooling. I stuck my head into the still-jammed sauna and got a full nude frontal of Janice Joplin slugging away on a bottle of Jim Beam. Her elderly male companions were just sitting naked in the extreme heat with their mouths open. Some of them looked dead. Outside, a throng of equally old ladies were yelling over my shoulder demanding that their husbands get out of there immediately. But nobody moved; maybe they were actually dead. I left and vowed I would never end up that way, or at least I hoped I wouldn't. I decided I would walk up the stairs and take a look at what was happening on each floor; the elevator's interiors looked like something Dante would appreciate.

There were parties going on everywhere and the rooms in which they were happening had their doors open. I looked in on a few and decided civilisation as I knew it was breaking down. There were many old people out in the hallway yelling at 'you hippies' to keep the noise down, without any success. All the rooms had old men sitting on the floor with stoned hippy girls, talking away, and I wondered just what strange language they must be using as all were smoking joints. One young top-less girl was braiding an old geezer's chest hair. I figured that I had better get out of there before the wives arrived. That floor had the potential for a blood bath.

I was looking for the Stones' room because Bennet had said the manager had mentioned them specifically. So far I had seen nothing I could do anything about. It would take the second coming of Christ to restore order in that hotel. Even he would have been hard pressed with that bunch of heathens. Singer Island had little or no police protection and an almost non-existent police department. Nothing much ever happened there, until now. My department was worn out from the festival and I would need at least ten deputies to carry out any arrests safely. I still looked like a degenerate drug dealer, except I was clean and dressed in clean clothes.

It seemed the festival-goers were determined to wear their dirt and filth all the way home to wherever they came from. Every floor was a mirror image of the first, and it never got better – old people, stoned rockers and hippies. The nervous manager caught up with me on a higher floor and dramatically pointed at the open door of a very large suite. 'There,' he said, as if he was about to show me the Holy Grail, 'do something.'

I hustled him to the stairs and told him to go down and stay in his office until I called him with further instructions. He hurried off like a man with a mission and I was glad. I had a big decision to make and he was not making it any easier. What I had on my hands was a tangled, intertwined mass of bodies who had drunk too much, smoked too much marijuana and then fornicated themselves to sleep.

I stood in the room for a long time considering my options, none of which were good. I could attempt to get juvenile officers out to help me, but I knew that would be futile. The chances of getting ten deputies to respond to the hotel were slim to none. So what the hell was I supposed to do? Everybody was passed out. The only possibility was to hike down the stairwell with a rocker over my shoulder and thereby place all of them in my undercover car, one at a time. I could imagine the commotion when the hippies and the paparazzi discovered some bearded guy lugging the icons of rock and roll down a hotel stairway. They probably would have killed me. I checked to ensure that all of them were breathing regularly and not experiencing a drug overdose. Then I decided to just walk away and go home, better that way for everybody.

# 12

# THE FUTILITY OF WAR

The force of the explosion blew the door of my car back, throwing me to the ground. I knew it was a powerful bomb. A cloud of smoke and fire rushed skyward. People were screaming and rushing everywhere. Madness had come to Dundalk, a town long accused of causing it elsewhere. Now it was here, in my home town.

I was home for a month-long vacation and was working in our bar from time to time, which I enjoyed. It was 5.30 p.m. on Friday, 19 December 1975 and I had decided to go to Kay's Tavern on Crowe Street for a pint of Harp before going to work. My father always told me that it was not a good idea to drink in your own pub and he was probably right. I dressed upstairs and heard my aunt Ina arrive to visit my mother.

When I got downstairs my mother and my aunt asked me a few questions about my life in America. It was after six when I finally broke away and drove my Volkswagen to town. Those few minutes I was delayed probably saved my life. I parked next to the Kelly Monument across from St Patrick's church. I opened my car door and it was then that it happened. The explosion from the car bomb was deafening, but I was completely unscathed.

Rescue services arrived on the scene and the injured were rushed to Louth Hospital. I did not know then that my sister Marna, a highly experienced Registered Nurse, had gone to the hospital to render assistance to the twenty-one badly wounded and maimed victims of the bombing; two died at the scene. I stood amidst the mayhem as people moved around, stunned – as they do after a horrific bomb explosion. Later, forensic experts estimated that the car bomb had contained a hundred and fifty pounds of sophisticated explosives. It was so powerful and expertly placed that it gutted Kay's Tavern and sent shrapnel into buildings hundred of yards away. My first reaction was that it must have been a military operation because no local group would have had access to such techniques or military-style explosives.

My instinct was to rush forward and assist the wounded, but almost immediately the police were on the scene and prevented anybody from approaching the bomb site. As I stood there watching the carnage, I suddenly had a chilling thought: our pub! If Kay's Tavern was a target, so was ours! If there were more bombs on the way, they were intended either for Mark's Bar, another republican pub, or ours. I drove there and found it dark and deserted, and there were no cars on the streets: Peter Mac Manus' pub was a target and everybody had fled when the bomb exploded at Kay's Tavern. Even the nearby houses were dark and deserted.

The barman stood in the back of the dark pub. His eyes were wide with tension, but not fear. 'They sent two bombs down to Dundalk, one was for Kay's and the other is either for Mark's or here. I'm thinking it's here. You get out of here – I'm going home.'

I had been around bombs before and had made bombs; I knew how they worked. I opened all the doors and windows so that the bomb's impact would not find a sealed target. I noticed that two cars had arrived and parked just down the street. I went outside and checked them and their trunks for C-4 or the tell-tale smell of marzipan, which has the same smell as C-4 in explosives; there was none.

I went back inside and waited in the small room in the back of the pub. It was Christmas week and bitterly cold. I had only dressed to work in the pub and normally it was very warm. It was eerie standing in the semi-darkness of the pub, the only light coming in the front door from a light across the street. I went under the counter where I had stored a bottle of Jack Daniels I had brought with me from America. I stood there sipping the whiskey and thinking about the insanity of it all. The barman, who had been imprisoned by the British for IRA activities, was right: our pub was a target.

I felt like I was on a dangerous military patrol or a police stake-out, but I felt no fear; experience will do that to you. After a while you begin to develop a fatalistic attitude about it all. If it's going to happen, it's going to happen and you can't do anything about it. There were no sounds out on the usually busy street and it was Friday evening, payday, and just five days to Christmas. No cars driving by, no children playing or on their way to buy sweets with their pocket money. It was deathly quiet as everybody waited in their darkened homes, listening, but not knowing for what.

One hour passed, then two. Then I heard a noise outside our darkened front door. It was the barman. 'Gerard, are you still in there.' I came around the corner and he shook his head. 'I thought you went home, your car is not outside.' I had parked my car down the street. He brought his bicycle inside and locked the door and began securing all the doors and windows. Then he said: 'There is nothing to worry about now; they lost their nerve at the border and exploded the other car bomb in Silverbridge at Donnelly's Pub. There are at least three dead and nobody knows how many injured.' We just turned on the small light in the back room and began to get the place heated up again. We left the pub locked. Nobody would be coming out again because they would not know that the danger had passed, but our barman knew.

There is no sense in my naming the barman because he has paid the price for what he did. Now all he wanted to do was to be with his family. For somebody with such a violent background, he could be a humorous man. The funniest episode involved his little front garden. He, his wife and their young children lived in a council house. It was a relatively new, two-storey home in a nice housing estate. The front garden was about ten feet wide by six feet deep, with no wall, and his neighbours had planted flowers in their small, well-tended gardens. Our barman, however, decided to plant some potatoes and cabbage to help with the food bill. The rich, black soil soon produced many potatoes and prodigiously sized cabbage plants.

The neighbours complained to the county council about his mini farm clashing with their rose bushes. He ignored their demands to conform, and then something happened during the night: his potatoes and cabbages began to disappear. The next time I visited him I nearly fell over laughing. He had constructed a three-foot-high military concertina barbed wire fence around his precious potatoes and cabbages.

I knew from experience that it was standard-issue, British army concertina wire. I have this mental picture of him pedalling his bicycle across the heavily guarded border and stealing the wire from some British army base, and hauling it back to his home, undetected. The uproar over this miniature copy of the British internment camp where he had been imprisoned was immediate. The council was petitioned that he be evicted. There was only one problem: nobody wanted to knock on his front door and serve the eviction papers; everybody knew what he had done to be imprisoned in the first place, and nobody wanted that done to them. His cabbages and potatoes remained and flourished. Eventually things settled down and people began waving at each other again.

Two nights after the explosion, he asked me to stay behind after closing the pub because he had information on the bombings. After cleaning up and locking the pub, we settled into the back room with the bottle of Jack Daniels. I was hoarding the contents as I still had a few weeks to go before I returned to America. When he said he had information, what he should have said was that he had the facts, because he was not into hearsay. He said that the Red Hand Commando group was responsible. This ultra-violent group is closely linked to the Ulster Volunteer Force. This explained where the explosives had come from and the precision of both bombings. They were British army operations. While the British have always vehemently denied these violent illegal activities, they have a long history of bombings, spying and sabotage in the Republic of Ireland. The mid Ulster group of the Red Hand Commandos, led by Robin 'The Jackal' Jackson, was the actual bomb crew. They were based in Portadown, County Armagh, and operated out of a farmhouse and large barn in Glenane. This is where the two car bombs were assembled. This location was well known to the British army. It was an established training base and bomb-making factory for the Red Hand Commando terrorist group. The British intelligence services and their army knew full well what was going on in that barn for years. That same bomb factory and the terrorists that operated there are also the only logical suspects in the massive earlier Dublin bombings.

# 13

# SOMEBODY IS MURDERING OUR CHILDREN

For those readers who doubt that dark angels exist, find a quiet moment and think about your own life, past and present. I guarantee that you have had them or they are in your life now. They come in all sorts of guises: relatives, friends, lovers, wearers of the holy cloth, and business associates. This chapter is about one such dark angel. One who became the worst mass murderer of children in the history of the world, and I breathed his air: I was that close to him. I know what a dark angel is, I truly and sadly do, and so should you.

The dark purple detective car was tucked in under the hanging limbs of an elm tree, in the dark, and I wondered about that. I was back in Atlanta patrolling my beat on the midnight shift on Atlanta's south side, a far cry from the Palm Beaches. My beat was about the same size as the city of Dublin, and I was alone, the result of the never ending racial law suits that have crippled the Atlanta police department for decades. I was driving with my lights out as this area was a free-fire drug zone. I slowed and watched the car. I wondered why the detectives had not coordinated with me prior to whatever they were investigating. It was a dangerous area: bandit country.

The darkened car was hard to see on the dirt road under

the tree, but I knew it was a detective car. The only light was from the moon, but it was enough. Parking on small dirt roads in this drug-infested neighbourhood was a risky business. I was on the road checking for street drug deals. While I was normally too busy on crime calls to do this, when things quietened down I always liked to drive down those dirt roads and see the customers and dealers scurry away, like cockroaches when a light is turned on. When my marked patrol car passed, they would come back out on the roads and continue what they were doing. We did that because we knew that if we did not at least show them that the law was there in their neighbourhood, they would be shoulder to shoulder up on the main streets flagging customers down. Then everybody would know we had lost the battle, which we had anyway, but they did not know that we knew that; it was all a game, except that people got killed. Life on these streets was like Kleenex: disposable.

While we were in sight of Atlanta's skyscrapers, we might as well have been on Mars. The adjacent road, Lee Street, was a major north–south thoroughfare. A small dirt road ran off Lee into the dirt road without a name, where I was with the detective car. There were no street lights, but plenty of ordinary black people lived there in small, shotgun shacks, held hostage in their bolted homes by the drug dealers. Poverty kept them there also, and anyway there was nowhere to go.

The narcotics squad would set up a dragnet operation there sometimes and arrest dozens of dealers. As soon as the last paddy wagon left, more dealers would emerge from the shadows and it was as if nothing had happened. And when the jailed dealers got out of jail they would go back to reclaim their 'selling' location, and somebody would get killed, so the homicide squad would be called. It was a never-ending cycle of drugs, violence and death.

Those small dark dirt roads would see more public service

vehicles in a week than any other street in Atlanta would in a year: police cars, including detective cars of all varieties; ambulances; fire trucks; the vehicles of animal control people and nervous government inspectors; and those of even more nervous meter readers. Those roads ran all through Atlanta and were a virtual no-man's land. They were like a secret network that allowed people who did not want to be seen to circulate freely, as long as they belonged there. And that is the key: belonging there. As violent and dark as those streets were, everybody knew everybody and anything strange, like a new face or a car, and the word went out in this claustrophobic world.

What was this detective car doing hiding in the darkness on this dangerous street? I was parked behind the car and I gently touched my brake pedal which momentarily turned on my brake lights; but there was no response from the dark car, which was unusual. Why had he not responded with a similar signal? He could clearly see my marked police car in his rearview mirror.

It was then I became cautious; was the detective asleep or injured, or worse? I could see the outline of a man's head, and it was not moving. I eased out of my patrol car, drew my weapon, and walked up to the driver's side door, and shined my strong beam flashlight into the car. It was occupied by a young black man wearing a suit. But he did not move and gave no sign of recognition. I knocked on the car's window and he turned his face in my direction, and gently smiled.

I was about to knock when he rolled the window down. There was a mobile radio in the car like mine and a clipboard lay on the seat beside him. He raised an identification folder, and it contained an Atlanta Public Safety identification card, also like mine, yet he said nothing. I took the card from him and examined it. The card had been signed by public safety commissioner Reginald Eaves. The man in the car was named Wayne Williams.

I was growing concerned by his odd behaviour and asked: 'What are you doing here?' He gave me that relaxed smile again and said: 'I am a fire department photographer and I am waiting for a call.' Normally that would have set off alarm bells, but a drug dealer's car had been torched earlier that night by a competitor just around the corner, and we were expecting a reprisal torching. Still, we were only about a quarter mile from a fire station on Lee Street – why had he not parked there? So I asked him. Again that easy smile as he said: 'I like the privacy.' That made sense too because fire stations were crowded and claustrophobic. Relaxed now, I leaned closer to him and told him I did not want him parking there because I did not want to have a murder case on my hands on this busy night. He nodded and that was that.

I was close enough to him to notice his breath, and it smelled like boiled vegetables. He wore glasses and had an old style afro haircut and a round soft face, and I smelled just a slight touch of cologne. His physique was soft and feminine and he had small blemishes on his face. I wanted to get a good look at him because, in spite of his credentials, I felt uneasy about him and I trusted my gut instincts. I had been on the streets a long time, and there was something about him that was just not right. This was weeks before the child murders began: he was rehearsing!

I was dispatched on a call, and when I returned he was gone. I checked the fire station parking lot and his car was not parked there. Then it got busy again. That young man with the easy smile turned out to be Wayne Williams, the Atlanta child killer, now convicted and in prison. I can see his soft face and smile even now, and I can smell him, and the evil in him. Some things just never go away, no matter how hard you try. Dark angels are like that; they become part of you. And ordinary people never understand that.

When I reported for duty the following night, I asked around the midnight shift if anybody knew anything about this fire department photographer. All I got was shrugs, though I noticed a flicker of recognition in one officer's blue eyes, but he said nothing. After our routine briefing on the current situation on the streets, we went outside to switch with the evening shift. As I stood there waiting for my patrol car to drive in with the evening watch officer behind the wheel, I sensed somebody standing close behind me: it was the young officer who I suspected knew who the fire department photographer was. He stood directly behind me and said: 'Wayne is alright.' I turned and only then did I notice the deep scratch marks on his neck, very visible under the harsh outdoor lighting. I looked directly into his eyes and asked him what had happened to his neck, and he said, 'My wife,' and then walked away. I caught up with him and asked him what he knew about Wayne Williams and he just repeated the same thing: 'Wayne is alright.'

The big problem I was having was that the car the officer was driving was identical to the car I drove when I was a detective; it just made no sense. I knew the city sold the detective cars when they reached a certain age as surplus vehicles, and that car looked and 'felt' like my old detective car. If that was the case, why was he driving a surplus city car if he worked for the fire department? He was a quiet, intense and somewhat remote officer who kept to himself, and did his job as far as anybody could tell. I would hear him acknowledge the radio dispatcher and answer his calls. Then after a while he would check back in and that was that. That young officer was later to commit suicide.

Between 1979 and 1981 thirty-one black children and young adults were murdered in the Atlanta metropolitan area over a period of twenty-two agonising months. These slayings were to become known as the Atlanta Child Murders.

This was the same period the Atlanta Organised Crime Squad was feverishly working to jail me for the attempted murder by bombing of a police detective sergeant, a member of the same squad. Since I was intimately involved with both situations, I will provide deep insights to both nightmares which to this day have not been revealed.

Never has a series of murders produced such a volume of news stories, books, television series, shows and films. The investigation was to become the largest and most intense in the annals of the American law enforcement community. Wayne Williams was found guilty of two of the murders, yet was blamed for all thirty-one.

If there is one thing that I am sure of in my heart of hearts, it is that Wayne Bertram Williams was not responsible for all of those murders. While I am convinced of his involvement, the real mass murderers walk the streets of Atlanta today, as free men. Wayne Williams was, and is, a spoiled man-child with the softness in his body of a young girl. He just does not have the mental and physical toughness to overpower, strangle, and shoot thirty-one young men and girls. Williams must have had help, because many of his victims were stronger than he was.

Never has a major American city been so ill prepared to manage a police investigation of such enormous proportions. Let me start from the beginning. On 20 July 1979, Edward Hope Smith, a fourteen-year-old boy, left his home; five days later his friend, thirteen-year-old Alfred Evans, also left his home. These children were the end product of a poor community, where children come and go; nobody paid any attention to them because they always came home, some time. But they didn't this time.

On 28 July, a woman scavenging for aluminium cans on rural Niskey Lake Road in southwest Atlanta found both boys dead in the shrub grass and weeds, together in death, as in life. Their bodies had been thrown out in the open with no attempt at concealment. Smith had been shot with a .22 calibre pistol and Evans had been strangled. Atlanta and the nation's nightmare had begun.

I knew Niskey Lake Road well as I had patrolled Zone Four, where it is located. Within a mile or so are the large Kimberley Court projects, a government-subsidised housing development. This was Atlanta's solution to cleaning out the downtown so-called 'ghetto' neighbourhoods and moving the residents as far away from the public eye as possible. What they created was a concentration of poor blacks out in the woods, where there is zero employment and substandard transportation. They swapped urban ghettos for suburban ghettos and everybody still stayed poor and desperate. But at least they were hidden, and that made Atlanta's developers very happy.

Somebody had to know the city well to have known where Niskey Lake Road was. When blacks began to migrate from the city to the undeveloped suburbs, the whites fled farther north, south, east, and west and that stopped the developers dead in their tracks; they followed the white migration out of the city limits. There are obvious signs that developers had plans to build a subdivision in that area. Roads had been plotted out, and a big attraction would have been Niskey Lake itself.

At the time of the Smith and Evans murders, the developers had cut their losses and the area had become an eerie, overgrown wasteland. Once in a while when I patrolled the zone I would check those roads for stolen cars. And sometimes I would drive out by the lake and sit for a moment. I would take off my sweat-soaked, bullet-resistant vest and tee shirt and try to dry out my body in the slight breeze that always seemed to be there. I carried extra underwear in my equipment bag and it felt good to get the heavy vest off and stretch. I would do this standing beside the lake, leaving my patrol car's engine and air conditioner running at full blast, and the doors open. This way, when I got back into the car, the stink of what had been in the back seat on and off all night would be gone.

No, somebody had to know just where Niskey Lake Road was because it was so well concealed by trees and undergrowth, somebody like me, who worked in the area. I am not going to detail the rest of the killings because the Smith and Evans murders set the stage and the modus operandi. The victims were universally poor, young, black, strong street children. Wayne Williams could not have done it alone. He had help.

I know how much strength and determination it requires to subdue these young black males because I have had to do that hundreds of times as a patrol officer. There is nothing worse on a boiling-hot southern day than to chase down a teenager in the alleyways of Atlanta. We would be chasing them for auto theft, burglary, larceny and shoplifting. To me it was important to take down and arrest the suspect in a manner where the boy was not injured. It was hard enough to catch these budding criminals, but when you did, they would squirm, struggle and fight you all the way to the custody of the patrol car's back seat. It took a well-trained person in excellent condition to get them into the patrol car, and Wayne Williams was not that kind of person.

Many of those boys ended up dead later on, but not all. When I was in Zone Four I was also a field training officer. Our job was to observe police academy recruits at the end of their training to ensure they were ready to strap on a gun and go out on the mean streets of Atlanta. I didn't like this assignment because I had got used to being alone in a patrol car, and there was nothing worse than having some wide-eyed rookie trailing behind me as I went into crisis situations. But it all worked out one way or the other. The recruits either stayed or left the department.

One recruit I remember in particular was a young black trainee who displayed remarkable abilities at running down suspects and subduing them without injury. On about our third night as we sat in a deserted supermarket parking lot cooling off, he said: 'You don't remember me do you, Mr Mac Manus? I'm Pewee.' I had chased him down as a teenager many times. 'You never hurt me and I remember that, thank you.'

To comprehend why these murders were allowed to occur in the first place, it is necessary to understand the complex social and political situation at the time. The atmosphere of racial tension within the Atlanta police department and the city itself had paralysed the police force; it was dysfunctional. Controversial black public safety commissioner Reginald Eaves had to be eased out by the black administration. They then went in search of a new commissioner and police chief. Lee Brown, a highly educated black, was hired as commissioner and almost immediately began to polarise the department. Then they hired George Napper, another highly educated black, as the new chief, and things grew worse. Brown and Napper were at loggerheads almost immediately.

The theory had been that if you hired black police administrators for a majority black city, everything would be all right. The only problem with that was that the black population itself was sick and tired of the incompetence of the senior levels of city government. They wanted effective leadership, no matter what colour they were. Brown and Napper were not even close to being effective. They squabbled like adolescents and left the Atlanta police department leaderless.

Just prior to this, major law suits were filed by black police officers who claimed racial discrimination was practised in the promotion process. New promotional tests were administered by the then commissioner, Reginald Eaves, but answers to the tests were provided to the black candidates. With Eaves out, Brown and Napper administered a new battery of tests and the end result was an unmitigated disaster. The two academics promoted inexperienced patrolmen to captain and departmental morale hit the bottom. Overnight the Atlanta police department went from being a demoralised organisation to one fraught with racial tension and disgust in general. Nobody seemed to care any more and there was distrust everywhere.

All of this was going on when Atlanta's children began to be slaughtered. The killers could not have chosen a more opportune time, for there was nobody to stop them. And within the department itself, corrupt officers saw their chance and chaos reigned. All of those senior police administrators and politicians who allowed this to happen must share the responsibility for those children's deaths. They are as guilty as the child killers, and the children's blood is on their hands.

In the beginning it was not apparent that child killers were on the loose. Then girls began to be murdered. As the number of murders increased it was obvious something had to be done. Murder cases are normally assigned to the homicide squad. But either Napper or Brown or both decided that what was needed was a task force dedicated to the investigation of the children's murders. This would have been a good idea if the task force had been effectively staffed. But it wasn't.

Chosen to lead this force was Captain Johnny Sparks, a young ex-Marine Corps officer like Chief Napper. I personally never had any contact with Captain Sparks other than seeing him around. I once received some raw intelligence on a possible suspect and drove over to police headquarters to give him the information. He had a reputation for being arrogant and brittle. I sat in his office and never in my life had I encountered such hostility from a man whom I have never even spoken to before. I can only assume that he wanted only his task force to handle any incoming information. I was heading the Crime Network and had contacts throughout the country. After that meeting I stepped across the hall into the office where the investigators were sitting. All shook their heads and told me not to worry about Sparks. They also said I had no idea how bad it was working there.

Of all the commanders to place in this critical position, Johnny Sparks was the worst possible choice. Apart from having absolutely no experience of working in homicide, his antagonistic, confrontational style of leadership was the opposite of what the task force needed: a team player who could draw the many squads together and get everybody motivated. So in the first critical months the task force was dead in the water, and children were being murdered.

An even graver error was that the initial task force was not even staffed by homicide detectives, who were excluded by Sparks. While Sparks' leadership might have, and I stress *might* have, inspired a Marine to give his life for his country, it gutted the task force. It destroyed any possibility of the detectives digging in and getting a grip on the basic facts and solving the first child murders.

All veteran homicide detectives will tell you that if a murder is not solved within the first twenty-four hours, the investigation will bog down and probably end up in the backlog file. In other words, time is on the killer's side. The more time passes, the better chance the killer has of not being detected. This aspect of the investigation has never been discussed. Captain Ken Green, the chief's administrative assistant, told me one day that he was sick of the bickering between the chief and the commissioner, and said that the commissioner had even sent a memo saying that Chief Napper 'had fools working for him'.

As the frequency of the child murders increased, so did the

confusion and conflict within the police department. Then, in a move that was ill-conceived, the commissioner removed the task force from the police department and relocated it to a long-abandoned, run-down, used-car building on Spring Street. It was obvious that the commissioner did not trust his own police chief to manage the child murders investigation, and had had the task force moved out under his supervision.

There was a secret parallel investigation into the murders being conducted by the state Georgia Bureau of Investigation. They were convinced that the Ku Klux Klan, or KKK, was involved. This investigation never saw the light of day. The KKK's motive was supposed to be that the black child murders would incite a race war.

The GBI had received information that black groups were actively raising funds to have guns shipped into Atlanta to arm a black militia. Since some of the murder victims had been thrown over bridges spanning the Chattahoochee River, surveillance teams were set up under and around many of the bridges. One night a splash was heard under a bridge spanning the river in north Atlanta. The officer under the bridge radioed to the team up on the road and a car was stopped. The driver was Wayne Williams. After being interrogated, he was released. During a period of time when Williams was being openly followed around Atlanta, the body of Nathaniel Cater floated to the surface under the bridge where Williams had been stopped. Williams was eventually arrested and, on 27 February 1982, he was convicted of two counts of murder and sentenced to two terms of life imprisonment. The prosecution presented a vast array of circumstantial evidence, including fibre evidence and witnesses who had seen him with scratches on his neck.

There is no way that soft person could have murdered those children unaided. I looked into his eyes at a distance of inches and smelled his breath. He was a weak man-child and I sensed no physical threat. When you work the streets you become attuned to the people who get into your comfort zone. If you don't, you get hurt or killed. It's as simple as that. Animals in the jungle do that instinctively, just like street cops.

# 14

# THE NUNS' CHORUS

The small room began to feel like it was closing in on me and my chest constricted so that it was hard for me to breathe. 'You are the suspect in the bombing and attempted murder of Detective Sergeant Wesley Derrick. I will read you your rights. You have the right to an attorney' – now the room was spinning – 'you have the right to…' After the officer had finished reading me my rights, he stood up: 'Give me your gun and badge.' His words seemed to echo all over the room, and inside my head. I tried to stand up, but my legs failed me.

I knew then that organised elements within the Atlanta police department were controlling an attempted murder investigation against me. A great rage began to build up in me and I wanted to strike out at these people. These were corrupt police officials who were charged with the protection of the citizens of Atlanta from organised crime. Yet they were worse than anything organised crime ever produced, and the police department's administration knew that, but did nothing.

I took the polygraph test and got a hundred per cent pass. I still have the original paperwork from that test confirming this. Yet I had been painted with a broad brush of the worst hue. I was a potential cop killer. Once it sticks to you, the stink never goes away, no matter how hard you try to prove your innocence, or even if a polygraph test conclusively proves your innocence, as mine did. When your accusers are veteran officers and wear the gold braid of ranking officers, the accused is doomed, and with no way open for vindication.

I had worked hard to come to America, and worked doubly hard when I got there. I believed in America and all it stood for, I truly did. All things in America were on the up and up and right would always prevail. That's what I used to believe; not now, not ever again. Anger and despair welled up in me; where could I go for help? I was on Chief George Napper's staff and was head of the Atlanta Criminal Information Network, both trusted positions.

Now I was steps away from being indicted for the attempted murder of a fellow police officer, the most heinous crime any cop can be charged with. I would be ostracised within my own department and police departments all over America. And that is exactly what the organised crime elements within the Atlanta police department wanted. They desperately wanted to either control or destroy the Atlanta Criminal Information Network, and to do so they had to destroy me. The why of it all is simple: the network gave me access to law enforcement agencies all over America and the world, and information flowed freely, because I was trusted.

When I flew around the US to various intelligence meetings, I would hear things, bad things, about my own department. And after the official meetings, I would go out to eat or have a beer with colleagues, and I would hear worse things about 'dirty cops' in our Special Investigations Section, or SIS. This section was located in a discreet office far away from any police buildings. While many detectives worked there, they were in plain clothes in an ordinary office complex and did not look out of place. This was the elite unit within the Atlanta police department and only veteran detectives were assigned there. The unit investigated white-collar crime, narcotics, gambling and organised crime.

The Atlanta Criminal Information Network was also part of that unit. Apart from being the coordinator of the network I was the administrative assistant to the unit's commander. In essence, I created the frequent progress reports of all of the units on major investigations, which were then handed-over to the commissioner, chief and critical department heads. This was probably the most trusted position within the police department; but I knew things, and had to be eliminated. I also handled the arrest statistics for the units, and, if prepared correctly, they do not lie, and I instinctively knew something was going on, something bad. Many arrests were for show and volume, but there was little substance there; it was all smoke and mirrors. Organised crime was getting a free ride, and very senior officers within the unit were obviously orchestrating this criminal activity.

They had another reason to fear me. I had been away for six years in south Florida, so I was an outsider. I could smell a corrupt policeman or unit a mile away, and the corrupt cops in SIS knew that; I was not part of their conspiracy, and they knew I never would be. The first step they took was to have me removed from my position as the administrator for SIS. It was then that the dark angels felt strong enough to emerge from down below and reveal themselves, and they had good reason to do so, for they were now effectively in control.

The commander of this unit was Major Herman Griner, an end product of the discrimination law suits filed by black police officers, which produced woefully under-qualified administrators.

My other options were far worse. Chief Napper was a carbon copy of Griner. He looked good on paper but was basically useless. The commissioner was so remote and engrossed in his hate war with his chief that he was worse than useless, if that is possible. So there I was with nowhere to go. I could have gone to the federal government, but where? The FBI was worse than all three put together. I could have gone to the media I suppose; but I suspect that would have ended up with me floating in a river as soon as the first headlines hit the streets. Under these incompetent administrators it was open season of corrupt officers at the Atlanta police department.

A very senior black woman administrator in the detective division was caught on a television newscast wearing a burglary victim's expensive jewellery. When the victim went to the media and complained, the administrator became an invisible person. She was protected from all external inquiries, and nothing happened.

The jewellery came from the department's property section. This was the mother lode for corruption in the department. Here, even today, you can find millions of dollars in cocaine, jewels and other valuables, all for the taking, which corrupt cops did, and I am certain still do today. Millions of dollars' worth of confiscated cocaine is replaced with flour; valuable diamonds are taken out of their settings and replaced with cheap stones and solid gold jewellery is replaced with gold-plated junk.

The property section is charged with disposing of the cocaine after the trial. When the victims arrive to sign out their valuable jewellery, and protest that it is not theirs, all they get is a shrug and an explanation that the criminal must have replaced the real jewellery with fakes. What are they to do? There is nowhere to go because the police themselves were the perpetrators.

This is a critical department where all property custodians should be given a lie-detector test on a monthly basis, and not just in the Atlanta police department, but in all police departments nationwide. The confiscated cocaine should be tested on a regular basis by an outside agency for dilution. Cocaine is far more valuable than gold, and people have been known to do some terrible things for gold.

Another reason that the criminal element in the department wanted me out of SIS was probably just as critical, and that was that the Atlanta police department had apparently been thrown out of the National Intelligence sharing community. This disgrace was headlined and I knew who the culprits were: it was our own organised crime section. They did not want any external communications because that would threaten their criminal enterprises. That paranoia also explained why they wanted me out of the section which would make it easier for them to gain control of the Atlanta Criminal Information Network. But there was another factor at play here – racism. For the first time in the history of the Atlanta police department, blacks were in total control. Many of the racist policemen were infuriated by having to report to and obey a black supervisor.

Those who find that difficult to believe should remember that the KKK was alive and well in the department. A certain Atlanta police officer took great pleasure in joking with me about the Klan and even divulged some of their secret language. One night he laughingly asked me 'AYAK?' That meant: 'Are you a Klansman?' He told me my reply should be 'IAAK', which means 'I am a Klansman'. He was on his way to a Klan vocation at Stone Mountain, which is a traditional Klan meeting place, even today.

That Atlanta police officer went on to become a very senior administrator within the department. Yes, I believe that the Klan is alive and well, only now under a different name: the Aryan Brotherhood. They are armed with high-tech weaponry and possess a high degree of military skills; but their objectives remain the same as their Klan founders – white power.

I would be shocked if anybody said that there were no racist white police officers in the department at this very time. I worked with a veteran detective who knew I was a catholic and a foreigner, and I knew he was a Klansman. It was an odd relationship, but one that worked on the streets. He was ex-military like me and Ranger-trained, and that went a long way in our close relationship on the streets, otherwise I suspect this story would have been very different.

This man literally hated catholics, blacks and foreigners, and he had names for us all. Catholics were 'papists and queers', foreigners were 'ignorant scum', and blacks were 'blue gum niggers' or 'water heads'. It was a real joy spending night after night in the close confines of a detective car with that piece of work. He knew my background because he went to records and browsed through my file. At first he refused to work with me, but he had no choice: we were severely short of detectives due to a hiring freeze.

We were involved in a series of extremely violent situations where I literally saved his prejudiced rectum, and that was that. All of a sudden I was acceptable to his red-neck presence. Frankly I could not have cared less; he was one sick man.

Returning to the Atlanta police department's uneasy relationship with the National Intelligence networks, the chief authorised me to fly to New Jersey for a meeting of all the nation's intelligence agencies. I had a long-standing good relationship with all of the agencies in attendance. I had one-on-one meetings with the principals and we soon realised that Atlanta's real problem was internal, and existed within the Organised Crime Unit. I was shocked to learn that Atlanta had not been kicked out, and that the rumour had been circulated to the Atlanta media by members of the unit.

I called Major Griner and wrote a letter to that effect. This was announced to the media and upon my return all hell broke loose in my life. Elements of the Organised Crime Unit were out for my blood.

Both Chief Napper and Major Griner then authorised the Internal Affairs Squad to go after me on the attempted murder charges.

Furious that their ploy had been discovered, elements of the Organised Crime Unit had Griner order them extremely expensive and sophisticated wire-tapping equipment. The justification was that they needed it to monitor organised crime in Atlanta. They neglected to mention that I also was a target of their surveillance. I detected that my office and home had been wire-tapped almost immediately. They were not very good.

Since its inception, the Atlanta Organised Crime Unit had not investigated organised crime in the city nor had it made a single organised crime arrest. The upper echelons of the department had to be involved in this obvious cover-up of a crooked relationship between the two: organised crime and the organised crime squad itself. How else could such inactivity exist or be explained? It was not as if there was no organised crime in Atlanta; it was, and is, saturated in it; inter-state gambling, car theft, narcotics, stolen property and big-time prostitution.

The easiest, safest money for crooked cops to get their hands on is from the mega-million-dollar Atlanta prostitution rackets. Atlanta vies with Chicago and Las Vegas for the title of convention capital of America. As for naked bodies, Atlanta has no peer because totally nude clubs are everywhere, with private rooms for high-paying customers. It is not unusual for a millionaire NBA star to drop ten thousand dollars in one of those rooms. For well-heeled athletes and conventioneers, Atlanta is the Mecca of beautiful flesh, and I do mean beautiful.

It is also the Mecca for recreational cocaine, because the two go hand in hand, especially with beautiful naked girls around. All of this amounts to staggering amounts of cash. Nobody wants to use their credit cards and leave a paper trail of their weaknesses to their owners – guys with bent noses and serious mob connections. While that segment of the flesh trade rakes in millions, there is an even bigger flesh-trade cash cow: escort services. Atlanta has more escort services than anywhere in the world, also staffed by thousands of beautiful young women.

In one of my daily meetings with Major Griner, I mentioned that the mob could be caught easier by wire-tapping the escort services. Catch the principals and 'squeeze' them for information. It seems somebody was listening to our conversation. Almost on cue, the Organised Crime Unit began a 'massive' investigation into the Phil Romano prostitution escort services. He was based on the south side of the city along with the majority of the escort services.

Romano's organisations raked in millions, tax free. But there was an even bigger escort service: Penelope's. Romano and Penelope were fierce competitors for both the best girls and customers. But for some mysterious reason both operated for years with impunity. I wondered why Romano's organisation and not Penelope's had been targeted. She was the logical target because her organisation was larger and with more mob connections. I was to discover why in a very short time: Penelope had very close connections within the Organised Crime Unit itself – a drinking and personal relationship with one of its commanders, Sergeant Wesley Derrick, soon to be a deputy chief of police. The first and only organised crime investigation conducted by the Atlanta police department was nothing more than an expensive and elaborate charade.

At great expense the unit began a twenty-four-hour surveillance of the Romano organisation's operations, and much overtime was expended for these surveillances and wire-tapping. Lieutenant Fred Townley, the commander of the Organised Crime Unit, began to report that he was receiving death threats at his home. The chief approved an expensive video-surveil-lance system for his home and more overtime for detectives to protect Townley and his family. Griner discussed this with me and I told him that from my experience the odds against organised crime threatening a police lieutenant and his family were astronomically high. The mob never likes to draw attention to themselves because they have found it easier over the years to just grease the palms of corrupt cops, and they have apparently been very successful in that endeavour.

Equally mysterious was that each dramatic episode of this 'Godfather' saga, featuring an almost daily account of the harrowing experiences the cops were having at the hands of the mob, was being displayed in the daily papers. The investigation of the Romano organisation reached comedic heights when the commissioner issued a statement that nobody was going to get away with threatening his organised crime investigators. It seemed that everybody was forgetting the fact that Townley's investigation was supposed to be a highly secret undercover operation. Instead, it might as well have been a daily television soap opera. Poor old Romano must have been shitting in his pants when he read his morning paper. He was being pre-tried by the newspapers and whoever was leaking them the inside information. He had to know his worthless criminal ass was being screwed and he might as well pack his bags for prison.

Then, when just about everybody thought the investigation could not get more bizarre, it did. The detectives who had staked out Townley's home reported that there was something wrong with the newly installed surveillance cameras. They 'discovered' that 'somebody' had spray-painted the lenses of the cameras. As this was done with the cameras in plain sight of the detectives, we figured it must have been ghosts, or aliens.

The laughing stopped, however, when Townley announced that a horse's head had been discovered in his garage, just like in

*The Godfather* movie. The laughing stopped because the investigation had become a farce. I received a call from Lieutenant Bill Pope, the commander of the robbery squad. I sat at his desk and he looked me squarely in the eye and said: 'I heard about the problems you have been having with Townley. That horse's head came out of our own evidence room. And last night Sergeant Wesley Derrick was drunk on his ass with Penelope.'

Lieutenant Townley and his unit arrested Romano in a burst of publicity. Townley had a 'star' witness, a notorious biker. I was stunned when Townley paraded him through our offices because I knew him well. He was none other than simple-minded 'Tiny', the pretend biker. He was no more a biker than I was the Pope. I came across Tiny when I worked Atlanta's south side and Stewart Avenue in particular. Stewart Avenue was a second-tier, miles-long amalgamation of nude bars, biker bars and porn parlours. It was easy to police that beat at night because everybody was up to something, or thinking about it, or had just done it, or was on the way to do something.

I first met Tiny when I received a call to go to an adult book store under the Cleveland Avenue bridge. A drunk was bitterly complaining that the quality of a bestiality video he had purchased was very poor. I called a paddy wagon to transport him to the city jail before somebody administered him a serious, good old southern ass-whipping, for which Stewarts Avenue was famous. The degree of pain was commensurate with your level of resistance and stamina.

While I was filling out the paperwork a gigantic biker kept giving me the 'bad eye', which I did not appreciate. When you work alone in an urban combat zone, bad eyes have to be put down immediately. If you don't, they escalate into something physical, and somebody gets hurt. You have to establish your 'space' with the denizens of the night, otherwise they will eat you alive. I rousted the biker outside and behind the building. I laid down the law: no bad eyes on me. Then I noticed that his lower lip was beginning to jut out and tremble, just like a baby who was about to cry.

I studied this giant of a man, who, at first glance, looked like a biker; but his phony patches told me otherwise. In spite of his patch-laden denim jacket, biker boots, chains and cap, this man was an imposter. I had ridden undercover with biker gangs in south Florida and this was no biker. I jerked him up by his belt, and he cringed; he said his name was Tiny.

I got to know Tiny and his childlike worship for cops. He was always calling me to tell me about this person or that who were involved in serious criminal activity. I did check out his information but it was just figments of his imagination. I was so busy that I told him to meet me behind a supermarket one night so that I could tell him to stop calling me. He drove up in a little, red, dinky pick-up truck and not a Harley. I looked his truck over and it contained a police scanner, a police hand-held searchlight, a nightstick and official-looking notepads. Poor Tiny was a hopeless police groupie, and a simple-minded one at that.

While the horse's head incident stretched everybody's credulity, worse was to come, far worse, and even more unbelievable. On a balmy evening a small bomb exploded in the trunk of Sergeant Wesley Derrick's detective car as he was driving along Peachtree Street. He was being closely followed by Lieutenant Fred Townley. The explosion caused little or no injury to Derrick, but did cause massive publicity. While I did not believe that the incident was related to the Romano investigation and that the entire thing smelled to high heaven, I assumed that they were setting Romano up for serious jail time. But that was not the whole story. Romano was one of two targets of the people who staged the phony explosion. I was the other.

I was charged with the attempted murder of Derrick, and

Romano was found guilty in a sensational trial. It was then that the third motive for this deadly charade raised its ugly head. With Romano out of the way, Penelope became the owner of all of the escort services. She conveniently died, and whoever is in charge now remains hidden in the shadows. But I have a strong suspicion who it is.

For the second time I went to the chief's office and resigned. He kept his door closed. I then tried to turn in my badge and uniforms to the property officers but they just shook their heads; they knew what had happened, again. They had taken my first badge. If the Atlanta Police Department wants my gold detective shield, police identification card and uniforms they know where to find them. But before I hand them over, I want to look them straight in the eye, if they can find anybody with the gall to do that. If they want to do the right thing they can have somebody calculate what my retirement benefits would have been. Make it retroactive and forward the cheque to me. I know a school that needs desks and books. I could have sued, and called a press conference. But enough disgrace had been brought on our badges by criminal Atlanta police officers. At the end of that last day I went to P. J. Haley's darkened pub. I sipped Jack Daniels and listened to the 'Nuns' Chorus' on their jukebox, alone, and felt at peace with myself. I played the chorus over and over. That way I could not hear the frenetic rustling of the dark angels down below as they celebrated their victory with corrupt Atlanta cops.

# 15

# HIGH STAKES

I experienced an almost physical rush of relief when I awakened the day after I had resigned. I lay in bed staring at the ceiling and realised the knot in my guts was gone. I showered, ate breakfast and went for a walk around the lake I lived on. I felt like I was beginning my life all over again, and it felt good. It was only during that first week that I understood just how much pressure I had been under. Lieutenant Townley had been ordered to take a polygraph test. Sergeant Brown, the examiner, called and told me they could not get a 'true reading' because they suspected Townley had taken medication to mask his responses. No effort was made on the part of the administration of the Atlanta Police Department to contact me or address the polygraph issue. Townley remained Commander of the Organised Crime Unit. The charges against me simply disappeared when I passed my polygraph test. I have often been asked by friends still wearing a good badge just what went wrong in Atlanta. It's simple really. When organised crime controls vital investigative units within any police department, they control the department. To the honest but naïve Atlanta police officers who take exception to this book, I am sorry. Not that I have upset you, but that you are swimming in a sea of sharks and you just don't know. I feel sorry for you and those you are supposed to protect. The solution? Give the members of the Vice and Organised Crime Units a monthly polygraph test.

I began to enjoy my new life and the sense of freedom that came with being away from the cesspool I had been in for so many years. I did some well paid work for an upscale corporate security company, and life was really good. Then Sal De Pasquali came into my life, and it got even better.

Sal had attended a number of conferences I had coordinated and I was drawn to his intelligence, wit and warm personality, and we became friends. He was employed by ADT, the world's largest security company, as a consultant. Out of the blue he called me for lunch. He said he had an interesting proposition for me. At lunch he proposed that I apply for a new executive position with ADT as the banking division coordinator.

I knew ADT. They were a one hundred-year-old company that manufactured, installed and protected most of America's Fortune 500 companies and just about all of the nation's secret military facilities. I was very interested, but for one problem: banking? I knew as much about banking as I did about brain surgery. But I was willing to listen. What followed was a series of interviews, one in a room with about ten ADT executives and managers. They were frank with me and said that while ADT was the major player in the security marketplace they had no real presence in the banking industry. They had some old accounts with banks in the New England area and New York, but no growth. They asked me if I thought I could bring some new thinking to the table and develop a banking programme. While I knew nothing about electronic security for banks, I knew how to organise national programmes and I could learn the technical aspects of the job.

They also told me that they needed a person with a strong reputation for integrity. I needed to hear that because I knew they were aware of my difficulties at the Atlanta Police Department. They also knew how corrupt the department really was. They hired me and my new life began, with a clean slate. So there I was, once a cop, now a real life American business executive with pin-striped suits, mobile phones, a company car, an expense account and a great salary. But I was under no illusions because I had a significant challenge ahead of me.

I reported directly to the regional vice president, Bill Welch. He was an administrator who listened more than he talked and when he did talk whatever he said made sense. He simply asked me what I needed and then left me alone to formulate the banking programme. The first time I sat down at my nice desk in my nice, very empty office, I knew I had a tough nut to crack; but I was not intimidated. I had been in far worse places and cracked bigger and harder nuts. My area of responsibility was vast and included the entire southern United States and the Caribbean. I began my analysis of the banking industry in those areas. I ordered the banking digests for the banks which did business there. After a few weeks I began to form a mental picture of the banking industry and where it was going. Dramatic changes were in the offing and I sensed that almost immediately. But I could not put my finger on what that change would be, so I kept researching and went out and met some banking officers. They were nice but were of no help. They all had long-term relationships with other security companies and had no intention of switching to ADT. I understood that because we had some stiff competition.

Some of these relationships dated back nearly a hundred years. Firms like Wells Fargo, Honeywell, Mosler and Diebold were synonymous with bank security; ADT was not. These companies were not about to allow an ex cop from ADT to waltz in and squire away multi-million-dollar accounts. It promised to be a battle royal in the business sense of the word.

As with any business, personal contacts were critical, and ADT had none in the banking industry. ADT knew before they hired me that I had contacts all over the United States and took a gamble that I could open some doors for them, and I understood that. The first step in penetrating any bank's organisation to sell security equipment is to gain the confidence of the security officer. If they refused to open the door for me to senior bank officers, the ADT banking programme was dead in the water.

That first bridge was not as difficult to cross as I thought it might be. All of the security officers were former law enforcement. That experience was gratifying and gave my heart and soul the boost I needed. The bank officers were well aware of my problems in Florida and Atlanta. They also made it clear that they were satisfied as to who was right and who was wrong.

I returned to my research and began to realise that there were literally thousands of one-bank operations scattered all over the southern states. Their assets ranged from three to five million dollars. These banks were located in small towns and served the rural and farming communities in their areas. The next tier was the banks with four or five branches and then you had the big dogs like Citizens and Southern, with hundreds of branches. There was something that interested me about that whole arrangement: it was not very cost efficient. But while it was not an ideal situation, there were good reasons for that. Some of those banks had been where they were in those small towns since they were incorporated. There was only enough money in that town to support one bank. While the big banks would like to penetrate the rural areas, it was just not cost effective. It was then that I began to understand just what that change I knew was coming would be: consolidation. The big banks would buy out the small banks and grow their assets and area of financial influence. But when?

The first clue that consolidation within the banking industry was beginning came in a small article in the *Wall Street Journal*, hidden away in the back pages. A medium-sized bank out west had merged with a small number of rural banks. The bank's president was quoted as saying that it had worked out well and the customer base was satisfied. In the next few months I found more and more small banks merging and I knew it had started. All of the mergers had been small, and all were out west. Nobody paid much attention. I called these merged banks and after some cautious back and forth, they told me that the reason they had merged was to prepare for a major bank coming into their area and buying up the banks one at a time. Apparently some of those country bankers got together and figured out that they would get a better deal if they presented a unified front. That would translate into more stock options.

I had identified the Tampa area as an ideal location for takeovers. The west coast of Florida had many single banks and was cash rich. I flew there and talked to the security manager for Flagship Bank, the largest bank in Tampa. The manager had had a good experience with ADT at another bank he worked for up north, and that helped.

I knew we had to get a toehold in the banking industry sooner rather than later. I made a number of trips to Tampa and began to build up a relationship with the bank officers. Then I noticed that the pace of small bank consolidations out west was accelerating and that meant time was running out for me. On one of my visits, ADT's regional managers were having an organisational meeting there. This was an excellent opportunity to gain their confidence and ask for their support. Without the area manager's support, the bank programme would fail. I had nothing to show them before and really no marketing plan; now I had. But I knew I would be speaking to an extremely sceptical audience. Each of them had, over the years, attempted to penetrate the banking industry in their respective areas and had failed. All of the southern states managers were represented in the room when I stood up to speak. So was the regional marketing manager, Wendell Thomas: he would be difficult to convince. I started by showing them copies of the *Wall Street Journal* with the bank mergers outlined. I explained my theory that one day there would only be a few superbanks instead of the thousands that then existed. I explained that ADT had to secure a foothold now or the richest mother lode in the security industry would be lost forever. The managers listened intently. They wanted to be involved in the banking industry but felt ADT had nothing to sell them, and they did not know how to train their sales personnel to approach the bankers. Wendell Thomas smiled, and I knew I was home free.

I then went on to explain my plan of action. All banks had alarm systems that were connected either to local alarm companies or police departments. For the rural banks that was no problem; but for the major banks with many locations it was a nightmare because they had hundreds of branches connected to hundreds of locations. While this made it easier for the bank robbers, that was not the frugal bankers' real concern, which was liability. Employees and customers who got killed or hurt during these robberies hired silk-stocking lawyers who had no difficulty convincing juries that the bank's outdated security systems were to blame. Awards were in the millions. On top of that, the cost of dedicated phone lines to all of the branches was astronomical.

ADT had developed the Centrascan computer-driven electronic security system. It was ideal for large military and industrial applications, why not banks? This system would all but eliminate line costs and effectively gut the lawyers' claims that the banks were negligent. ADT had provided me with the equipment, now I had to convince the banks to use our system.

My competitors had somewhat similar systems, but upon examination I was convinced that our rugged, highly sophisticated Centrascan was head and shoulders above theirs. My competitors made comments like: 'An ex cop, what the hell does he know about banking?' This was good for it allowed me freedom to market the Centrascan system to their banks. When I signed up Flagship Bank in Tampa to a major contract, the jokes stopped. I then signed up Central Bank, Southtrust Bank and First Alabama Bank in Birmingham.

I flew two million air miles and, while I was successful, I knew that there were bigger plans out there. A major bank – Citizens and Southern Bank, or C&S – had plans to buy all of those banks, and they were a solidly Diebold bank. All of the progress we had accomplished would go for nothing if we did not secure that bank as a client. There is no point in detailing the intense battle that was waged by every major security company in America for that contract. I had it signed, and that was a good day's work on everybody's part.

Today C&S Bank is known as the Bank of America, one of the world's largest banks. I had hired skilled banking executives to assist me and ADT was finally recognised as a major player in America's banking industry. Then I received my reward – one beyond my wildest dreams. I was going home to Ireland on a two-year assignment as managing director of ADT Ireland. ADT had purchased an alarm company there and it turned out to be a disaster. It was a money pit instead of a profit centre. The only way ADT could possibly survive was to buy the two Irish security companies, Magnum Alarms and the highly successful Allied Alarms, that were not part of an international consortium. That was to be my mission, to buy them both.

We bought Allied Alarms, and then later, after I had left Ireland, Magnum Alarms. Those two years back home were pure magic. I was an emigrant who had returned home young enough to enjoy my accomplishments. Those times with my family are still cherished moments, fresh still in my mind. I bought a home on the water in Skerries. I would walk down to Joe May's for a pint of Harp, read my paper and look out at the fishing boats. It was truly the best of times. None have ever been better, before or since then. I was home.

# 16

# LOVE AND DANGER

**W**hen I returned to America to resume my corporate career, I was emotionally and financially secure. I had learned that these are two of the vital factors if one is looking for happiness in one's life. The other is love and that I did not have. I had an itch in my mind and heart because I had been home for two years. That itch kept telling me to take the final step and break free.

The urge to do what my father had done grew stronger by the day. He had struck out and started his own business. The years I worked in his businesses taught me that it takes real guts to gamble everything and trust that customers will walk through the door of your business every day, keeping you afloat. My father had those, and more.

I am forever grateful to ADT for opening the gate to the new life I lived, which was diametrically opposed to the dangerous and tense life of a cop. But I knew that I wanted to take the last step out that door and attain total personal freedom. I had the guts because my father taught me well.

While I was still in Ireland on my ADT assignment, the germ of an idea that some day I would open my own business was planted in my head. I knew how to run a business – my father had seen to that; and I knew the business world – ADT had seen to that. Now I needed a unique quality product. Ireland had such products, but just about everything that met that description, such as Waterford crystal and Aran sweaters, had already found a market place in America.

There are two cultures in any American corporation. There is the regional culture where branch offices usually develop according to the management style of the local executive. Then there is the corporate culture. This tends to be a more free-swinging, power-driven culture, where all great ideas and original thinking are supposed to originate. Sometimes they do, sometimes they don't. When my banking programme began to expand and prosper, I came to the attention of corporate officers. I remember well having the use of a luxury penthouse apartment in a high-rise overlooking the Hudson in New York. This 'apartment' had more floor space than the average American home and was decorated with furniture whose price tags were way beyond my resources. It belonged to the president of ADT, Raymond Carey, a good and honest man.

While my salary and lifestyle dramatically changed, there was a price to be paid: I came under corporate scrutiny. Some of that scrutiny was welcome; some of it was not. As in any corporation, programmes that spring up from nowhere 'out' in regional offices and become highly successful, tend to become targets of corporate types, who want to affix their names and their management style to those programmes. They 'glom onto' these programmes and attempt to 'improve' them. I was not to know that then. I was just too busy to think about it, or get involved in corporate politics. In fact I was totally naïve as to the machinations of these corporate types, with their smiling, sincere faces, firm congratulatory handshakes, and expensive suits. I was used to being able to detect instinctively a scumbag on the streets when I was a cop, and when I became a business executive, I turned that radar off: a big, big mistake.

When my banking programme was at its zenith and I had signed up the largest banks in the region, I began to get requests to fly to other parts of America since ADT is a nationwide corporation. I felt good about myself and life in general. The only thing missing in my life was the most important thing: somebody to love and be loved by.

My happy little bubble was burst in an almost comical way. I received a call from corporate headquarters to meet two executives in Miami. They wanted to talk to me and the account representative who handled the banking business there for me. ADT did not do much banking business in Miami, and, after reviewing the situation, I immediately saw what the problem was: the local ADT branch just did not want the business. Believe it or not, many managers in ADT thought that the banking business was just too high maintenance. This is far from the truth. The real reason was that they had tried for years to penetrate this complex industry and had failed.

What I found strange was that the meeting was being held in Miami. It would have been logical to hold the meeting at regional headquarters in Atlanta. The trip for the two corporate executives would be far shorter and the Miami rep needed to come to Atlanta for a meeting with me anyway.

I flew to Miami and checked into the hotel that the executives recommended, which in itself was unusual. How would they even know about the hotels in Miami? New York perhaps, but hardly Miami. That is, unless they were spending more time in Miami than anybody in our region was aware of, and that would be highly unusual. I was advised that there would be a meeting in the morning in one of the executives' hotel rooms.

At this point money had been wasted on extended airfares and time. We had arrived early, expecting to conduct our meeting at the local ADT office which was the normal procedure. I sensed something fishy was going on, to put it mildly. The two corporate executives were John Genatempo and Francis Onofrio. They reported to Vice President Anthony Grosso in New York. Onofrio began the meeting by advising us on some mundane banking facts. What he was saying meant little to me. As I sat there I kept wondering what this expensive little charade was all for; I was about to find out. Alan Marguilese was the representative handling what little bank business there was in Miami. He and I were sitting, and Genatempo and Onofrio were standing.

I have had years of undercover experience as a cop, and I sensed that whatever these two were up to was about to 'go down' as cops call scams. I thought I was back as a cop again, or in an episode of the *Sopranos* or in a *Godfather* film. These two characters obviously did not know just who was in the room with them, and what they were all about. That is critical if you are about to do something illegal, which they were. I knew it, and it was hard to keep a straight face as Onofrio 'set up' the scam. He was talking to us like we were village idiots, and then he showed his real colours.

Out of the blue, in an emotional outburst, he yelled: 'All bankers are whores, all bankers are whores!' Genatempo said nothing, he only nodded vigorously. This time I began to feel like I was in a third-rate Mafia movie made in Salerno. I wish I had a video of that pair going through their little act – it would have won an award at the Sicilian annual movie awards.

After that dramatic announcement, I wondered just where Onofrio was going with all this. Perhaps he was going to suggest that ADT help rehabilitate these 'whore bankers'. It was all I could do to keep from laughing out loud. Then he played his hand and I immediately understand their dirty little scam. 'All bankers are whores. Buy them prostitutes and charge that on your expense account as taxi-cab fares.'

I did not feel like laughing any more. By openly declaring that buying prostitutes for banking customers was corporate ADT policy, and in an open meeting, they directly implicated me. Marguilese just sat there with a sly smile on his face. I had known for some time that his weakness was exotic lap dancers. Now he had the perfect cover to conceal these expensive inter-ludes: he would just charge them as taxi fares for the bankers, as obviously Onofrio and Genatempo did.

I flew back to Atlanta and sat down with Bill Welch, my boss and the regional vice president. I told him in no uncertain terms that there was no way I was going to provide prostitutes to ADT banking customers. Since this was the first time he had ever heard of such a thing, he sat there with his mouth open and his eyes as big as silver dollars. I had to get it on record that I was in no way involved in this scam. I can just imagine any of my senior banking officer customers' reaction to the offer of a cheap, road-whore prostitute. One in particular would have shot me out of hand. What those two characters were up to was clear: the falsification of their expense accounts to buy prosti-tutes for their own personal gratification. They chose Miami because I, as the regional banking manager, rarely went there; there were no witnesses.

I was sad and disappointed in Genatempo as he stood there nodding his head in agreement. He had been one of the cor-porate executives I had liked and respected, but he obviously condoned this corrupt and dangerous behaviour. I was not sur-prised that Onofrio had shown himself for what he was. I al-ways had a queasy feeing about his veracity. It must have been the cop in me. I remember when he had called me to pick him up at Tampa airport when I was there on a visit to Flagship

Bank. He said he was flying in from New York to assist me on a technical presentation. There was something odd about his flight number, so I checked if it was correct. It was from Miami and not New York. There was absolutely no justification for a corporate engineer to fly all the way from New York to Miami for what little banking business ADT did there. I asked him what was going on and he was evasive. This was a long time before our little sleazy meeting in his hotel room. Apparently he had been operating his scam for some time.

English tycoon Michael Ashcroft bought ADT and folded it into what is known today as Tyco/ADT. Ashcroft, who later became Lord Ashcroft, invited his European executives to a lavish dinner at Kensington Palace. This was to be a dinner in aid of the London Ballet and Princess Diana was the guest of honour. The entire affair was somewhat mind-boggling. The princess was seated at the head table with Ashcroft and Richard Burton's widow, and the London Ballet performed in between the two rows of tables in the Great Hall. It seemed each guest had their own personal waiter. The food was delicious and delicate. The guests were then led through the long hallways, where minstrels played their flutes and danced around the guests.

We were led outside to the front of the palace where we were seated on park benches. Princess Diana sat on the bench next to mine. She was a beautiful woman, very genteel, and appeared shy. The massive grounds in front of us were in darkness and it was very quiet. Then the night erupted into bedlam as a massive fireworks display commenced. If that was not enough excitement, bright lights suddenly illuminated the Welsh Guards regimental band as they began to play and parade in front of the guests. The entire evening was almost surreal and the ending somewhat unreal. A dark green Jaguar eased in front of our benches, just feet away, and the rear left door opened. The princess stood and stepped into the car and she was gone, just like that, all in a matter of seconds; then there was silence, and the evening was over. But the weekend was not over. The following evening we were treated to a ride and cocktails on what they said was a royal barge down the Thames. It took me a few days to come down from all that.

The culture of corruption was to become very public when Tyco/ADT's chief executive officer was indicted on multiple corruption charges. Dennis Kozlowski and his chief financial officer, Mark Swartz, basically looted the company to the tune of $600 million. Their machinations cost Tyco/ADT $90 billion in stock value. Kozlowski and Swartz nearly brought down their giant conglomerate, which had a quarter of a million employees and $40 billion in annual revenues. Using corporate funds, Kozlowski had his New York apartment decorated with such things as a $7,000 shower curtain, and he spent $2,200 on a gilded wastebasket, $2,900 on coat hangers, and $15,000 on an antique poodle umbrella stand. All this was a drop in the ocean compared to his mansions and homes around America. His taste in expensive and exotic toys included a helicopter, a yacht, Harley-Davidsons and whatever else met his fancy.

Kozlowski's new wife, a former waitress named Karen Lee Mayo, enjoyed her fortieth birthday party, which is not surprising since it cost $2.1 million in plundered funds. The party was thrown on the island of Sardinia, and wealthy guests and celebrities were flown in from all over the world. Circulating through the crowd were scantily clad young men in togas. The centrepiece of the festivities was a life-sized, vodka-spewing ice carving of Michaelangelo's *David*. Yet this orgy of indulgence was nothing compared to Kozlowski's art collection valued at $13 million and bought with stolen funds. His collection included works by Renoir and Monet. But all good things have to come to an end in the criminal world. On 17 June 2005, after a very public trial, both executives were led away in chains to begin serving their twenty-five-year sentences.

I wonder what life is like for them in prison, where hardened criminals feast on soft, corrupt people like them. Because of that, they are probably segregated and share a cell. What do these two con-artists talk about all day and night, as they pass away the time of their twenty-five-year sentences in a small cell, together?

Apart from the corruption, ADT is an excellent corporation. When I left it, I did not consider buying an alarm system from any other company. They are the best. I really believed that once away from law enforcement, I would see corruption in my life come to an end. I learned that the dark angels were even busier in corporate America. After my experiences as a law enforcement officer and corporate executive, I am convinced that corruption in America is institutionalised.

It was a long way from sitting on the jetty in Ireland to where I ended up. Life had been good to me. To be sure, there were a few rough spots here and there, but when one chooses the roads I have travelled, there are going to be a few pot-holes. But I was ready to live my life in a more sedate manner, and travel a nice quiet country road with no pot-holes.

On a visit to see my mother in Dundalk, she told me about Joe Lennon and his three sons. He was renovating antique pine furniture and she thought I might be interested. I had dated his sister Helen when I was a teenager and we had tried to continue our relationship when I emigrated, but vast distances and infrequent communications saw our love wither on the vine.

I remembered Joe as the younger brother and he was always very quiet. He got a raw deal in life when, at a very young age, he went to work as a farm labourer for a relative. They worked Joe from sun-up to sundown, and I know for a fact he did the work of four men, but never complained. He had been promised a few good acres of his relative's vast farm when he reached eighteen, but they reneged on the deal. Basically Joe had been an unpaid slave for many years, and then they threw him out when he asked for his due.

I visited Joe at his home and found that he had prospered and had a wonderful family. He also had a farm, but did not farm it. I think he just wanted to have that farm he had worked so hard for and never got. Helen had married well and had four children. Joe talked me through the process of restoring the old pine furniture and I was reassured by his offer to help me if and when I set up a business in America. Each of his sons was as hard a worker as their father was.

I returned to America and resumed working at ADT, but my mind was elsewhere. I wanted to establish a viable business importing from Ireland that would allow me to visit home as many times a year as I wanted to travel. So I left ADT. For the first time in my life I experienced total freedom as I walked to my car. I had had a wonderful experience at ADT, but it was time to go. I was financially secure, and now I had time to create my own business. After much consideration I incorporated the company as 'Irish Country Pine'. I had done the basics and estimated the initial cost of the product, shipping and store rent. I would not become a millionaire, but I would live well and net more money than I had ever done before.

The greatest challenge was to locate a store for rent in Atlanta. Since I would be shipping in forty-foot containers I would need a large parking lot. And the furniture at times would be bulky, requiring easy access to the showrooms. It had to be in an up-market area with good visibility. I provided those specifications to a number of leasing agencies and all responded that such a location did not exist in Atlanta, and if it did, the rent would be outrageous. So they suggested a warehouse location. My image of what I wanted my company to look like did not include a warehouse, so I kept looking.

When I was not fruitlessly wandering around Atlanta searching for a home for Irish Country Pine, I was trying to improve my social life. Concerned friends, aware of my blessed single status, began to introduce me to concerned young ladies – concerned, that is, that they would never find a suitable husband. After a few dates I put an end to that little nightmare. One more-astute and less-concerned friend called me and said he had a cousin he would like me to meet, and he assured me there would be no complications. She had just graduated from college and had relocated to Atlanta. He warned me that she was a free soul and very independent, and did not date. The deal was he would invite her to one of his frequent soirées and we could see if we hit it off.

Following my last few disastrous dates, I feared the worst, and for good reason. Marriage-hunting American women should be required to walk around with the theme song from *Jaws* playing in the background.

I arrived a little late for the party and I asked my friend where my 'date' was in the milling crowd. He replied: 'You go figure it out.' He explained that if it was meant to happen, it would happen when we met. I roamed around the many floors of his party house and saw many beautiful girls, but nobody that seemed to be looking for somebody in particular. I did see many girls who were looking for anybody, period. Then the front door opened and every male in the house stopped talking bullshit to their intended bedding mates for the night. She was tall and looked like a fashion model, which she was, part time. She had a pixie hair style, a beautiful face and dark eyes. Long legs and a body to die for brought instant sneers from the less-endowed females in that lusty bunch. I watched as she accepted a glass of white wine and began to circulate through the crowd, a horde of horny studs trailing behind, whom she politely ignored.

I had been standing in an alcove waiting for my friend's cousin to show her face, when I heard a voice: 'You are Gerard, are you not?' It was the vision of loveliness with the long legs. I do not rattle easily – my background took care of that – but she had sneaked up on me, and that was unnerving, especially with those liquid eyes. I assumed my friend had pointed me out. 'No, I knew you by your body language,' she said. 'My cousin told me about your background. You stand in a corner and watch everybody and everything. You are a dangerous man.' Her entourage slunk off, grumbling.

We dated for a few times and I explained my dilemma about finding a suitable location for my business. It turned out that her family had many business connections in Atlanta, and she told me to stop looking – she would take care of my location problem. Normally that would have raised red flags. When somebody does something for you there was an unspoken understanding that they will expect something in return; that's the American way. She never to this day asked anything other than loyal friendship.

The next day she called and asked me to meet her at one of the most expensive restaurants in Buckhead, where all the money is in Atlanta, period. If Mercedes – yes, that is her name – had found me a location in Buckhead, there was no way I could afford the rent. Besides, no such location existed there. It was wall-to-wall fine dining and up-market everything. She introduced me to the owner of the restaurant and I recognised him immediately. He owned many of the best restaurants and millions of dollars' worth of real estate in the Buckhead area.

We met in his office and he seemed to understand my dilemma. He had a proposal. There was a very large Victorian-style home on the corner of East Paces Ferry Road and Maple

Road that was in a severe state of disrepair. It had three floors and an extremely large parking lot at the rear. I knew exactly where it was and always admired its old-world charm with its mature oak trees. He asked me if I was willing to renovate the property, and I told him yes. I had renovated three homes, including Harbour House in Skerries.

This location was in the highest-visibility spot in Buckhead. There was no way I could afford the rent. Sensing my trepidation, Mercedes just widened her beautiful eyes and smiled gently; she already knew. The rent for a five-year-contract was unbelievably low. I signed on the spot.

What followed was the best ten years of my life. The third floor of the building was actually a residence, but in disrepair. My priority was to renovate the bottom two floors as showrooms, and I enjoyed doing that. Then I created a Parisian-style apartment upstairs, and moved in. It was just like our home over our businesses in Dundalk.

It was not easy but the business flourished. Many people were interested in Ireland, so I contacted the Irish Tourist Board and they shipped me boxloads of quality brochures on visiting Ireland. Delta had just started direct flights from Atlanta to Ireland. I have no idea how many American tourists I have been responsible for encouraging to visit Ireland, but it's got to be in the thousands, and I felt good about that. The only flaw was that I was emotionally alone. Mercedes and I were friends and other things, but there was no emotional attachment other than a close friendship.

Then something Irish happened. The Dublin-based Irish Pub Group opened 'Fados' in Buckhead just down from my business. They had shipped in container-loads of Irish antiques and an Irish staff. I was ecstatic because their attention to detail was outstanding. It soon became a hang-out for the Emory University crowd. I got to know the staff and they were from all over Ireland. It was a great place to go to eat and have a pint of Harp, but I still did not have anybody to share it with. Mercedes was a sushi person; a pile of spuds, vegetables and Irish ham was not her thing. They had a fireplace, and I shipped over a few bags of turf and set fires in the winter months for them. There was an Irish-born professor who used to frequent the bar and I got to know him. Often he would bring in his students and talk to them about Ireland.

One evening I was eating a bowl of Irish stew when he tapped me on the arm. 'I have a student here who would like to speak to you; why, I don't know; she talks to nobody.' I glanced across the bar and a tall, beautiful Asian girl was smiling at me. I had no idea what was going on, but she certainly was more appealing than a bowl of Irish stew, so I crossed the bar and introduced myself. She replied: 'I heard you speak at a conference some time ago, and you have some different points of view.' I had been coaxed out of 'retirement' and been giving occasional terrorism lectures around the country. I had no idea where she had heard me speak, but it had to be a large venue, because I would have noticed this exotic beauty. She was, as my friend had noted, quiet and reserved, and younger than me; but we started dating. We found ourselves in a symbiotic relationship where I was transported to another culture and a gentleness I had never experienced before, but one I longed for.

Eva was a Filipino and lived on one of the islands located on the Pacific Ocean of the Philippines. She wanted to complete her studies and go home, which was to be in a month. She and I dated often during that last month and she postponed her return home for a few months at my request. I was falling in love and for the first time in years felt complete, and that was a good feeling.

I was due to travel to Ireland for another container-load of furniture and invited her along. She loved Ireland and Ireland loved her. She and my mother became fast friends and spent a lot of time together just talking and going for walks along my jetty. Because of her unusual appearance, tanned skin and round eyes she came under close scrutiny. The wife of a friend asked permission to touch her face. I asked my friend later what his wife was doing. He said she wondered if the colour of her skin was make-up.

Eva loved Irish food, all the stuff that I liked. A fry in the morning and a hearty dinner and tea in the evening was her regular routine. We had a great time driving around and she was fun to be with, but she steered away from any talk of a permanent relationship. She was going home and that was that. I had been to the Philippines in the past and genuinely liked the people and the country, but never considered living there; now I was not so sure. We discussed that possibility and she replied that I had better give that some serious thought. We exchanged telephone numbers and internet information and said goodbye.

Four months later I pulled up in front of her house in a rental car and when we embraced in front of her family and friends, that was that: we got engaged. She joined me in Atlanta a month later and we drove to Florida and got married. I owned a condo there, and had planned to relocate to it and write when I had sold my business.

The condo was situated directly on the Gulf of Mexico and the sunsets were magnificent, as was the fishing. Eva loved the beach and the water as much as I did. She was happy, but I knew where her heart was. I was an immigrant also and understood what she was going through. At that point in my life, home was where I hung my hat, but Eva was far from that stage. I saw no sense in her suffering as I did. I sold my business and the condo and we moved to the Philippines. We constructed a home on the beach, and life was good, but war clouds were gathering over our island.

Muslim separatist groups had launched a bloody series of raids and kidnappings, targeting foreigners. The island of Mindanao is large and we lived on the extreme north end, where it was peaceful. I paid little attention to the raging conflict until one day the fanatical Abu Sayyaf group kidnapped a large number of European tourists for ransom. This was still a long way from where we lived, but I started to pay closer attention to the growing crisis.

With all that going on you might wonder why I would choose to live in the Philippines and not go back to my Florida condo. Frankly I loved living there. The Filipino people are better to coexist with than most of the races I have encountered in my travels around the world. While I can't explain why, there is a similarity between the Irish and the Filipino people and their cultures. Maybe it is as simple as the fact that we are two predominantly catholic countries or that we are family oriented. I just know that I get along well with Filipinos even from the remote island provinces. Anyway, I did not want to mentally rot away in my condo. And I have a suspicion that is exactly what would have happened to me. There was little chance that would happen to me in the Philippines; the place kept me mentally alert.

The archipelago of the Philippines comprises some 1,100 beautiful islands stretching from east of Vietnam to north of Australia. There is no recognisable national language, and there are about seventy dialects. The closest to a national language is a mishmash of English and Filipino called Taglish. Spain occupied the islands for hundreds of years, as did America. So English is widely spoken and understood. The country has a population of approximately ninety million people. Ninety-five per cent are Christian, and the rest are Muslim. While the

Muslims were late arrivals in the Philippines, they insist they should be awarded vast tracts of land as they have historical domain rights. Therein lies the crux of the war that has cost lives in six figures: the Muslims have one history book and the Christians have another, and they don't agree. This is not a war being waged by a ragged peasant army, far from it. The Muslim separatists are heavily armed, well trained and wear combat uniforms just like the Filipino regular army. They receive aid from many Muslim countries and have trained and fought in Iraq and Afghanistan. Osama bin Laden's influence is particularly strong in Mindanao.

While the Filipino soldiers are among the best in the world, they are woefully under-equipped. The media constantly report that this is because the generals are corrupt. Many foreign countries donate aid to the Philippines, but where the money goes is anybody's guess: it never reaches the soldiers fighting the war.

There are four Muslim separatist armies, ranging from ten to fifteen thousand heavily armed and uniformed combatants. Then there are splinter groups that are nothing more than criminal gangs who extort money through terror. The Abu Sayyaf is the most violent. A countrywide problem is the NPA, or the New People's Army. They profess to be communists but are nothing more than extortionists. Businessmen who do not pay their 'revolutionary taxes' have their businesses burned and their employees terrorised. Cell phone companies have their transmission towers blown up on a regular basis. Impoverished farmers are forced to hand over a large portion of their crops to avoid being murdered. Norway has been providing sanctuary to the NPA leadership for years, much to the justified frustration of the Philippine government.

The Abu Sayyaf claim to be a splinter group from one of the main Muslim separatist armies, but they are afforded safe sanctuary in these armies. They also carry out the dirty work for the larger Muslim National Liberation Front, or MNLF. Recently, hundreds of MNLF combatants ambushed a Filipino marines patrol and captured ten marines in spite of a signed peace accord. The decapitated bodies of the marines were found the next day.

As usual the MNLF denied any knowledge of the beheadings and blamed the Abu Sayyaf. The Abu Sayyaf used their victims' cell phones and transmitted pictures of the marines being beheaded and castrated to the marines' families. The reason the marines were captured was because of faulty munitions.

Many senior Filipino military and police officials train annually in the United States. When I was addressing a conference in New Orleans I met a senior Filipino police official and we struck up a rapport. After we had moved to the Philippines, I went to check on my mailbox one day. The police station was next door. I had just picked up my mail when a voice said: 'My friend.' It was none other than my pal the police officer, now a colonel and police chief. Over time we became close friends and he called on my expertise once in a while on different cases.

One of the problems for foreigners in the Philippines is that you cannot own a firearm. And in a country like that, it is a good idea to be armed. The colonel suggested I become a member of the local intelligence unit and the national police. I was taken aback by that, but went through the process, somewhat sceptical that it would be approved.

After submitting extensive documentation I received my local and national police identification cards. I was a cop again, an Irish/American/Filipino one. One immediate benefit was that I then had an Ingram sub-machine gun, a .45 and .38 calibre revolver, and enough ammunition to protect the White House.

I made many Christian and Muslim friends and, what with

my police contacts, a very disturbing picture began to emerge of what was really happening in the southern Philippines in regards to international terrorism. It was scary because nobody in the outside world seemed to be aware of what was going on in the vast, sprawling island of Mindanao and the surrounding islands: the islands had become an international training base for terrorists.

# 17

# EXTREME DANGER

International terrorism was not what I had in mind when I moved to this island paradise, not at all. I had envisioned a blissful time, with Eva and I enjoying life and writing being my priority. We talked about raising a family then slowly but surely I felt myself getting sucked into a deadly nightmare where life was the cheapest commodity. I thought about the situation I found myself in and decided to keep my head down and mind my own business; life was too short. I had spent my life risking myself; now I had another person, and possibly a third to consider. Eva sensed my inner turmoil and just said: 'Be careful, you do what you think is right. I am here by your side.'

I was frankly shocked to hear that Osama bin Laden had fathered a son by his fortieth wife on our island. Then I discovered that his brother-in-law had opened a Saudi-funded 'charity' here also. That meant that Saudi Arabian oil money was also fuelling the fires of terrorism in southeast Asia. In the guise of paying ransom for the release of Europeans being held prisoners by the Abu Sayyaf, Libya handed over twenty million dollars in cash to the extremists. Our island was then awash in money to fund the various terrorist groups, and the outside world seemed blissfully unaware.

A further concern was that the Philippines had another entry and exit point besides Manila. It is called the 'southern backdoor'. Through the many islands, big and small, there is a heavy, unrestricted, daily traffic of good and not-so-good people in and out of the Philippines. We know of office workers who travel back and forth every weekend to Malaysia. This ease of movement is also available to the Indonesian, Malaysian and Filipino terrorists who are now fighting Australian, American and Filipino army troops.

I used to sit in native-built bamboo Nipa huts and drink *tuba*, a coconut wine, and talk to my friends in the police and the military. What they told me left no doubt that outside intelligence agencies did not have a clue as to the scale of the growing crisis in Mindanao.

One evening I asked if they were sharing any of this vital raw information with the Americans charged with assisting the Filipino government in fighting terrorism. This was a mega-million-dollar operation. They all just laughed and agreed that both the American and Filipino agencies charged with this mission did not even come to Mindanao. One senior officer shook his head and said: 'They stay in their offices in Manila, where it is safe. We feed them bullshit information so that they can do their monthly reports.' Another officer said that they spoon-fed the Americans whatever they wanted to hear: 'We treat them like mushrooms and keep them in the dark and feed them shit.' So there it was, nothing of tactical value ever reached the FBI, the American agency charged with combating terrorism in the Philippines.

The Philippines is the training ground for terrorists who fight for Bin Laden all over the world. Where is the FBI? In 2007 I communicated with the American ambassador and advised her that her agents did 'not have a clue what was going on in Mindanao'. She had a letter in her possession from the US

Senate regarding me and knew of my existence in the southern Philippines. She managed to pry a few moribund FBI agents out of their chairs and sent them to Zamboanga City. This was as far away as they could get from the real action, but it had an exotic name and sounded good in their reports. The news media ridiculed the 'undercover' sweaty agents stumbling around in suits and that was the end of that little FBI 'front line' effort to combat terrorism.

Then the Abu Sayyaf kidnapped Americans and beheaded one. They then grabbed two missionaries, the Burnhams, for ransom. They were out of control and the situation was worsening. There were strong indications that Filipino army generals were involved with the Abu Sayyaf in the division of ransom monies. I had a choice to make: leave or do something about the situation. On 1 October 2001, I entered the US embassy in Manila for a meeting with the FBI and 'other unidentified' American intelligence agents, to provide vital raw intelligence information. I spoke with a 'Mr Colleta' and a 'Frank', then was ushered into FBI agent Nixon's office. Nixon was a hostile, pompous ass who did not want to hear anything I had to say.

I flew back to Zamboanga Del Norte and picked up the phone and called Washington; enough was enough, and I had had enough. I contacted Duke Short at the US Senate Armed Services and faxed reams of reports. It was not much later that the US Rangers and Green Berets descended on the southern Philippines. They were directly involved in the operation that killed Abu Sabaya, the bloodthirsty leader of the Abu Sayyaf. They set up a permanent base of operations there.

Why did I get involved? If I had not done anything we would have had to move out of Mindanao, and we were not ready to do that; Eva is built from strong timber. My only concern was that somebody would leak the fact that I was communicating directly with the powerful Armed Services Committee. If that had happened, it would have sealed our death warrants.

Then I began to become sick on a daily basis, very sick. Local doctors could not diagnose my problem. But I was growing weaker and began to collapse for no apparent reason. Then, in the middle of the night, a phone call came from a high-ranking police official friend: 'You have to get out as quickly as possible; they are looking for you – get out,' and he hung up the phone. I trusted him and his voice told it all. I was a doomed man.

We had a beautiful home on the beach, filled with a lifetime of personal possessions and antiques. We sold it for a fraction of its value and fled with the clothes on our backs. I remember little about our flight back to America and Florida. We had called ahead and rented a furnished condo in Panacea on the Gulf. I collapsed there and our friend Bob Sperri helped Eva get me to Tallahassee General Hospital. I remember little of that. I felt like I was sinking into a black hole. I was later to learn that I was dying.

I spent a week in intensive care and six doctors performed every test available in a modern hospital. They desperately tried to discover what had happened to me in southeast Asia. My entire body was shutting down: kidneys, liver and other vital organs. I would surface every now and then and always I would see Eva sitting by my bed, haggard, weary and still wearing the same clothes she was wearing when I was admitted.

I have over $25,000 in hospital receipts but no clue as to what happened to me. I slowly became aware of my surroundings after about a week. It seemed I had been some place else for a very long time. They drove us back home and I rapidly recovered.

We made new friends and settled in for a year so that I could recover. We constructed a home out in the woods and that was nice. It was not unusual to awaken and find deer in our front yard, and our bird feeder was a busy place. We went to the beach, fished and just enjoyed life.

By this time, the Philippines had quietened down and we often talked about returning, but not to Mindanao. Then something magical happened: Eva woke one morning and said she 'felt funny'. She was pregnant! We did all of the preliminary tests and had comprehensive pre-natal care; a boy was on the way. We had dreamed of this so long that we had already agreed on a name, Logan Shane Mac Manus.

That decided the issue of returning to the Philippines – we were going! We had already contacted a state-of-the-art hospital in a city north of Mindanao and we were on our way. We first had to visit Eva's parents in Mindanao to share the excitement of Logan's impending birth. He would be an American and a Filipino and, when things slowed down, an Irish-American-Filipino. That's a lot of passports.

While I was there for that week, I visited my police and military friends, and it was then I found out what had happened to me: somebody had tried to kill me. Cyanide leaves no trace but breaks down the body's organs. The source of the poison was from the red fish I ate almost daily. I would go down to the fishing boats each day and buy my red fish fresh, and everybody knew that. I was the only one in the house who ate red fish. How did they find that fact out? In the Philippines it is always the maids who will betray you, whether you are a Filipino or a foreigner. It took a year for my friends to discover who leaked my activities to my assassins. He was based in Manila and was not a Filipino, but we all know his name.

We are happy now, safe and far away from danger, and enjoying life. We live in Europe and Asia and I am writing full time. Eva also writes and Logan keeps both of us busy in our down time. At the end of the day, we are blessed and thankful for everything we have, which is a loving, caring family and peace of mind.

# A NOTE FROM THE AUTHOR

**M**y wife and my close friends started me down the path to this book. It was a path I dreaded and would never have gone down were it not for them. It has been a gut-wrenching experience but, oddly, now that it's over, I can't seem to let go. It has also been a cauterising experience for me.

My life has seen many happy moments and accomplishments, and I've been lucky to have so many wonderful people in it. I am at peace in my heart and soul as my wife of many years stands by my side as I write these last few words. I hold no grievances in my heart and I forgive those honest cops who remained silent, even knowing what they did – they will punish themselves.

I forgive those corrupt people who tried to destroy me. They will suffer a terrible fate when the Devil comes to collect their damned black souls – and he will come for them.

So, I will close out *Dark Corners* on a positive and happy note. I am writing full-time now, maybe I will see you down the road.

# ACKNOWLEDGEMENTS

To Mary and Clodagh Feehan, who opened the door and let me through. To Eoin Purcell, Commissioning Editor at Mercier Press, an insightful man with a writer's soul, thank you. To Brian Ronan, Managing Editor at Mercier Press, thank you for your navigational skills. To James Harpur, my editor, who gave this book direction, thank you for your patience. To Lisa Daly, who brought *Dark Corners* to life with your artwork and graphics, thank you.

To my mother and father, Peter and Maureen Mac Manus, thank you for the strength you gave me. Without that, I would not have survived to have written *Dark Corners*.

To my siblings and their spouses, Marna and Michael Fleming, Canice and Jannett, Terry and Pat Mac Manus, thank you for being in my life. While we are a world apart, I love you.

To my beloved sons, Christopher and Logan, please choose an easier road than the one I travelled. If you go down my road, listen to my written words and remember, I am there beside you, shoulder to shoulder, whether you can see me or not.

To the friends who have stood by my side in good times and bad, you know who you are, so thank you. To all of the honest cops who try to do their jobs in spite of corruption, thank you and hang in there! To my former comrades-in-arms who have to fight wars without conscience, stay strong and come home alive.

To the anchor in my life, Eva, my wife of many years, you are even more beautiful in body, heart and soul than the first day I met you and lost my heart. We have travelled the world and have seen some wonderful times and some very dangerous times. I would not be alive today if it were not for you. You are the true warrior in our family.

# APPENDIX

**A** handwritten note from Duke Short to the author. The last two lines are carefully written, and refer to the author's previously transmitted frustration as to the slow arrival of American Special Forces to assist in the rescue of US hostages.

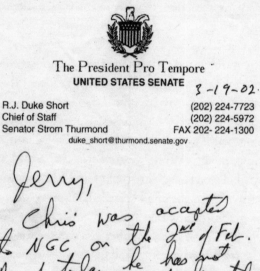

The President Pro Tempore
**UNITED STATES SENATE**

8-19-02

R.J. Duke Short
Chief of Staff
Senator Strom Thurmond

(202) 224-7723
(202) 224-5972
FAX 202- 224-1300

duke_short@thurmond.senate.gov

Jerry,

Chris was acapted to NGC on the 2nd of Feb. As of today he has not responded & I wrote him today. and advised him to contact NGC.

Hope all is well – we continue to do what we can

Take Care.

Duke